Anne Finch and Her Poetry

Anne Finch

and Her Poetry

A CRITICAL BIOGRAPHY

Barbara McGovern

The University of Georgia Press · Athens & London

© 1992 by the University of Georgia Press
Athens, Georgia 30602
All rights reserved
Designed by Betty Palmer McDaniel
Set in 11 on 13 Fournier by Tseng Information Systems, Inc.
Printed and bound by Braun-Brumfield, Inc.
The paper in this book meets the guidelines for
permanence and durability of the Committee on
Production Guidelines for Book Longevity of the
Council on Library Resources.

Printed in the United States of America

96 95 94 93 92   C   5 4 3 2 1

Library of Congress Cataloging in Publication Data
McGovern, Barbara.
Anne Finch and her poetry : a critical biography / Barbara
McGovern.
     p.   cm.
Includes bibliographical references and index.
ISBN 0-8203-1410-2 (alk. paper)
1. Winchilsea, Anne Kingsmill Finch, Countess of, 1661–1720.
2. Women and literature—England—History—17th century.
3. Poets, English—Early modern, 1500–1700—Biography.   4. Poets,
English—18th century—Biography.   I. Title.
PR3765.W57Z77   1992
821′.5—dc20
[B]   91-23862
                              CIP

British Library Cataloging in Publication Data available

"Apollo Outwitted" by Jonathan Swift is reprinted by permission of the
publishers from Collected Poems of Jonathan Swift, Joseph Horrell, editor.
Cambridge, Mass.: Harvard University Press; London: Routledge. ©
1958 by Joseph Horrell.

"Impromptu, to Lady Winchelsea" by Alexander Pope is reprinted from
Minor Poems, edited by Norman Ault and John Butt. London: Methuen,
1964.

Title page illustration: Miniature of Anne Finch, Countess of Winchilsea,
by Laurence Crosse. National Portrait Gallery, London

FOR MY CHILDREN, NICK, BRIGID, JIM, AND TARA,
AND FOR BOB, WHO

. . . to the World, by tend'rest proof discovers
They err, who say that husbands can't be lovers.

Contents

Contents

Acknowledgments

J am grateful to many people within the scholarly community for their repeated acts of kindness and generosity while I was working on this project. John F. Sena has given me his valuable advice and support at all stages of this undertaking. David O. Frantz, Albert J. Kuhn, Marlene Longenecker, Julian Markels, Ann Messenger, and Barbara Hill Rigney have read my manuscript in earlier drafts and given me direction at crucial points. Paula Backscheider, Charles Hinnant, Roger Lonsdale, Catharine R. Stimpson, Janet Todd, and James Woolley have supplied information and offered encouragement.

I am indebted to the Earl of Winchilsea for answering my queries and the Duke of Northumberland and the Marquess of Bath for putting at my disposal family papers in their private libraries and allowing me to quote excerpts from them. I also wish to thank the numerous librarians and archivists in the United Kingdom and the United States who have provided assistance. I particularly want to thank Norman Evans, Head of Research at the Public Record Office at Chancery Lane, London, for his valuable aid in helping me locate and interpret some seventeenth-century legal documents; Kate Harris, Librarian and Archivist to the Marquess of Bath at Longleat House; Special Collections Librarian Ruth R. Rogers and her predecessor, Anne Anninger, at Margaret Clapp Library, Wellesley College; and Sherri Edwards and Patricia Markley of The Ohio State University Libraries. I also wish to thank Kerri Mellick, my faithful student assistant, and Charles Myers, whose computer expertise made possible the genealogical charts in the appendix.

The Alnwick Castle library in Northumberland, the Ashford Library in Kent, the Bodleian Library at Oxford, the British Library, the Folger Shakespeare Library, the Hampshire Record Office, the Kent Public Record Office, the library at Longleat House in Wiltshire, the National Portrait Gallery Archives, the Northamptonshire Record Office, the Public Record Office in London, the Society of Genealogists, the Victoria and Albert Museum National Art Library, the Victoria University Library in Wellington, New Zealand, the Westminster City Library, and the Dr. Williams Library in London have assisted me in locating materials and have allowed me to quote from them. In particular I thank Wellesley College for permission to publish poems from the Anne Finch manuscript in its English Poetry Collection.

I wish to express my appreciation to Philip G. Dormer for supplying me with many materials collected by him on the history of Eastwell and its vicinity, to George V. Allen for giving me extracts from Ashford Library papers and other local records regarding Godmersham, and to the management and staff of the current Eastwell Manor Hotel for their courtesy in providing me with historical records of the manor and for allowing me to explore the estate grounds and the churchyard.

A generous Seed Grant from The Ohio State University, as well as a Women's Studies Research Grant and several Professional Development grants, have supported my research. I acknowledge with appreciation John O. Riedl, Dean and Director of The Ohio State University at Mansfield, and Charles P. Bird, Associate Dean, for assisting me with travel funds for my research and for granting me a sabbatical.

Finally, I wish to acknowledge with gratitude and affection the support of my family, in particular my husband, Bob, who many years ago introduced me to the poetry of Anne Finch, and without whom this book would not have been possible.

Author's Note

*I*n the seventeenth- and eighteenth-century documents that I cite, and in the poems that I have transcribed from the Wellesley manuscript, I have preserved the original spelling and punctuation, including such customary abbreviations as "y^t" for "that."

Dates are a problem. Britain remained loyal to the Julian or Old Style calendar until 1752. In the seventeenth century the British calendar was ten days behind the New Style or Gregorian calendar used in most of Europe, with the New Year beginning on March 25. In 1700 the difference between the British calendar and the New Style calendar increased to eleven days. I have retained the Old Style dates for England but take the year to begin on January 1.

Abbreviations

Add. ms.	Additional manuscript, British Library
BL	British Library
Bodl.	Bodleian Library, Oxford
DNB	*Dictionary of National Biography*
F-H ms.	Finch-Hatton manuscript, Northamptonshire Record Office
HMC	Historical Manuscripts Commission
HMSO	Her (His) Majesty's Stationery Office
OED	*Oxford English Dictionary*
PCC	Prerogative Court of Canterbury records
PRO	Public Record Office, London
W ms.	Wellesley manuscript

Anne Finch and Her Poetry

"Alas! a woman
that attempts the pen"

nne Finch and her poetry are in many ways an ideal subject for a critical biography. A configuration of biographical circumstances aided her in becoming one of the earliest women writers to commit herself seriously to poetry. Moreover, during her life, which spanned almost the entire Restoration period and the first two decades of the eighteenth century, she was involved with some of Britain's most critical religious and political controversies, and she knew a number of the most famous literary figures of her age. Finch is arguably the best woman poet England produced before the nineteenth century, yet no full biography of her life has existed previously, no edition of her complete poems has yet been published, and no substantial analysis and evaluation of her entire poetic output has been attempted prior to this study.[1]

Despite being born into the privileged class, Finch had to contend with enormous vicissitudes throughout her life. She was orphaned early in childhood and then involved in two separate custody fights, so insecurity was familiar to her. As an adult she knew displacement from the court and public life, homelessness, and financial hardships. Her early married life was marred by the political intrigue and danger surrounding the Glorious Revolution—and the ultimate arrest of her husband on charges of treason. For years she endured grave bouts with a chronic illness that affected both mind and body. She struggled against the derision and censure directed toward all women who dared to write. And in the final years of her life she faced increased illness, new financial difficulties, and the return of an adverse, potentially threatening political climate.

Finch's struggle to achieve identity as a poet was not an easy one. Not only were most women in her day denied the education, social experience, and leisure necessary for developing their minds, but those few who, like Finch, overcame these obstacles faced one more insidious impediment. Having nurtured their talent as authors, they frequently found themselves denied opportunities for publication and serious public recognition, or had their writings denigrated and trivialized by a patriarchal literary world. Finch poignantly describes her plight in these lines from "The Introduction," composed at least seven years after she had begun writing poetry:

> Did I my lines intend for publick view,
> How many censures would their faults persue,
> Some wou'd, because such words they do affect,
> Cry they're insipid, empty, uncorrect.
> And many, have attain'd, dull and untaught
> The name of Witt, only by finding fault.
> True judges, might condemn their want of witt,
> And all might say, they're by a Woman writt.
> Alas! a woman that attempts the pen,
> Such an intruder on the rights of men,
> Such a presumptuous Creature, is esteem'd,
> The fault, can by no vertue be redeem'd.
>
> (4, lines 1–12)[2]

While one must always be cautious in treating such texts as a reflection of a writer's life, a revisionary biography, particularly of a woman author, cannot ignore them.

This book is a critical biography, combining an account of Finch's life with a critical study of her poems; its premise is that the poet's life and her poetry can best be understood by exploring the tensions that exist between authorship and textuality and between text and history. The narrative sequence is therefore interrupted at several points where a more comprehensive analysis of a thematic group of poems seems appropriate.

In reconstructing Finch's life I have tried to avoid the kind of historical approach that Lawrence K. Lipking calls "retrenchment" ("History of the Future" 166). Historical fact and reflections on political, cultural, and textual issues here inform each other. The results of Public Record Office sleuthing are presented along with the broader implications of discourses of power and other conceptual concerns of current theoretical studies. In bringing historical knowledge to bear on the readings of her poems, I examine the relationships among literary conventions and forms, history, and feminist politics.

My focus is on Finch's historical place and her displacement in early eighteenth-century England, and particularly on the methods by which she developed a poetic identity for her own artistic liberation. She was in many ways a displaced person. Katharine Rogers sees her as "a woman imprisoned in man-made conventions" (introduction to *Selected Poems* xv) and Sandra M. Gilbert and Susan Gubar similarly distinguish her as a woman poet struggling "to escape the male designs in which she feels herself enmeshed" (*Madwoman* 17). Her displacement, however, was due not to gender alone but also to political ideology, religious orientation, and aesthetic sensibility. She was a marginal figure, then, by virtue of a number of "differences" in the sense in which Felicity Nussbaum defines the term: "those interests which run counter to prevailing interests during the particular historical moment . . . , especially those of the state and of the dominant race, gender and social strata."[3] When she was determining her own identity through her poetics, however, ideologies of gender were foremost for Finch.

Finch is never avowedly autobiographical, yet her poetry reveals much about her life and the world around her as perceived and interpreted through her artistic sensibility. While sometimes her poems reflect her personal experiences, frequently they deal with experiences common to women's lives, though not necessarily a part of her own life. Thus she wrote with great feeling about the plight of women trapped in unhappy marriages, though she repeatedly gave evidence of contentment and happiness in her own marriage; she wrote of women being cruelly maligned by a society that set a double sexual standard, yet she was known throughout her life as a pious woman of impeccable virtue who remained free of the sort of scandalous gossip that plagued other contemporary women writers, such as Aphra Behn and Delariviere Manley.

Investigating and interpreting the relationship between a writer's texts and her life takes on an additional dimension when the subject is an early woman writer, for it raises many gender-related questions. How she was reared and educated, what sort of marriage she had, and what her daily domestic life was like are more significant issues when writing the biography of a woman than they are in the portrayal of a man's life because a woman's existence was more limited and confined. One must consider how she was able to create her own poetic voice and write about her own experiences, her own concerns, given a literary tradition that was almost entirely male-biased. What sense did she have of those female authors who had preceded her, and was she aware of any affinities with other contemporary women writers? Was there in her life and in her writing any sense of a connectedness with other women that enabled her to write? Are there marked differences in ideologies of gender and aesthetics/poetics between her poetry and that of contemporary male writers? Are there significant similarities? How did she use the literary traditions and conventions that she inherited? And, finally, what is innovative in her writing, and what are her contributions to the history of literature?

Many critics have recently called into question the significance of a tradition of women's literature and the reliability of the relationship between women's experiences and their representation in women's writings.[4] Certainly a variety of social issues complicate gender issues, so that in reconstructing the biography of a woman one must avoid viewing history as a monolithic patriarchal hegemony.[5] In some instances the differences in religious and political stance, aesthetics, class, and sexual orientation are great within that general category of "women." While recognizing these variables, and the fact that gender is itself both socially constructed and relational, I nevertheless treat Finch's femaleness as a quality that can sometimes be recognized in her poetry—a quality of voice, of metaphor, of poetic identity. In my construction of a framework for this study of her life and poetry I do not treat gender ideology as isolated from considerations of social and cultural patterns and the various discourses that inform that ideology. I avoid an essentialist position while yet recognizing the emergence of an identifiable female literary tradition in which Finch played an integral part.[6]

A large number of her poems deal with being a woman, both as a member of society and as an internalized poetic identity. Sometimes in her poetry she glorifies traditional "feminine" values. Other times, however, she subverts those values to create a radically feminist statement. Her own understanding of her "womanness" was in some ways very traditional and conservative, reflecting her aristocratic Royalist and Anglican background. As Ruth Perry has observed of Finch's contemporary Mary Astell, many Tory women of the time who decried some aspects of gender discrimination in their own societies remained loyal to established political and ecclesiastical authorities. They were also skeptical about the beginnings of democratization and the true motives behind the Glorious or "Bloodless" Revolution of 1688, which they feared to be greed and petty opportunism.[7]

Finch's poetry was published at a time when few women identified themselves as serious poets. In the entire first decade of the eighteenth century, prior to the 1713 appearance of her *Miscellany Poems, on Several Occasions*, only two women published collections of their poetry (Mary, Lady Chudleigh, and Sarah Egerton). However, in the last decade of the eighteenth century, as Roger Lonsdale has noted, more than thirty women did so (xxii). But for a woman writing and publishing in the early eighteenth century, the literary tradition she had to work with was almost exclusively male-oriented. The fear of public scorn and the reluctance to defy literary convention would therefore be great. Thus the issues of style and tone, of subject matter, of genre, and of masking strategies become very complex.

Finch's talent lay in her ability to use a variety of literary genres and conventions so as to achieve a freedom of expression that would not otherwise have been available for a woman. Writing from a marginal position in her social and literary milieu, she often viewed her exclusion from masculine traditions as a challenge to her creativity, rather than a repression of it. Although her writing can be overtly polemical, the feminism in her poetry often achieves a subversive force through a variety of rhetorical and stylistic devices, including the manipulation of literary conventions and the innovative use of dramatic techniques and persona.

Much feminist criticism has been directed toward documenting a connectedness in the female literary experience. Critics such as Elaine Showalter, Ellen Moers, Sandra M. Gilbert, and Susan Gubar argue that a female literature and culture existed by the nineteenth century, while others, most notably Marilyn L. Williamson, find even earlier evidence of a continuous feminist history in British literature.[8] Showalter writes in *A Literature of Their Own*, for example, that "women have always been self-conscious, but only rarely self-defining. While they have been deeply and perennially aware of their individual identities and experiences, women writers have very infrequently considered whether these experiences might transcend the personal and local, assume a collective form in art, and reveal a history" (4). Finch, writing at the dawn of the eighteenth century, was surprisingly aware of the need for a female literary subculture. Though not a separatist, she repeatedly identified with her literary sisters, alluding in her poetry to a diverse range of female writers, from Sappho to more contemporary writers such as Aphra Behn and Katherine Philips. She also wrote numerous poems that extol female friendship with a consistency and fervor seldom equaled in literary history. Furthermore, she often did "reveal a history" by couching even her most personal poetic expressions in morally conscious and often satirical commentary.

Finch's reflections on gender issues can help us better understand the Restoration and eighteenth century, especially the role of women in society and the problems confronted by a creative artist writing amid a world of men. It was not biology, she maintained, but custom that relegated women to an inferior and subservient position; women, she wrote, were "Education's, more than Nature's fools" ("The Introduction" 6, line 52). Thus she wrote, often satirically, of the inequities in the social status of English women. She was, moreover, a devout Anglican whose religious sensibilities formed the bedrock of her more feminist views. She believed that intellectual and spiritual endowments were not gender-discriminatory, and her poetic dicta about the responsibility of women to fulfill their individual and collective potential attain something of a moral imperative. But the strongest reflection of Finch's feminism is to be found in her concept of herself as a woman writer and in her commitment to writing. In poem after poem she eloquently and persistently defends her right, and the right of any woman, to take up the pen and to enter the world of letters.

The standard edition of Finch's work is the 1903 University of Chicago collection by Myra Reynolds, *The Poems of Anne Countess of Winchilsea*, though it is woefully incomplete. Reynolds was unaware of the existence of an unpublished manuscript containing a large body of later Finch poems; consequently, fifty-three poems from this manuscript, which is deposited in the Margaret Clapp Library of Wellesley College, are not found in the Reynolds edition.[9] These poems are a part of this study, as are other unpublished letters and poems that exist only in manuscripts scattered throughout libraries and private collections in England and the United States. Some of these poems are included in appendix A.

The significance of the Wellesley manuscript is enormous. This extraordinarily rich collection of her poems, most of which were written in the last two decades of her life, is essential to any evaluation of her work. These poems help define her contribution as one of England's earliest female writers, assure her prominence as the foremost woman poet of her age, and provide a valuable perspective on the politics of the woman writer in the early eighteenth century.

ONE

Childhood Years

nne Finch, countess of Winchilsea, was not the meek, closeted woman she has too often been portrayed as. Characterizing her as the gentle lady who wrote of "This soft, endearing life," Edmund Gosse, Myra Reynolds, and J. Middleton Murry all offered romanticized portraits of her that literary historians and anthologizers have perpetuated.[1] But the reality is that Finch was a tough-minded, courageous, highly principled woman, and neither her life nor her poetry was immune to the "shocks that flesh is heir to."

Finch's childhood years alone contained events sufficient to dispel the myth of the retiring poet of the "soft, endearing life." She was born Anne Kingsmill at Sydmonton in the county of Hampshire at the dawn of the Restoration.[2] The month of her birth, April 1661, saw the English people celebrating the reestablishment of the Stuart line with the consecration and crowning of Charles II in a two-day ceremony at Westminster. That event symbolized the promise of dynastic glory for the Stuart monarchy—a monarchy that was to play a profound role in Finch's life.

Her parents, Sir William Kingsmill and Anne Haslewood, were both descended from old and respected families noted for Royalist sympathies, pride in family heritage, commitment to hospitality, and orthodox Church of England loyalties. Such landed gentry as the Kingsmills and Haslewoods, and the values they embodied, were to be an important stabilizing force in early Restoration society and a significant influence upon Finch.

Finch's mother was the daughter of Sir Anthony and Elizabeth Hasle-

8

wood of Maidwell, Northamptonshire. Thomas Fuller's *History of the Worthies of England*, first published in 1662, categorizes the name Haslewood as "very ancient in a worshipful family in Northamptonshire" (1: 286). On her father's side the Kingsmills traced their lineage through more than four centuries of royal service, and they figured prominently in the history of Hampshire County.[3] The origin of the family name itself denotes a relationship with the crown: an ancestor, credited with saving the life of King John during a hunting incident, was rewarded with the lease for the Royal Mill at Basingstoke and thereafter assumed the name Kingsmill. By the middle of the sixteenth century the Kingsmills had acquired some valuable estates, primarily from Henry VIII, and Sydmonton Court near Kingsclere became the family seat (PRO patent Henry VIII; Doubleday and Page 4: 252).

Sir William Kingsmill married Anne Haslewood in 1654 during the Interregnum.[4] Though his Sydmonton estate had been briefly confiscated during the Civil War, he had survived the war with his lands essentially intact and therefore was able to provide for his young family.[5] Two children were born before Anne: Bridget in June of 1657 and William in late 1659 or early 1660.[6]

Five months after Anne Kingsmill's birth her father died, leaving his widow with three children, the eldest of whom was barely four.[7] It is unfortunate that Anne never knew her father, for he was himself a poet of at least modest competence.[8] It is tempting to speculate on the literary relationship they might have had as father and daughter, particularly since he appears to have wanted his daughters to be well educated and independent—an unusually enlightened view for the times.

In his will Sir William left the family estates to his son, but he also set aside bequests of two thousand pounds and fifteen hundred pounds for Bridget and Anne respectively, to be paid with accrued interest when each married or turned twenty-one (PRO PCC 135, May 1661, Prob. 11/305).

A bequest of fifteen hundred pounds, while not lavish, was certainly sufficient to allow a single woman to provide modestly for her own needs, or to offer a respectable marriage dowry.[9] Though it was not uncommon for men from well-to-do families to provide dowries for their daughters, it was unusual for a provision to allow those daughters, once they came of age, to retain control of their own money if they chose to remain single. (Two and a half centuries later, financial independence was still an anomaly for women, as Virginia Woolf was to note in *A Room of One's Own*.)

Also significant in Sir William's will is his emphasis upon the education of his daughters. Here, too, he deviates from customary practice of the times, for while aristocratic fathers frequently provided in their wills for the maintenance of their daughters, they did not usually concern themselves with their education. Sir William, however, specified in his will that the rents and issues of the estates left to his son were to go to his wife during his son's minority so that she would be able to provide for the care and education of all the children, daughters as well as son.

A year following the death of Anne's father, her mother took a second husband, a younger man named Sir Thomas Ogle.[10] From that union came Dorothy, whose intimate friendship with her half-sister Anne would years later inspire such poems as "Some Reflections: In a Dialogue Between TERESA and ARDELIA" and "To my Sister Ogle."

In 1664, when Anne was only three years old, her mother died. Shortly before her death, in a will dated September 1, 1664, Anne Ogle made her husband the sole executor of her will, left him all her possessions, and assigned to him the management of the estates from her first husband that were held in trust until her son, William, came of age. She also gave Sir Thomas Ogle full responsibility for the education and rearing of her children.[11] There is no evidence, however, that any of the children ever lived with him from the death of his wife until his own death in 1671. Little, indeed, is known about him during those intervening years, other than that he was made a major in His Majesty's Holland Regiment in 1665 and apparently pursued a military career (Reynolds, introduction to *Poems* xx). Upon his death his daughter, Dorothy, became a ward of Sir Richard Campion.[12]

Few details are available about the childhood of Anne Kingsmill. Much about her education and rearing must be surmised from what is known about her as an adult and from what is known about the typical upbringing for girls from upper-class families at that time. Relevant legal documents, including wills and Chancery records that involved custody fights and litigation over inheritances, provide some information. Whatever else one might say about the extended family of young Anne Kingsmill, it is apparent that they were a contentious, litigious group.

Shortly after the death of Anne's mother, a suit was filed in the Court of Chancery on behalf of William Kingsmill, said to be four years old, and his young sisters, Bridget and Anne (who would have been seven and three, respectively), against the children's stepfather, Sir Thomas Ogle. The complaint was brought jointly by the children's maternal uncle, William Haslewood, who is referred to in the court records as the children's guardian, and three other men: Sir Robert Mason, Kingsmill Lucy, and William Langham. Langham was, like Haslewood, a relative of Anne Kingsmill Ogle, having married her sister Elizabeth; he was a learned doctor of medicine and frequent visitor to Maidwell. Lucy was related to Sir William Kingsmill through Constance Kingsmill, Lucy's paternal grandmother. And Mason, who is listed in the court records as residing in Kingsclere, where the Kingsmill family had holdings and where Anne Kingsmill's father was buried, was also most likely either a relative or friend of Sir William.[13]

The case was argued before the Chancery on ten different occasions, from Michaelmas term in November 1664 until its settlement in May 1665.[14] In the suit the plaintiffs claimed that Ogle had been unlawfully using profits and interests from the estates left in trust by Sir William Kingsmill during the minority of his son and daughters. His widow, they further claimed, had assigned the estates to four men—the same Haslewood, Mason, Lucy, and Langham—so that they could carry out the trust specified in Sir William's will for the education and maintenance of the children until they should come of age.

Ogle claimed in his defense that the profits from the Sydmonton estates and other lands were assigned by Dame Anne Kingsmill, Sir William's widow, prior to her remarriage, and that in her will she had reassigned all these interests to him and named him solely responsible for the education and governance of all her children.

The court entries suggest that the lengthy trial was nasty at times, and Ogle did not fare very well. On one occasion he was found to be in contempt of court for refusing to answer the charges of the plaintiffs and was placed under arrest (PRO PCC, Nov. 7, 1664). Ogle was also charged with forging a document in order to gain control over one of his wife's estates and with retaining "for his own use" income from estates supposed to be held in trust for the children and used only for their education and maintenance. He was also accused of forfeiting the lease for the manor of Sandford by his refusal to pay legitimate debts out of the estate income. Finally, in the most devastating charge of all, it was alleged that if any will was made by his wife assigning all interests in the children's estates to him (and clearly the will was made, for it still exists), then it was "unduly obtained and not long before her death."

When the case was finally settled, the court found in favor of the Kingsmill children, as represented by their guardian and the others. The nature of the trial and the apparent acrimony of some of the testimony would suggest that relations between the Haslewood/Kingsmill families and Ogle were most likely strained, if not completely severed, from that time on; there is, at least, no indication that Ogle played any further part in the life of the Kingsmill children.

At the time of Anne Ogle's death, William Haslewood, her brother and now the guardian of her three younger children, was only twenty-one years old. He and his wife, Elizabeth, were the parents of an infant son born the previous October. Their manor, Maidwell, lay in a remote area of Northamptonshire, about fifteen miles from the town of Northampton. That Haslewood is referred to in the 1664–65 Chancery case as the children's guardian does not mean, however, that all the children resided with him after their mother's death. Haslewood's designation as "guardian," at least in the case of his nieces, was apparently essentially for legal purposes; that is, he managed all the children's financial affairs, overseeing the estates and apportioning funds for their education and daily care, but only his nephew actually lived with him in Northamptonshire. Anne and Bridget spent the next seven years in London with their paternal grandmother.

Bridget, Lady Kingsmill, widow of Sir Henry Kingsmill, maintained a home at 55 Charing Cross on the north end of the road. An engraving made sometime between 1720 and 1723 and printed in the London County Council's *Survey of London* reveals a good-sized three-story building with a brick exterior and sloped roof (16: 115–17, plate 85). The house was situated, then, on the crossroad where, Samuel Johnson was later to claim, one could encounter "the full tide of human existence." And it was undoubtedly to this Charing Cross residence that the poet Anne Finch would trace back her earliest memories.

During the time that she was living with her grandmother, Charing Cross was closely identified in recent memory with the violent Civil War and its aftermath. The Kingsmill house overlooked the exact place, perhaps no more than a hundred feet away, where a number of convicted regicides were executed in October 1660. Charing Cross, rather than Tyburn, had been selected as the execution site for its grisly theatrical possibilities. Following the hangings the bodies were drawn and quartered there as a public spectacle. And in that same spot Charles II later erected the equestrian statue of his father that still stands today. That grandly impressive monument to Charles I, which had been kept hidden during the Commonwealth, further invested this great crossroad with emotionally charged symbolic significance.[15]

Having spent a good part of her childhood at Charing Cross, Anne Kingsmill must have been aware of what had taken place a few years earlier just beyond her front door. What effect the tales of these bloody incidents had on a young girl is a matter for conjecture. Because she grew up in such temporal and spacial proximity to these events, she could not but be touched by them. Her childhood associations with historic dates and localities may well have been related to the way her adult life was closely intertwined with the fate of the Stuart monarchy, as well as to the subtle political strains that run through some of her most poignant poetry.

More than a highly politicized sensibility, however, may possibly be traced to Finch's early years. Lady Kingsmill was, to judge from her handling of the family's financial affairs and her efforts to protect the rights of her own daughters, a strong-willed, shrewd, independent woman. After the death of her husband she assumed control of the large Kingsmill holdings and began working to strengthen the family's financial security. She set about to increase the maintenance for her eldest son, William, and to provide settlements for her other sons. Even after William reached maturity and came into his inheritance of the estates, Lady Kingsmill continued to govern the family's affairs and to usurp what were traditionally patriarchal responsibilities, at one point even becoming involved briefly in a dispute with him over some land.[16] She also, significantly, sold the family manor at Shoddesdon in order to give her daughters ample marriage portions, for they had been neglected in their father's will.[17] It is quite likely, in fact, that her concern with providing for her daughters taught a valuable lesson to her son William, Anne Finch's father, and led him to provide in his own will for the education and maintenance of his daughters.

Lastly, the adult Anne Finch may have owed much of her strength of character, her disdain of female reticence, and her scorn for unquestioned female subordination to this dominant matriarchal figure who played such a major role in her youth.

Once again, however, the course of Anne's childhood was to be determined in part by the Court of Chancery. During Michaelmas term, 1670–71, Lady Kingsmill filed suit on behalf of William, Bridget, and Anne Kingsmill. Charged in the suit are the children's maternal uncle, Sir William Haslewood, and the other three men who had successfully won their suit almost six years earlier against Sir Thomas Ogle: Sir Robert Mason, Kingsmill Lucy, and William Langham.

According to court transcripts Lady Kingsmill, now listed as guardian of the children, sued for "management of the infants' estates" in order to have money for their education and care. As noted, the custody was split, although Haslewood had control of the trust. Several of the court transcripts refer to the children's different living arrangements. Thus the court ruled that William should "continue where he is at present" with his uncle, "in the country," but that the girls, "as is proper," should remain with their grandmother (PRO PCC, Jan. 31, 1671).

The source of the dispute appears to have been a matter of who would manage the estates held in trust and disperse money from rents and interest for the education and maintenance of the children—and again, education is a crucial issue. In the decision continuing the split custody the court decreed that "a fitting allowance for maintenance and education" be granted both to Lady Kingsmill and to Haslewood from the estates held in trust, to cover their expenses in rearing their respective charges.

A year after the trial, in August of 1672, Lady Kingsmill died (Isham 104 n23, 144 n35). Apparently, however, Anne and Bridget Kingsmill, now eleven and fifteen years of age, were already at Maidwell with their uncle. That Lady Kingsmill's will makes no mention of her granddaughters suggests that they were already under Haslewood's care.[18] A reference in a neighbor's diary suggests that they were at Maidwell at least by April of that year (Isham 103, Apr. 20, 1672). Most likely the girls were sent to Northampton earlier in the year because of their grandmother's declining health. After her death they remained at Maidwell, reunited with their brother.

Something about life at Maidwell and the nature of the Haslewood household can be learned from the diary just mentioned. It was kept by a teenage boy, Thomas Isham, who lived about two miles from Maidwell at the Lamport Hall estate. At the urging of his father, Sir Justinian Isham, the fourteen-year-old Thomas began the exercise of keeping a diary in Latin, with daily entries that started in November 1671 and ran through September 1673. This diary, now made accessible by its translation into English and its recent publication in a well-annotated edition, is a unique source of information for the historian of Restoration country life.[19] The diary, moreover, is of particular value for the biographer of Anne Finch, for it is written from the viewpoint not of an adult but of a youngster—one who was a contemporary of hers and who lived for a while in close proximity to her.

By the time Thomas began keeping his diary, Haslewood had already been knighted by Charles II at Whitehall and would shortly, in 1672, be appointed justice of the peace (Isham 91, Mar. 5, 1672). Thus he had achieved some stature in Northamptonshire. Following the death of his first wife he was married again, to Cecil Ayshford, so that the household, which included children from both marriages and an assortment of relatives, was a large one (Isham, introduction 27–28).

The Ishams and the Haslewoods were on very friendly terms as neighbors, frequently exchanging visits and participating in excursions and social events for recreation and amusement. Sir William Haslewood kept a stable of fine horses, and both he and his nephew, William Kingsmill, appear to have been interested in a variety of sports and to have enjoyed with their neighbors such activities as hunting, fishing, hawking, lawn bowling, and horse racing.

Haslewood made occasional trips to London and, like the Ishams, had frequent visitors from London at the family manor, so that there was always much news of Parliament and the court, as well as the latest gossip. It is noteworthy that the young people in both households were not sequestered from adults, but appear to have heard fully and often participated in discussions with family and friends, particularly at the dinner table. Indeed, Thomas's diary abounds in anecdotes and remarks gleaned from conversations in which the children obviously were permitted, and expected, to join in with the adults. Moreover, if there was no segregation of children from adults at the manors of Lamport Hall and Maidwell, in most instances there also appears to have been little segregation of females from males in the intellectual and social life of these two manors.

After one of these dinners, to which Anne and Bridget Kingsmill were invited, along with a bachelor neighbor, Edward Saunders, squire of Brixworth, Thomas made the following entry in his diary. At the time, incidentally, Anne would have been eleven years old. The passage is worth quoting in full, for it gives the flavor of the evening and suggests the extent to which the young people shared in the activities and conversation with adult visitors:

> Mr. Saunders came to dinner with Mistress Bridget and her sister; we played bowls with him for a while. After dinner he told us that a large cave had recently been found in Whittlebury Forest by a man who was looking for the stone quarries and nearly fell into it. Some gentleman or other heard of this new sight and went down into the cave with drawn sword. He was forced to stoop for some distance as the passage was so narrow, but came to a very confined space, where he saw whitened walls and an artificially constructed floor paved with stones. He also found a huge skull, bigger than those of two or three men of the present day. He saw other gloomy recesses but dare not venture farther. They think that it was once the den of a gang of deer stealers. (33, July 29, 1672)

The children heard everything at these gatherings, from the latest news about military maneuvers in Holland to accounts of political squabbles in London, from bits of gossip about court intrigues and *liaisons dangereuses* to sensational tales about petty crimes and macabre murders. The talk was entertaining, but it was also informative. The topics of discussion and areas of interest that Thomas reports include international events, local domestic affairs, ecclesiastical issues, antiquarian lore, recent scientific achievements, historical narratives, current musical and dramatic productions, and literature.

From these conversations, in the friendly, informal setting of a family or neighbor's home, Anne Finch received some of her childhood education. Her poetry indicates that she was unusually learned for a woman of her day, even for a woman on the fringes of the aristocracy. She was familiar with the classics and with Greek and Roman mythology; she knew some French and Italian literature, had enough facility with French to do respectable translations, and probably had at least a speaking knowledge of Italian; she was well versed in the Bible and frequently alluded to biblical stories from both Old and New Testaments; she had some knowledge of history, particularly English history; and she was very well read in contemporary English literature—both poetry and drama. How, then, did this orphan girl acquire such knowledge? ——

Thomas Isham has documented fairly extensively, in his diary and in his letters, the progress of his own studies and, to a lesser extent, those of his two sisters, Mary and Vere. What he has to say may suggest something about the type of education that Anne Kingsmill received. Given the close proximity of the Haslewood and Isham manors and the frequency with which their households shared activities, it is both possible and likely that Anne and her sister took lessons with the Isham girls at Lamport Hall.

In response to his father's inquiry about his studies, the thirteen-year-old Thomas wrote to report the progress he was making with his tutor:

Wee goe on in our Studies according as you directed in our weekly task of translating Tullies epistles, & making our own. Wee have almost conquered half ye first Iliad, in wch although we proceed slowly yet wee doe it with delight and perfectness. Wee are constant in our parts both in ye Greek & Latin Grammars, & getting ye Greek Testament, besides our daily repetitions in ye Colloquies, Tullies Epistles, & Aesops Fables: which books we have read so through & through, that they begin not to be so pleasant to us as they have bin, & therefore we intreat you will pleas to send us Tullies longer epistles & Ad Atticum, & some Histories of those times concerning wch we have already read Nepos & Justin; as Curtius de rebus gestis Alexandri & Valerius maximus & Florus of ye Latin story, or which other you pleas either for our Studyes or recreations. And since you command me to let you know what we desier to have from thence, Pray S^r pleas to send us some good books wch may be helpful to us for making verses. (Isham 15, June 4, 1670)

Elsewhere in letters between father and son and in diary entries there are references to training in mathematics, music, and dancing. Thomas also displays a keen interest in science, an interest undoubtedly stimulated by his father's own learning, for Sir Justinian was a member of the Royal Society, had been a student of Francis Bacon, and was on friendly terms with Sir Thomas Browne and Robert Boyle (Isham, introduction 34–35). Thus Thomas mentions in his diary inventions such as the stentorophonic trumpet for amplifying the voice (75, Dec. 28, 1671), the reflecting telescope (79, Jan. 29, 1672), a fire engine (229, Aug. 29, 1673), and the long, bowed, single-stringed musical instrument that Pepys "was mightly pleased with"—the marine trumpet (145, Aug. 27, 1672).[20] There are also a couple of references to his sisters' keeping of bees—a hobby that must have had some scientific basis, since Thomas's tutor, Richard Richardson, had translated into Latin Charles Butler's scholarly book on bees (Isham, introduction 16; 147, Aug. 29, 1672).

Sir Justinian Isham was atypical of the seventeenth-century male head of the household in that he took great care with the education of his daughters. Roger Thompson, in his study of education in Stuart England, examines the possibilities for young women from well-to-do classes and notes that apart from training by a parent or a tutor within the home, there was the option of sending a girl to a boarding school. Thompson found that such boarding schools increased greatly in number in the seventeenth century, but these were elementary schools, and Thompson concludes that girls, even from aristocratic families, were pretty much excluded from secondary education (*Women* 189, 194). Yet the Isham girls had an education clearly beyond an elementary level. Not only did they participate fully in family conversations about a variety of sophisticated topics, but they also received a thorough training in subjects not usually included in the curriculum for young girls of that time—if, indeed, young girls were fortunate enough to receive any education at all. Mary Isham, for example, became so proficient in Latin that she earned the praise of Sir James Langham, himself an accomplished Latinist (Isham 145, Aug. 26, 1672). And Vere Isham's skill in mathematics and algebra was outstanding enough to be noted on her tombstone following her death at the age of eighteen.[21]

Anne Kingsmill's education was probably quite similar to that of the Isham girls. Given the close friendship of Sir Justinian Isham and Sir William Haslewood, it is reasonable to suppose that their views on educating women were compatible. Thomas Isham reports that Haslewood did send his twelve-year-old nephew to Harborough School to pursue his education, an indication that he took seriously his charge to educate his sister's children (203, Apr. 16, 1673). One could expect, then, that Anne and her sister received a somewhat extensive education. There is evidence, moreover, of a family interest in the arts, or at least ancestral interest in accumulating books and artistic furnishings.[22]

Throughout her teenage years, then, after a childhood punctuated by deaths and wrangles in Chancery, Anne remained at Maidwell, enjoying the benefits of association with neighbors and relatives who were among the more sophisticated and learned members of the country gentry.[23] For information about her early adulthood, however, we must turn from a legal court to a royal one.

TWO

Court and Courtship

The year 1682 was one of great change in the life of Anne Kingsmill Finch. January saw the death of her uncle and guardian, Sir William Haslewood (Isham, introduction 28). That spring, following her twenty-first birthday, she abandoned country life in Northamptonshire to take up residence at St. James's Palace as a maid of honor to Mary of Modena. There she was immersed in an environment rich in lively talk and sophisticated wit and came into contact with some of the greatest literary figures of the age. There, too, she developed a devotion to the future queen of England and a loyalty to the Stuart monarchy that would affect the future course of her life. And, finally, there she met Heneage Finch, the man who would be her husband, companion, and lover for the remainder of her life.

Anne Kingsmill, orphaned at an early age and reared in at least three different households, had matured into a bright, witty, and learned young woman—all traits evident even in her earliest poetry. She was also very beautiful. The miniature portrait of her, painted in her late twenties by Laurence Crosse and now displayed in the National Portrait Gallery in London, reveals a slim, dark-haired woman with a lovely oval face, penetrating eyes, and an expression that suggests both sensitivity and strength.

Kingsmill began her service to Princess Mary of Modena around the time the future queen first arrived in London. When James, duke of York, had married the Italian princess in 1673, Mary Beatrice was barely fifteen years old. Her Roman Catholic faith, and James's subsequent conversion to Catholicism, led to a heightened fear of popery among an already nervous English people, culminating in such crises as the Popish Plot.[1] Nine years, therefore, passed before James, brother of Charles II and heir presumptive to the throne, was able to bring his wife to England, on May 27, 1682, and set up court at the Palace of St. James (Luttrell 1: 189; Ashley, *James II* 96–99, 144). Pregnant, lonely, and increasingly aware of her husband's frequent infidelities, this second wife of the duke of York was the princess to whom Kingsmill became an affectionate attendant.

Mary was only three years Kingsmill's senior. More than their shared youth, however, would account for Kingsmill's devoted attachment to the future queen consort. Mary, as her biographer, Carola Oman, records, had ample artistic and intellectual accomplishments: she was musical, well read, and fluent in four tongues (vi). Though noted for her piety, she could also be fun-loving; there are numerous anecdotes of her at play—pelting the duke of York with snowballs, delighting in theatrical productions and festive balls, and yielding to persuasion that she try her hand at gambling (Oman 45, 47, 70). This mixture of piety and playfulness is also characteristic of Anne Kingsmill Finch, even in her later years. Moreover, the satirical strain in Finch that expressed itself in a number of poems was apparently evident in Mary's temperament as well. Bishop Burnet, whose political inclinations led to harsh criticism of this Stuart queen, remarks in his *History of My Own Times* that occasionally her "satirical temper broke out too much, which was imputed to youth."[2]

Gregario Leti, official historian and biographer of Charles II, includes Kingsmill among Mary's six English maids of honor in the year 1683. Most likely these women had been in attendance since James brought his wife to England and set up court the previous year, especially if we take into account that she was expecting a child in August. Agnes Strickland, quoting Leti's original document in her *Lives of the Queens of England*, lists as maids of honor Frances Walsingham, Catharine Fraser, Anne Killigrew, Anne Kingsmill, Catharine Walters, and Catharine Sedley (9: 119). Most notable of the other five is Anne Killigrew, the talented poet and painter whose death from smallpox was mourned by John Dryden in his "Ode to Mistress Anne Killigrew." Though the extent of the friendship of these two young women is unknown, Strickland writes that both were "much beloved" by Mary and "were ladies of the most irreproachable virtue, members of the Church of England, and alike distinguished for moral worth and literary attainments" (9: 147).

Through her position in the royal household, Kingsmill was thrust into the midst of an exciting environment that included many of the most prominent literary figures of the day. Both Charles II and James II surrounded themselves with a coterie of spirited writers who earned for themselves the epithet "the Court Wits." Their most famous (and infamous) member, John Wilmot, earl of Rochester, set the tone for the group. He died just before Kingsmill joined the court, but the lively conversation of the other wits, men such as Sir George Etherege, Sir Charles Sedley, and William Wycherley, must have provided a most stimulating intellectual milieu for the young maid of honor. Furthermore, though hard evidence is lacking, it is highly probable that Kingsmill knew the foremost writer of the age, John Dryden, to whom she would later pay poetic tribute.[3] Dryden was, after all, included in the relatively small court circle, and he was at least casually acquainted with the other literary maid of honor, Anne Killigrew. Furthermore, Kingsmill had a family connection with Dryden, since her first cousin, the daughter of Sir Richard Kingsmill, had married Dryden's brother-in-law, Sir Robert Howard.

The court provided Kingsmill with an environment that must have sharpened, if not awakened, her artistic and intellectual sensibilities. Despite its reputation for denigrating women and flaunting sexual promiscuity, the courts of Charles II and James II were a valuable source for the furtherance of her education. The paradoxical manner in which the Restoration Court Wits helped to liberate women is succinctly expressed by Katharine Rogers in *Feminism in Eighteenth-Century England*: "The court wits surrounding Charles II, already disposed to ridicule the morality of female subordination because it was associated with middle-class puritanism, extended to women the right to plain-speaking and pleasure-seeking they claimed for themselves. Thus, without systematic concern for the rights of women, aristocratic literature challenged traditional restrictions upon their freedom and supported women in evading them" (54).

More than thirty years later Finch wrote of those court days in one of the few autobiographical references in all of her poetry. In "On the

Death of the Queen," an elegy following Mary's death in 1718 (see
app. A), Finch describes herself as one who

> . . . in Her Domestick train hadst stood
> And seen her great and found her warmly good
> Duely maintaining her exalted place
> Yet condescending with attractive grace
> Recall'd be days when ebon locks o'erspread
> My youthfull neck my cheeks a bashfull red
> When early joys my glowing bosom warm'd
> When trifles pleas'd & every pleasure charm'd
> Then eager from the rural seat I came
> Of long traced Ancestors of worthy name
> To seek the Court. . . .
>
> (W ms. 69)

There are a couple of points of biographical interest in this poem.
First, it includes Finch's brief physical description of herself as a young
girl, cheerful and carefree, with long black hair flowing about her shoul-
ders. Then there is the reference to "long traced Ancestors of worthy
name," which suggests a pride in her forebears. Having lost both parents at such an early age, she could not have had any real memory of
them. Therefore, the identification with an ancestral line in which she
could take pride was probably important in shaping her self-esteem and
independent character.

Her affection for Mary and the sense of loss that she expresses in
this poem differentiate it from the highly stylized, less personal elegy
she wrote in 1701 for James II. Unlike "Upon the Death of King James
the Second," the Queen Mary poem has an intimate poignancy that
underlies its tone of quiet, formal dignity. Moreover, "On the Death of
the Queen" offers a rare picture of Kingsmill at court:

> Bles't my attention was when drawing near
> (My places claim) her crouded audience chair
> I heard her by admiring States addrest
> With embasies in different tongues exprest
> To all that Europe sent she gave replies
> In their own speech most eloquent & wise.

Here, then, is the mature Anne Finch, reminiscing about the queen she idolized in her youth and remained loyal to throughout her lifetime. The iconographic representation in these verses of the young maid of honor, positioned near her mistress as she holds court and converses learnedly in foreign languages with heads of state, is highly suggestive. And as if to reinforce the symbolic bond between the two women and the sense of a female unity, Finch follows these lines by a passage linking the Italian Mary of Modena with illustrious Roman women of the past. Portia, she writes, forced Brutus "to applaud her worth," and Livia so influenced Augustus that his accomplishments in world dominion were brought about only "thro' a woman's wit."

Another notable maid of honor from Finch's court days was Catharine Sedley, daughter of Sir Charles Sedley. She was James's mistress and, according to Strickland, "an object of great uneasiness to her royal highness, on account of her illicit tie with the duke" (9: 119). One can well imagine that Catharine Sedley was the source of some anxiety in the court and that her presence might have been disturbing to Kingsmill and other attendants who were devoted to Mary. Sedley bore James two children prior to his ascension to the throne and continued to be his mistress even after he became king and created her countess of Dorchester (Ashley, *James II* 191–92).

Among the other women Strickland records as part of Mary's retinue was Penelope Obrien, countess of Peterborough, who was noted for her fluency in French and who had been with Mary ever since her marriage to James. Lady Susan Bellasyse, one of the ladies of the bedchamber, had been wooed by James following the death of his first wife, but he had to abandon his suit when Charles II refused to consent to the marriage.[4] Strickland notes that James "had vindicated her character from all aspersion, by making her lady of the bedchamber to his young consort, Mary Beatrice d'Este, who never expressed the slightest jealousy of her" (9: 119). Also a lady of the bedchamber was the countess of Roscommon, wife of the poet Wentworth Dillon, earl of Roscommon—the "Noble Piso" whom Finch was to praise years later in her satiric poem "Ardelia's Answer to Ephelia" as a talented poet and man of true virtue (42–43, lines 133–62). The remaining Englishwomen in Mary's court were Lady Harrison, who held the position of mother of the maids; Lady Jones, who was chamber-keeper; and the bedchamber women Mrs. Margaret Dawson, Lady Wentworth, Lady Boucher, and Lady Turner.

There were also four Italian women in the household: Madame Molza, Pelegrina Turinie, Madame de Montecuculi, and Madame de Montecuculi's daughter (Strickland 9: 119). The inclusion of these Italian women at St. James's Palace, and the fact that Mary was also Italian, may explain Finch's attraction to the Italian language. There is no evidence that she read the language, but she was interested in Italian verse and most likely had some facility in conversational Italian. In the prose preface she affixed to the privately circulated folio manuscripts of her poems but withheld from publication during her lifetime, she writes of her early rendering of the first act of Tasso's *Aminta* into English verse "from the verbal translation that I procured out of the Italian" (10).

Finch's earliest known poems date from this period.[5] As stimulating as this court environment may have been, however, it would be misleading to imply that it was anything other than hostile toward women who made any claim to literary talent. In the preface the following poignant statement appears: "itt is still a great satisfaction to me, that I was not so far abandon'd by my prudence, as out of a mistaken vanity, to lett any attempts of mine in Poetry, shew themselves whilst I liv'd in such a publick place as the Court, where every one wou'd have made their remarks upon a Versifying Maid of Honour; and far the greater number with prejudice, if not contempt" (7–8). Certainly the treatment of her court companion Anne Killigrew supports the accuracy of this judgment. The pain of thwarted ambition, coupled with the shame of being wrongly accused of plagiarism, sears through the lines of Killigrew's very personal poem "Upon the Saying that my Verses Were Made by Another." Encouraged at first by the good words of a close confidant or two ("I writ, and the judicious praised my pen: / Could any doubt ensuing glory then"), Killigrew bitterly records the results of her ensuing bid for recognition:

> Emboldened thus, to fame I did commit
> (By some few hands) my most unlucky wit.
> But ah, the sad effects that from it came!
> What ought t'have brought me honour, brought me shame!
> (Bernikow 79)

For Kingsmill, however, court life proved happy, even without any acknowledgment of her writing, for it was at St. James's Palace that she met Heneage Finch. At that time he, like Kingsmill, was attached to the court, serving as a gentleman of the bedchamber to James. And, also like her, he had strong Tory principles, with staunch allegiance to the Church of England and the monarchy—principles that would shortly cause both of them great distress and traumatic upheaval.

Born on January 3, 1657, Heneage Finch was the second son of the second earl of Winchilsea, also named Heneage. His mother, Lady Mary Seymour, was herself the second daughter of William, second duke of Somerset, and she was the earl's second wife (F-H ms. 282, 16; *DNB*; HMC, *Finch* 1: xxx). The repeated "second" designation in Heneage Finch's familial position is indicative of his limited expectations with regard to inheriting either land or title. Like Kingsmill's, his ancestry on both sides of the family contained many notable persons, and therefore many privileges of class were available for him. Moreover, as the younger son of an earl, he would have been regarded for all purposes as a noble, rather than a commoner.

Mary Seymour, his mother, was descended from a daughter of Henry VII. She married the earl in 1653 following the death of his first wife, who was childless, and bore him eleven children before her own death when Heneage was about fifteen (I'Anson 56; *DNB* "Finch").

The Finches traced their lineage back to the Norman Conquest. Bryan I'Anson's *History of the Finch Family*, which contains the most complete information, notes that the family was descended from the famous house of Herbert, from which the earls of Pembroke are also descended. The surname Finch was adopted in the thirteenth century by Herbert Fitz-Herbert after he became, through marriage, lord of the manor of Finch in Kent (9–11, 19–20). It was only in the seventeenth century that the Finches acquired the Winchilsea title, and the circumstances are worth noting, for they suggest that the Finch family, like the Kingsmills, had a tradition of strong matriarchal figures.

Sir Moyle Finch, who owned the thousand-acre estate of Eastwell in Kent, had served in the House of Commons as a member for Weymouth and later for Wincheslea, was knighted by Queen Elizabeth, and was created a baronet by James I in 1611.[6] Prior to his death in 1614, it had been rumored that he would be elevated to the peerage.[7]

His widow, Elizabeth, had been the only heir of Sir Thomas Heneage, vice-chamberlain of Queen Elizabeth and chancellor of the duchy of Lancaster, and she had inherited some very valuable estates from her father. Following her husband's death, she spent years negotiating and bargaining her lands to obtain a peerage. Her efforts were finally successful. In 1623 she was made viscountess of Maidstone, and five years later Charles I created her countess of Winchilsea, with both titles remaindered to her male heirs. Thus she achieved the extraordinary distinction of being only the second woman in all of English history to be elevated to a countess in her own right (T. Fuller 1: 526).

Upon the death of the countess in 1633, her second son, Sir Thomas, became first earl of Winchilsea, and her grandson Heneage succeeded to the title of Viscount Maidstone. With the death of the first earl in 1639, the viscount succeeded to his father's title. The unusual circumstances in which the peerage was created are responsible for frequent confusion about whether the first countess's son should be counted the first or the second earl of Winchilsea. Other confusion results from the preponderance of Heneage Finches in the seventeenth century.

Heneage Finch, second earl of Winchilsea and the father of Anne Finch's husband, distinguished himself during the Civil War as a Royalist. For his loyalty he was rewarded at the onset of the Restoration with the additional title of Lord Fitz-Herbert of Eastwell—an acknowledgment of his descent from the house of Herbert (I'Anson 88–89). He was also appointed lord lieutenant of Kent and then ambassador to Turkey, where he remained for eight years during his son Heneage's early years (HMC, *Finch* 1: xxx).

Anne Finch's future husband remained at Eastwell under the care of his grandmother, the duchess of Somerset, until he was sent to school at Chelsea in Middlesex.[8] His father, however, continued his interest in the education of the sons he had left in England, even providing their tutor, Mr. Dodson, with a rent-free vicarage (HMC, *Finch* 1: 302). He also encouraged his sons in antiquarian studies, frequently sending home items of historical interest that he picked up in Turkey (HMC, *Finch* 1: xxxv–xxxvi). The interest in history was to remain with young Heneage Finch throughout his life, and in later years he became a founding member of the Antiquarian Society.

In 1672 Heneage Finch's older brother, William, Viscount Maidstone, was killed at the battle of Sole-bay, leaving Heneage the eldest surviving son of the earl.[9] Under the terms of the Winchilsea title, however, it was Viscount Maidstone's son, Charles, who was next in line to ascend to the peerage.

Heneage Finch was trained as a courtier and soldier and early appeared destined for a public career. At the age of twenty-one he was already serving as a colonel in the foot militia in Kent and had received, at his father's request, an appointment from King Charles II as a deputy lieutenant for Kent, where his father was lord lieutenant.[10] He remained in Kent for the next few years and in 1680 was registered as a freeman from the city of Canterbury (Cowper 316). His military career continued to advance, and in 1682 he was appointed captain of the Coldstream Guards (Henning 2: 324).

Kingsmill probably first met Heneage Finch in 1683 when he was appointed groom of the bedchamber to the duke of York. That same year he was also appointed a justice of the peace for Kent and earned distinction at court for his accomplishments.[11] When the duke and duchess of York visited Oxford that May, the trip concluded with the bestowing of the honorary degree of doctor of civil laws on several men, including Heneage Finch.[12] Since the duke and duchess were accompanied by their retinues on that visit, Kingsmill most likely was present at the ceremony that honored the promising young man.

Kingsmill was apparently at first reluctant to yield to her suitor's entreaties. Several of her early songs from that period express a strong disdain of love and its tendency to trap the unwary female and rob her of her freedom. Most telling are some lines from "A Letter to Dafnis April: 20 1685," a poem discussed in more depth in the following chapter. In these love lyrics, written almost a year after her marriage, she describes Heneage as the man "whose constant passion found the art / To win a stubborn, and ungratefull heart" (20).

What happiness Kingsmill had during this period of courtship, as she grew to love Heneage Finch, was marred by another traumatic event in her life. On November 13, 1683, her only brother, William, killed his cousin William Haslewood in a duel and was arrested on charges of manslaughter. The boys, it should be remembered, had been raised together at Maidwell by Kingsmill's uncle, who also took in the eleven-year-old Anne and her sister shortly before their grandmother's death.

Hence the Kingsmill and Haslewood children had grown up together in the same household, more like siblings than cousins.

The death and the circumstances surrounding it must have torn the family apart and caused extreme anguish to Kingsmill. Her brother, who had been knighted two years earlier when he reached his majority, applied to the king for a pardon on the grounds that "this unhappy act did not proceed from any malice aforethought but was occasioned by the great provocations and sword of Mr. Haslewood drawn on the petitioner." However, the dead cousin's two sisters, Elizabeth and Penelope Haslewood, also filed a petition to the king, claiming that their brother was "inhumanely slain" and requesting that Sir William Kingsmill be brought to trial.[13]

The attorney general ruled on January 29, 1683, that the trial should proceed and that any plea for a pardon should be considered only after all the evidence was brought forward and a verdict reached. Sir William was subsequently found guilty of the manslaughter charge, but on June 14 of that year, King Charles II granted him a full pardon.[14]

Amid the torment of this family tragedy, Kingsmill was able to choose to love and to know joy. As the trial of her brother drew to a close, she consented to become the bride of Heneage Finch, and on May 15, 1684, they were married in the Chapel Royal of St. James's Palace.

The marriage license, taken out the previous day, reads as follows:

14 May, 1684. Appeared personally Collonell Heneage Finch of Eastwell in ye County of Kent, Batchelor, aged ab. 27 years, and alleadged that he intends to marry with Madam Anne Kingsmill of ye Parish of St. Martins in ye fields in ye county of Midd'l a spinster aged ab. 18 years at her own disposal he not knowing any lawful let or impediment to hinder ye said intended marriage of ye truth of which he made oath and prayed a Lycence for them to be married in the Chapple of St. James in ye parish of St. Martin in ye ffields after.[15]

After her marriage Anne Finch resigned her position as maid of honor, though her husband continued to hold his post as gentleman of the bedchamber (F-H ms. 282, 47; Hearne 7: 155).

Upon the death of Charles II the following February, the duke of

York became King James II. An anecdote about the April 23 coronation of the new king and queen offers another indication of the affection that existed between Anne Finch and her royal mistress. During the preparations a list was drawn up of those gentlemen who would bear the canopies over the heads of King James II and Queen Mary as they processed from Westminster Hall to Westminster Abbey. Heneage Finch, whom James had nominated to stand for his new Parliament from Hythe, was to assist the king in the procession, but Mary, seeing that she knew none of the sixteen men who were afforded the honor of carrying her canopy, requested that she be allowed to make two choices of her own. The request was granted, and Anne Finch's husband, dressed in scarlet breeches with crimson satin waistcoat and velvet cap and shoes, carried the queen's canopy—a fortunate substitution for him, since the frame of the king's canopy broke during the return from the abbey.[16]

The Finches, who now lived in Westminster Palace, continued to be closely connected with the court. Heneage Finch served one year as a member of Parliament from the Cinque Port of Hythe, and he was also promoted in 1687 to the rank of lieutenant-colonel.[17]

From all indications Anne and Heneage Finch, who remained childless, sustained during the entire thirty-six years of their married life an intimate, happy relationship. Many of her poems from this period deal with love and reflect the delight she found in married life. Some, such as the verse epistles to her husband, are personal, while others, including some of the songs, are of a more general nature. Particularly beautiful is the song "Love, thou art best of Human Joys," written within the early months of their marriage:

> Love, thou art best of Human Joys,
>   Our chiefest Happiness below;
> All other Pleasures are but Toys,
> Musick without Thee is but Noise,
>   And Beauty but an empty Show.
>
> Heav'n, who knew best what Man wou'd move,
>   And raise his Thoughts above the Brute;
> Said, Let him Be, and let him Love;

That must alone his Soul improve,
Howe'er Philosophers dispute.
(131)

But not all of Finch's poems present such a blissful picture of love. The topic of love is one that she returned to again and again in her writing, from her early twenties, when she wrote poems such as this song, to the last years of her life. Her poems on love and marriage offered her an opportunity for introspection about her own relationship with her husband, a relationship that she saw as atypical for the times. But even more important, perhaps, these poems on love and marriage and the relevant themes that they raised provided her with a means of reflecting on crucial gender issues and, in particular, on the role of women in Restoration and early eighteenth-century society.

THREE

"*Hymen's* Endearments and Its Ties": Poems on Love and Marriage

inch wrote of love and marriage in a number of poems that are sometimes tender and personal, sometimes satirical and coldly objective. Some of her intimate love poems to her husband, while expressive of her own marital delights, also contain ironic social commentary. Even her most personal poems often reveal a dynamic tension created by her awareness of, and rebellion against, a literary and social world that perpetuated the subservience of women.

The view of marriage and the role of women that prevailed in most literature of the early eighteenth century was primarily of two types. On the one hand there was the disdain for women evidenced in the verse and plays of the Restoration Court Wits and in the impulse toward antifeminist satire that extended well into the middle of the eighteenth century. The preponderance of these misogynistic views in the literature of that time has been well documented by such scholars as Katharine Rogers, Roger Thompson, and Felicity Nussbaum.[1] At the other extreme, but just as debilitating, was the sentimental concept of women, a concept that prevailed as the female image Virginia Woolf later termed "the angel in the house."[2] One source for part of this image was the large number of seventeenth-century miscellanies containing poetry in the Petrarchan convention. The traditional deification of women in these Petrarchan conceits, moreover, was analogous to the portrayal of women in the literature of sensibility that developed toward the end of the seventeenth and beginning of the eighteenth century. This sentimental image is expressed repeatedly in that widely popular periodical the *Spectator*. In 1711, just two years before the publication of the only volume of Finch's poetry to appear during her lifetime, Richard Steele wrote that "a right Woman should have gentle Softness, tender Fear, and all those parts of Life, which distinguish her from the other Sex, with some Subordination to it, but such an Inferiority that makes her still more lovely" (no. 144, Aug. 15, 1711). And a year later Steele wrote that all a woman "has to do in this World, is contained within the Duties of a Daughter, a Sister, a Wife, and a Mother" (no. 342, Apr. 2, 1712).

Despite what might be termed antifeminist elements in much of the contemporary literature, some women authors of the day expressed strongly feminist views about the situation of women in general, especially with regard to marriage. Aphra Behn, Mary, Lady Chudleigh, and Margaret Cavendish, duchess of Newcastle, for example, wrote disparagingly of marriage and the subordinate position of women in English society. Others, such as Mary Davys in her play *The Northern Heiress, or the Humours of York*, and Mary Astell in her book *Some Reflections upon Marriage*, advocated celibacy for women as a preferable alternative to the all-too-common tyranny of marriage.[3] None of these writers, however, could present a more harshly satirical and negative view of the role of women in marriage than could, on occasion, Anne Finch.

In a poem entitled "The Introduction," which she chose to withhold from publication but which was affixed to the manuscripts she circulated privately among friends, Finch bitterly describes the typical male concept of a woman's role:

> They tell us, we mistake our sex and way;
> Good breeding, fassion, dancing, dressing, play
> Are the accomplishments we shou'd desire;
> To write, or read, or think, or to enquire
> Wou'd cloud our beauty, and exaust our time,
> And interrupt the Conquests of our prime;

> Whilst the dull mannage, of a servile house
> Is held by some, our outmost art, and use.
>
> (5, lines 13–20)

Mindful of the danger of being relegated to "the dull mannage, of a servile house," Finch nevertheless married, and the relationship that she enjoyed with her husband informs much of her love poetry. Thus there is often a startling discrepancy between the passion and playful domesticity of her private love poems and the stark portrayal of contemporary marriages and the plight of women found in her more public poems. A number of critics have argued recently and convincingly that the distinctions between private and public literature are less sharply delineated than has traditionally been assumed.[4] In Finch's poetry the two voices, the private and the public, are sometimes combined within a single poem, so that an ironic contrast is created. "To Mr. F. Now Earl of W.," a poem that later in this chapter will be discussed more fully, provides just such an example. In it she writes that her love verses must be spoken in private, where her husband "alone might hear," because "the World do's so despise / *Hymen's* Endearments and its Ties" (20).

As noted in the preceding chapter, Finch's earliest poems date from the period when she was attached to the court. Charles II, notorious for his licentiousness, cultivated a coterie of ribald Court Wits whose love lyrics, unlike those of their Cavalier predecessors, were lusty and often outrageously obscene. And their attitude toward love and "*Hymen's* Endearments" was probably more cynical, negative, and openly hostile than that of any other group of court figures in English history, at least if the literature provides any accurate reflection of their thinking.

Underlying many love lyrics of the Court Wits is a disdain for women and a conviction that inconstancy is the norm for both sexes. Sir George Etherege, in his song "Ye happy Swains," gives advice to young men who have not yet been trapped by love's chain; in a series of metaphors of destruction, he warns young lads to "Fly the fair sex," for love can only bring pain:

> How faithless is the Lover's joy!
> How constant is their Care!

> The Kind with Falsehood do destroy,
> The Cruel with Despair.
>
> (Pinto, *Restoration* 33)

And Rochester, the most harshly sardonic of the Court Wits, begins one of his best-known songs with this quatrain:

> Love a woman? You're an ass!
> 'Tis a most insipid passion
> To choose out for your happiness
> The silliest part of God's creation.
>
> (Rochester 51)

The poem is replete with crude images that not only demean women but also degrade love as nothing but raw lust. Furthermore, Rochester's antifeminism is underscored by a homosexual suggestion in the poem's conclusion: when he cannot overcome a base sexual urge, he continues, then he makes use of "a sweet, soft page" who "Does the trick worth forty wenches."

If many Court Wits depicted love and courtship in negative terms, their views regarding marriage disturbed Finch even more. Almost without exception Restoration comedies savagely attack marriage.[5] The songs and love lyrics from these plays portray marriage as a restrictive social institution marked by mutual deceit, infidelity, and bitter disillusionment. It was not, then, to Etherege, Wycherley, or even much of Dryden that Finch could turn for a love poetry compatible with her own views.

Poems by writers associated with the Stuart courts condemn "*Hymen's* Endearments and its Ties" in tones that range from a lighthearted masculine jauntiness to a sardonic grimness. "No, hang me if I ever marry," the rake declares in Charles Cotton's "Was ever man of Nature's framing" (Bullen 13), and the young man in Sir Charles Sedley's "When first I made Love to my Cloris" declares that he'd "rather Dig Stones in a Quarry" than marry (Stead 68–69). Dryden's well-known "Why should a foolish Marriage Vow," on the other hand, argues in almost philosophical solemnity for mutual adultery.

In addition, women in these marriage poems are often not only depersonalized but also brutally dehumanized. Katharine Rogers, commenting on the reaction against Puritanism in the last part of the seventeenth century, finds evidence in the literature of that time of "a rivalry between the sexes which was overtly playful but frequently descended into sadism" (*Troublesome Helpmate* 160). In the Cotton poem just mentioned, every woman, the poet declares, is but the hulk of a ship in whom he will "tarry" only long enough to "trim and launch her." And in "Against Marriage," attributed to Rochester, we encounter what has to be the ultimate misogamist poem. After cataloging all the things that the poet insists marriage destroys (business, pleasure, wit, virtue, wealth, youth, and sleep), he insists that "a cunt has no sense of conscience or law." But if you must "have flesh," he continues, then find "a generous wench," for though venereal diseases are a danger, they "will admit of a cure, / But the hell-fire of marriage none can endure" (Rochester 159).

Dorothy Mermin, in her perceptive essay "Women Becoming Poets: Katherine Philips, Aphra Behn, Anne Finch," credits the sexual context of the Restoration with allowing women to speak as erotic subjects. Marilyn L. Williamson similarly concludes that the spectrum of late seventeenth- and early eighteenth-century ideology had a liberating effect upon women's attitudes about their own sexuality and helped make it possible for women writers to develop their own discourses of sexuality.[6] Yet despite the salutary effect that late seventeenth-century sexual concepts may have had upon women's writings, there is no conclusive agreement that the status of women had improved any by the end of the century.[7] Historian Christopher Hill observes that though the Court Wits and some radical religious sects of the late seventeenth century advocated less restrictive sexual codes, their discourses generally ignored the needs of women (*World Turned Upside Down* 257). And Harold Weber's study of Restoration rake and libertine attitudes similarly concludes that "such attitudes, with their emphasis on the arbitrary nature of social restrictions and the naturalness of the passions that people shared with beasts, might seem as applicable to women as men. Yet the men who fashioned such doctrines reveal a hostility and ambivalence towards women that appears little different from the misogyny of society at large" (146–47).

This was the literary and social environment in which Finch began to write. All of the poets and dramatists cited here were closely associated with the courts of Charles II and James II, and it is likely that she knew a number of them personally; it is certain that she was well acquainted with their writing, for references to these authors are scattered throughout her poetry.[8] Their views helped shape the backdrop of contemporary social attitudes against which she delineated her own reflections on love. Sometimes her poetry reflects the world of the Stuart courts, especially with regard to political and religious ideologies, but often, particularly in those poems that treat of love and marriage, she is reacting against that world. Small wonder, then, that while at court she kept secret her preoccupation with writing.

Finch's attitude toward her social and literary environment is evident in her poem "The Prodigy." Written in heroic couplets, the poem offers a satirical look at Restoration attitudes toward love. As part of the lengthy subtitle indicates, its topic is "the admiration that many expressed at a Gentleman's being in love, and their endeavours to dissuade him from it." Drawing on the original meaning of the word "prodigy" as an extraordinary thing from which omens are drawn, Finch opens her poem with a whimsical petition. "Protect the State, and let Old England thrive," she pleads, enumerating those things that might threaten it, and in the preceding few decades already had done so: the death of crowned heads (Charles I, England's last monarch to rule by "divine right," was beheaded in 1649); destruction from wind and flame (the Great Fire of 1666 had destroyed about four-fifths of London); destruction of naval fleets (the Anglo-Dutch Wars, which lasted until 1667, had threatened English maritime forces); and the Scots (keep "the Scotchmen tame," she adds as a last, humorous request, alluding to the long-standing friction between the two countries, which was particularly strong during the period of the 1688 Revolution).[9] All these terrible things that might befall the empire could be imminent, she continues, because England has been exposed to a "prodigy": "a man in love!" Not only a man in love, but a man who writes about his love in amorous verses, an act so astonishing that other men view him with pity or with scorn, while

> Maids so long unus'd to be ador'd
> Think it portends the pestilence or sword.
> (143, lines 11–12)

In decrying contemporary attitudes toward love, Finch does not reserve her admonishments solely for men. Whether primarily didactic, as in "The Prodigy," or predominantly satiric, as in "Ardelia's Answer to Ephelia," her moral pronouncements are frequently directed against women as well as men. However, even when criticizing women for their failure to embrace traditional values of chastity and marital fidelity, she differentiates between the situation of men and that of women, calling attention to society's double standards.

Against this background of flouted marriage vows, flaunted adulterous behavior, and indifference toward one's spouse, it is necessary to remember that marriages among the upper class were customarily arranged, and often for purely mercenary motives. A marriage such as that of Anne and Heneage Finch, which was based upon companionship, mutual respect, and love, was, as Lawrence Stone has found, still a rarity during the Restoration.[10] There is ample evidence that even in their youth they were fiercely independent individuals, each with a strong sense of personal integrity, so that a "convenient" or financially advantageous marriage would have been repugnant to both. Furthermore, Anne Kingsmill was an orphan and Heneage Finch had little expectation of title or inheritance, so that both were "free agents," unencumbered by any parental pressures for a marriage of convenience.

Yet Kingsmill was, by her own acknowledgment, reluctant to marry, and only the persistent pleading of her future husband convinced her to abandon her commitment to a single life, as her poem "A Letter to Dafnis April: 20 1685" attests.

In its intimate expression of love and conjugal fidelity, "A Letter to Dafnis" is very unlike what one would expect from a Restoration poem, and indeed, the poem builds some of its tone from a conscious contrast with contemporary popular views of marriage. Deceptively simple, as much of her poetry is, this seventeen-line verse epistle to her husband of almost a year, to whom she gives the poetic name "Daphnis,"[11] is worth quoting in its entirety:

> This to the Crown, and blessing of my life,
> The much lov'd husband, of a happy wife.
> To him, whose constant passion found the art
> To win a stubborn, and ungratefull heart;

And to the World, by tend'rest proof discovers
They err, who say that husbands can't be lovers.
With such return of passion, as is due,
Daphnis I love, Daphnis my thoughts persue,
Daphnis, my hopes, my joys, are bounded all in you:
Ev'n I, for Daphnis, and my promise sake,
What I in women censure, undertake.
But this from love, not vanity, proceeds;
You know who writes, and I who 'tis that reads.
Judge not my passion by my want of skill,
Many love well, though they express itt ill;
And I your censure cou'd with pleasure bear,
Wou'd you but soon return, and speak itt here.

(19)

The poem opens with two pairs of couplets that are something of a salutation, an extended "Dear Daphnis" that identifies him in relation to his wife, the author of this letter. He is told that he is "the Crown, and blessing" of his wife's life, "The much lov'd husband, of a happy wife," and the crown metaphor carries a rich multiplicity of meanings. As an emblem of monarchy it would hold special significance for Finch and her husband. In addition to its suggestion of nobility, "crown" also denotes an object usually treasured for its great value, as well as a wreath or garland worn as a sign of honor or reward for glory achieved. Daphnis is therefore, by his identification with the crown, acknowledged for his precious worth in and of himself; but he also becomes the crown of his wife's life, thereby achieving yet higher value as the pinnacle of her life. And, he is told, he is also the "blessing" of that life, and hence achieves consummate worth to her in both an earthly and a heavenly or spiritual sense.

In the next line Daphnis is told that he is the "much lov'd husband" and, as in the previous line, that sense of great value flows not merely to him but from him as well; he is "much lov'd," but he has given much in return, so that the giver of that love is also the receiver of his love and is therefore "a happy wife," again an intensification of the tribute.

In the next couplet Daphnis is further identified as "him, whose constant passion found the art / To win a stubborn, and ungratefull heart."

39

The reason for this "stubborn, and ungratefull" resistance is not given until a few lines later in the poem, but we are at least told that it was not his raw passion but, rather, passion artfully conveyed that ultimately won the heart of his future wife.

Up to this point the poem has been an intimate, private address to Daphnis by his spouse, but in the following couplet the poem suddenly becomes a public one as well:

> And to the World, by tend'rest proof discovers
> They err, who say that husbands can't be lovers.

By moving out from an intimate conjugal epistle to one addressed to the world at large, the poem takes on social implications, and the tributes of a wife to her husband become more generalized. The then-current notion of the passionless marriage and the contradiction between "husband" and "lover" can now be declared false, at least in the poet's own experience. And because her own experience so sharply contradicts that concept of marriage which the world maintains, as evidenced in its maxim about husbands and lovers, a level of ironic social commentary heightens her personal testimony to the worth of Daphnis and their relationship, while at the same time building a subtle satiric portrait of that world.

In the lines that follow, the poet then defines (for Daphnis and the world) the nature of the conjugal relationship and her responsibilities as wife. In declaring that she will return passion "as is due," we hear echoes of Cordelia declaring to Lear that she loves him according to her "bond," with all the etymological implications of that word. Certainly Finch chose her words deliberately to imply a responsibility that borders on the contractual, thereby emphasizing the social implications of marriage. Like Cordelia's, her love is defined by the nature of the relationship and the obligations inherent within it, though it is her love for Daphnis, as well as her promise (her marriage vows), that informs the fulfillment of that duty. Expanding on the subtle social commentary already introduced into the poem, she further states that she will fulfill this duty despite the fact that she censures in other women the surrender to a man of all "thoughts," "hopes," and "joys"—those very things that she herself now willingly surrenders to Daphnis. And this censure of women who give up their individual identity helps clarify the cause of that "stubborn, and ungratefull heart" earlier alluded to. The poet's initial reluctance to join her life with that of Daphnis is due to her disdain of the loss of female identity—a theme we see repeated elsewhere even more strongly in such poems as "An Epilogue to the Tragedy of Jane Shore."

Having moved out into the world at large, the poet now begins to move back to the personal, telling Daphnis that it is not from "vanity," but from "love" that she proceeds, and she reminds him, "You know who writes; and I who 'tis that reads." It is not, then, from any motives that turn inward upon the self that she proceeds (with this letter and with the fulfillment of her marriage commitment), but from love, which is directed outward, to the "other." A personal tone is established once again in the poem, as it was in the beginning, only this time it is more intimate and therefore transcends the limits of the poet's skill:

> Judge not my passion, by my want of skill,
> Many love well, though they express itt ill;
> And I your censure cou'd with pleasure bear,
> Wou'd you but soon return, and speak itt here.

These final lines offer a turn on the Renaissance and seventeenth-century tradition of imparting immortality to one's beloved by the poem itself—the sort of thing Shakespeare does in Sonnet 18 ("So long as men can breathe, or eyes can see, / So long lives this, and this gives life to thee"), or Donne in "The Canonization" ("And if unfit for tombs and hearse / Our legend be, it will be fit for verse"). In an unexpected reversal the poet here undercuts her own poem, choosing the reality of love and her beloved's presence over art. Daphnis's censure of the poem she has so carefully crafted would be accepted "with pleasure," could he but return swiftly to her.

This passage is one of a number of instances in which Finch responds with ambivalence to literary conventions that are decidedly gender-specific and that involve power-related issues. The claiming of power to confer immortality through one's poetry—quite common among male writers, even very obscure ones—is almost nonexistent among women poets. And Finch does not here claim such power for herself—at least not directly.

Some critics, including Teresa de Lauretis and Peggy Kamuf, have recently questioned what it means to write "as a woman" and, indeed, whether or not one *can* do so. Particularly relevant here are the observations of de Lauretis, who argues that strategies of writing may be "forms of cultural resistance" for women writers who are the repressed victims of patriarchal language (7). In the conclusion of "A Letter to Dafnis" Finch offers just such a strategy; she rejects the conventional language for bestowing immortality through poetry, yet her "art," her poem, despite her disclaimer, does survive—as she might well have expected. She manages, then, through the strategy of equivocation, to have it both ways.

Instances of a similar equivocation where the politics of gender is strongly evident may be found in Finch's application of the convention of the apology. The differences between male and female disclaimers and their general functions have been noted by several critics, and both Jean Mallison and Dorothy Mermin have commented on Finch's specific use of the apology.[12] As Mermin observes, the Renaissance tradition of amateurism, marked by appropriate apologies for one's literary inadequacies, "provided a framework for participating in the literary world without admitting any such intention" (337). In poems such as "Upon my Lord Winchilsea's Converting the Mount in his Garden to a Terras," "To the Honorable the Lady Worsley at Longleate," and "The Appology," Finch skillfully claims a lack of skill—again having it both ways. Her protestations against her own poetic abilities provide a protection against possible charges that she has usurped the authority/power traditionally reserved for male poets. Through the strategy of equivocation she creates an ambiguous space between her self-effacing stance and her well-wrought poems, and it is precisely this space that provides her with artistic freedom.

In "A Letter to Dafnis," one of Finch's most intimate and private poems, even very personal sentiments are juxtaposed with contemporary social views. Although she lived in an age that presented many barriers to female artistic expression, Finch was nevertheless able to develop her own individual talent, and nowhere more strongly than when writing of love and marriage. By innovative use of literary traditions and prosody, and by a variety of dramatic devices and subversive strategies, she responded to her times with a poetic stance that was at once both private and public.

Finch's poems are remarkable not only for what she has to say, however, but also for how she says it. Through innovative use of prosody, exploitation of generic traditions such as the pastoral, and experimentation with masking strategies and dramatic techniques, she continually and successfully struggled to achieve, as a woman, the greatest possible freedom of artistic expression.

In many of her most bitter and sharply satirical poems, Finch makes effective use of a persona or employs dramatic devices to convey her views. Indirection was one means by which she might speak openly about topics presumed to be acceptable only for men, or employ a tone of voice that would traditionally be considered inappropriate for a woman. One such poem that deals with marriage is "Ralph's Reflections," a narrative portrait cast almost entirely in the form of a dramatic monologue delivered by a man on the occasion of his wedding anniversary. Here, as in a number of poems, Finch demonstrates that the dramatic impulse that led her to write two verse plays could serve her well in poetry.

After introducing Ralph in the opening line of the poem, the poet withdraws, leaving Ralph on stage to offer his reflections; and as in a dramatic monologue, we gain special insight into his nature because we see him at a moment of heightened awareness:

> This day, sais Ralpho, I was free,
>   'Till one unlucky hour
> And some few mutter'd words by me,
>   Put freedom past my pow'r.
>
> (150)

Ralph's initial remarks seem at first to be no more than a statement of personal discontent, perhaps even a halfhearted utterance of the male stereotypical ball-and-chain metaphor about marriage. Even the metrical feeling created in this quatrain, with its ballad stanza form of iambic alternating tetrameter and trimeter lines and the "hour/pow'r" rhyme of its second and fourth lines, lends a slight element of levity to the opening of the poem. The next three lines, in which Ralph recites for himself some phrases from the marriage ceremony, also offer nothing to suggest that he has any more profound meaning in mind: "For better or for worse, / Till death us part. . . ." Suddenly, however, the monologue takes a different turn, for in remembering his vow ("I take thee Nell"), Ralph acknowledges to himself that what he took in reality was "a Purse."

Finch does not limit her poem to a didactic reflection upon the hypocrisy and greed that were the basis of many arranged marriages, nor does she limit her portrait of Ralph to a simplistic one. As the monologue unfolds, the poet probes the depths of a mind that is trapped in its own ambivalence:

> 'Tis Gold, must make that Pill go down,
>   The Priest without his Fee,
> Nor simple Clerk, but for half-crown
>   Would Execution see.
>
> Rubands, and Gloves, the standers by
>   To patience must encline,
> Besides the hopes of a supply
>   Of Bisquits, and of Wine.
>
> The Friends that wait us to our Beds,
>   (Who could no longer cross itt)
> But throw our stockins at our heads,
>   Or drown us with a Posset.
>
> O! happy state of human life,
>   If Mariage be thy best!
> Poor Ralpho cry'd, yet kiss't his Wife,
>   And no remorse confess't.

Ralph begins to rationalize his own motives in agreeing to the marriage by attributing similar avarice to the rest of the world. If he compromised himself, he observes, then so did all of those who partake in such wedding ceremonies: the priest who demands his fee, the clerk who for his payment would as soon authorize an execution as a wedding, and the friends themselves who hypocritically endure a tiresome and meaningless ceremony in order that they might enjoy some wine and refreshments afterward. Ralph has attempted to excuse himself by drawing into a circle of universal greed the church, the state, and even his personal friends, and he concludes his monologue with an ironic exclamation:

> Oh! happy state of human life,
> If Mariage be thy best!

In the final lines of this poem the poet again intercedes, stepping back out of Ralph's mind to offer this terse observation:

> Poor Ralpho cry'd, yet kiss't his Wife,
> And no remorse confess't.

Through use of the narrative voice, Finch offers the reader a double-angled objectivity. We know that Ralph is rationalizing, yet there is enough truth to his reflections to make us consider their larger implications for the society that fosters such cupidity and that manipulates an institution that forms the basis of the family structure. While we may find Ralph weak, at least initially, the poet has let us feel his pain keenly, and we empathize with him. His anguish, conveyed through his own words, is intensified by the brief authorial comment. Ralph remains trapped—a silent, self-justifying individual—yet his quiet compliance and dutiful kiss signify that he will probably try to make the best of an unfortunate marriage. The poet's final words, then, that he "no remorse confess't," echo in our ears in poignant and rich ambiguity.

Another poem that deals with the frequently devastating effects of marriage is "The Cautious Lovers." Here, in addition to dramatic devices, Finch also makes use of the pastoral genre to comment on contemporary issues. The poem is cast in the form of a dialogue between lovers and opens with a traditional plea to Silvia to flee the world and come live with her lover in seclusion:

> *Silvia,* let's from the Croud retire;
>   For, What to you and me
> (Who but each other do desire)
>   Is all that here we see?
>
> Apart we'll live, tho' not alone;
>   For, who *alone* can call
> Those, who in Desarts live with One,
>   If in that One they've All?
>
> (147)

Through use of the pastoral, the poet subtly creates expectations in the reader that she can then play against as the poem develops its true theme. After all the familiar arguments to his mistress to renounce the world for love, the lover suddenly turns to a brutally dark description of that world. Few in thousands, he tells Silvia, find "The happy mutual Way," for it is a world

> Where Hands are by stern Parents ty'd,
> Where oft, in *Cupid's* Scorn,
> Do for the widow'd State provide,
> Before that Love is born. . . .

Furthermore, he warns her, since monogamy is against nature, the only way for the two of them to avoid infidelity is to isolate themselves from all temptations. In short, what he offers Silvia is not a life of idyllic pastoral simplicity in which they would all the pleasures prove, but a negative, cynical escape from a world in which marriages are seen only as institutions for the perpetuation of mutual misery—business arrangements customarily devoid of love and companionship, and in such conflict with human nature that adultery is inevitable.

But Silvia, decidedly an enlightened nymph, has the final word. If her lover's fears are so great, she admonishes him, then there is probably good cause for her to fear the worst. Therefore, she decides, she will "not trust too far," and the poet reminds us, in true Augustan fashion, that

> *In Love, in Play, in Trade, in War*
> *They best themselves acquit,*
> *Who, tho' their Int'rests shipwreckt are,*
> *Keep unreprov'd their Wit.*

(149)

In "An Epilogue to the Tragedy of Jane Shore," written for Nicholas Rowe's play, Finch uses another dramatic device. Undoubtedly having learned much from Aphra Behn's prologues and epilogues (see Behn 6: 398–403), Finch uses the epilogue here as a vehicle for transcending limitations imposed upon her sex and speaking more directly to the audience.

As the subtitle indicates, the Jane Shore epilogue was written to be spoken "the night before the Poet's Day" by the actress Mrs. Oldfield in the character of Jane Shore. Though there is no hard evidence that

the epilogue was delivered by Oldfield on the eve of the traditionally designated Poet's Day, it is very likely that it was. Finch's literary
relationship with Rowe, author of *The Tragedy of Jane Shore,* was a long-
lasting one of apparent mutual admiration. The Jane Shore tragedy,
moreover, was first performed in 1714, two years after Finch became a
countess and a year after she published the only volume of her poetry
to appear during her lifetime.[13] It is likely that the playwright would
have enjoyed being associated publicly with a literary countess (albeit,
in this epilogue, a chiding one).

The play depicts the fate of Jane Shore, former mistress of Edward
IV and object of public derision by Edward's brother and successor,
Richard III, who forced her to do open penance by riding through
town in shame. The female protagonist of this "she-tragedy" (Rowe's
term for this form of sentimental-pathetic drama) dies at the play's
conclusion and is made the object of a moral lesson. Rowe's own epilogue, also designated to be spoken by Oldfield, addresses all "modest
matrons" and "virtuous wives" in a patronizing tone. Shore did wrong,
Rowe writes, but so have many who "look demurely," and Oldfield's
final words are, "Be kind at last, and pity poor Jane Shore" (75).

In her epilogue Finch examines the effect of aging upon women and
ironically contrasts it with the effect of aging upon men. In a tone of
good-natured humor she scolds the playwright, through the voice of
the actress, for showing Shore only in her time of disgrace, after she
has lost her youth and beauty, rather than "In the first triumphs of her
blooming age" (Reynolds ed. 100). She had hoped, the actress persona
declares, that his purpose would be

> To make her lavish, careless, gay and fine;
> Not bring her here to mortify and whine.

And the satiric jab at inequality in the sexes is unmistakable:

> There is a season, which too fast approaches,
> And every list'ning beauty nearly touches;
> When handsome Ladies, falling to decay,
> Pass thro' new epithets to smooth the way:
> From *fair* and *young* transportedly confess'd,
> Dwindle to *fine, well fashion'd,* and *well dress'd.*

47

Thence as their fortitude's extremest proof,
To *well as yet;* from *well* to *well enough;*
Till having on such weak foundation stood,
Deplorably at last they sink to *good.*
Abandon'd then, 'tis time to be retir'd,
And seen no more, when not alas! admir'd.
By men indeed a better fate is known.
The pretty fellow that has youth outgrown,
Who nothing knew, but how his cloaths did sit,
Transforms to a *Free-thinker* and a *Wit;*
At Operas becomes a skill'd Musician;
Ends in a partyman and politician;
Maintains some figure, while he keeps his breath,
And is a fop of consequence till death.

(101)

Through a progression of epithets Finch depicts the fate of women; with increasing age they lose their beauty and, thereby, the only means by which they can receive the admiration of others. The fate of men, by contrast, is quite different. A male whose ego is no longer sustained by praise for his physical appearance may expand into cultural and political realms for adulation. Thus, though he degenerates into a fop, the aged man may be admired as a wit and freethinker, may talk himself into a reputation as a talented music critic, and may even enjoy a transformation into that most visible of public figures, the politician.

In "The Unequal Fetters" Finch adopts the persona of an angry woman who rejects the double standard inherent in the commonly held male view of marriage. So strong was this double standard in the attitude toward "wenching" and in the acceptance of a man's adulterous behavior that young Restoration women were advised discreetly to disregard their husbands' illicit liaisons. Thus Sir George Savile, marquis of Halifax, gave the following advice to his twelve-year-old daughter in a letter written in 1688:

> You are to consider you live in a time which hath rendered some kind of frailties so habitual, that they lay claim to large grains of allowance. The world in this is somewhat unequal, and our sex seemeth to play the tyrant in distinguishing partially for ourselves, by making that in the utmost degree criminal in the woman, which

in a man passeth under a much gentler censure. . . . Remember, that next to the danger of committing the fault yourself, the greatest is that of seeing it in your husband. Do not seem to look or hear that way: If he is a man of sense, he will reclaim himself . . . if he is not so, he will be provok'd, but not reformed. . . . Such an undecent complaint makes a wife much more ridiculous than the injury that provoketh her to it. (279–80)

So popular was this letter, published as *The New-Year's-Gift: or, Advice to a Daughter*, that it had gone through fifteen editions by 1765 (Day 47).

In the opening stanza of "The Unequal Fetters," Finch cleverly plays upon the tradition of the *carpe diem* poem, employing some of the imagery and meter of Herrick's famous "To the Virgins, to Make Much of Time," and even using the same feminine rhymes, "flying" and "dying," that occur in Herrick's opening quatrain. But she reverses the *carpe diem* theme and uses the passage of time and the subsequent loss of youth and feminine beauty as an argument for *not* yielding to love:

> Cou'd we stop the time that's flying
> Or recall itt when 'tis past
> Put far off the day of Dying
> Or make Youth for ever last
> To Love wou'd then be worth our cost.
>
> (150)

Since men are enticed only by physical beauty, she argues, as the passage of time brings loss of beauty, they will inevitably "seek for [it] in new Faces." In the first two stanzas and the final one, this very contemporary-sounding feminist speaks for all women ("our cost," "our ruine"), answering not an individual male suitor but all men who have perpetuated false myths through traditional seduction arguments. In the third stanza, however, she breaks through in a direct use of the first person and defiantly asserts her own right to freedom:

> Free as Nature's first intention
> Was to make us, I'll be found
> Nor by subtle Man's invention
> Yeild to be in Fetters bound
> By one that walks a freer round.

49

A frequent experimenter with poetics, Finch uses in this poem a verse form that apparently was of her own invention. The quintet stanzas are of alternating eight and seven syllable lines, with the first and third lines ending in feminine rhymes that propel the movement of the stanza forward, while the second, fourth, and fifth lines all end in sharp masculine rhymes. The unusual syllabic and accentual patterns imitate the sense of confinement and entanglement that the poem conveys. In the first three stanzas, a metrical tension is heightened by the primary stress at the beginning of each of the first four lines ("Cou'd we stop the time that's flying / Or recall itt when 'tis past"), but this tension, in both meaning and meter, is resolved in each stanza in the final regular iambic line ("To Love wou'd then be worth our cost"). In the concluding stanza, however, this pattern is unexpectedly broken:

> Mariage does but slightly tye Men
> Whil'st close Pris'ners we remain
> They the larger Slaves of Hymen
> Still are begging Love again
> At the full length of all their chain.

The opening primary stressed lines again create tension, enforcing the ironic contrasts upon which the poem is built: the metaphoric marriage knot "but slightly" ties men, while women are fettered as "close Pris'ners." Here, moreover, there is no final resolution to the tension but, rather, an intensification of it; the poet will not give us even the slight rhythmic relief we have come to expect in the previous stanzas. That final monosyllabic line begins with a harsh accent, rather than the softer iambic foot of the other stanzas, and the line is dragged out in heavy, slow, unrelenting beats ("At the full length of all their chain"). The reader, then, experiences through sound and meter the entangling, burdensome, and "unequal" fetters that bind a woman and man in marriage. And this poem becomes ultimately a bitter antiseduction statement.

Though Finch could be harsh in her satirical condemnation of contemporary marriage customs, she could also be tenderly passionate and even playfully sensual in her poems celebrating her own marriage. Her poems speak often of delight in married life, often juxtaposing blissful conjugal love with the marriage norms of the day, in which discontent and adultery were both accepted and expected.

In "To Mr. F. Now Earl of W.," alluded to earlier, Finch offers a warm, lighthearted tribute to her own marriage. The poem, as the subtitle indicates, is for her husband, "Who going abroad, had desired Ardelia to write some Verses upon Whatever Subject she thought fit, against his Return in the Evening." In the poem, Ardelia (the poetic name she frequently gave herself) requests aid from the Muses of poetry, here portrayed as polite aristocratic ladies who reflect the shallowness and moral laxity of the times. Upon learning that the object of Ardelia's poetic effort will be to praise her husband, they respond with bewilderment and shock. Erato, the Muse of lyric and love poetry, cries out in amazement that not since the days when people wrote of ancient Troy, or penned medieval ballads like "Chevy Chase," has there been such a request. It is the duty of the Muses, we are satirically told, to keep quiet this connubial relationship, for in such times of adulterous intrigues and illicit liaisons, who, Erato inquires, could put up "With mention of a *Spouse*?" (22)

The Muses decide not to aid Ardelia, but they feel that they at least owe her excuses, and here Finch aims some very pointed gibes at the literary fashions of her time. The winged horse Pegasus has been so "spurr'd" recently by the writers of extravagant eulogies that he refuses to budge, and Thalia, the Muse of comedy and pastoral poetry, has sold out to current taste, being so well paid for her services that she "durst not for her life" aid Ardelia. Melpomene, the Muse of tragedy, having given a bond "by the new House alone to stand," has prostituted herself to the new monarchy and will write only "of War and Strife." This sardonic reference to the Bloodless Revolution and the coming to power of William and Mary is one that Finch takes care to particularize for us, as evidenced by her notation under the subtitle that the poem was "Written in the Year 1689"—in the aftermath of the revolution. (The effect of the revolution upon Finch's life and her poetry is the subject of the next chapter.) Her aligning the new monarchy with "War and Strife" is one of many instances throughout her poetry in which she alludes to current historic events to build a public poetic voice coexistent with her private one.

Though the other Muses in the poem each offer excuses, Urania, associated with Aphrodite and with virtue, is sympathetic to Ardelia's plea. Echoing Sidney's first sonnet of *Astrophel and Stella* (" 'Fool,' said my Muse to me, 'look in thy heart and write!' "), Urania whispers to

Ardelia to look within her own heart for inspiration. In a passage with delightful sexual overtones, Ardelia decides, finally, that her words of love must remain silent until she meets her returning husband that night "In some neighb'ring grove":

> For since the World do's so despise
> *Hymen's* Endearments and its Ties,
>   They shou'd mysterious be;
> Till We that Pleasure too possess
> (Which makes their fancy'd Happiness)
>   Of stollen Secrecy.

Such tender joy seems reminiscent more of the Cavalier poets, or of Robert Herrick in such lyrics as "The Night-Piece, to Julia," than of any of Finch's contemporaries.

Finch's poems about love and marriage deserve special attention. Some of them are among her finest poetry. Moreover, reflections on gender issues in these poems provide a valuable perspective on the position of women in Restoration and eighteenth-century society. In a chapter from *The Court Wits of the Restoration* that he entitles "Love Songs to Phyllis," John Harold Wilson examines the antifeminine strain found in much love poetry of the period. Commenting on the many harshly satirical songs that must, he acknowledges, have been upsetting to women of the time, he concludes that nevertheless, "Phyllis has left us no record of her reaction to these various attempts at seduction by erotic songs" (102). How wrong he is. Anne Finch has left a record, and it is one worthy to stand in the body of the best poetry of the Restoration and early eighteenth century.

FOUR

The Revolution
and Its Aftermath

The first few years following her marriage were good ones for Finch, to judge from the contentment evident in her early poems. She and her husband resided at Westminster Palace and continued to be closely involved with court activities as Heneage's career advanced. Undoubtedly she shared in the excitement when the duke of York became King James II early in 1685 and her former mistress now presided over court as her country's queen.

Around the time of her marriage Finch began to take up writing more seriously. Between 1684 and 1688 she wrote between twenty and twenty-five poems, as well as her first play. Some of these poems were love lyrics to her husband, including "A Letter to Daphnis from Westminster" and "A letter to Mr. Finch from Tunbridge Wells." The majority were songs—a poetic form widely popular at the time. John Harold Wilson's *Court Wits of the Restoration*, one of the best general studies of that court milieu, records that over 150 songbooks were published between 1660 and 1700 (88). Many Restoration songs were given musical settings by such eminent composers as Henry Purcell and Henry Playford, and as we shall see shortly, one of Finch's early publications was a song set by Purcell.

The play that she wrote during this period, a tragicomedy entitled *The Triumphs of Love and Innocence,* also owes much to contemporary literary tastes. From her arrival at court in 1682 until she and her husband left six years later, over forty English plays were performed at the court theater (Boswell 288–92). Particularly popular were Shakespeare and Beaumont and Fletcher, and *The Triumphs of Love and Innocence* shows the influence of these authors.[1]

Set at the court at Rhodes, the play strikes an authentic chord in the court scenes; some of the dialogue is particularly crisp and witty. The complicated plot is mirrored in a subplot, and both contain clearly de-marcated good and evil characters. Unlike the monarchs that Finch was personally acquainted with, Charles II and James II, the hero, Aubus-son, great master of Rhodes, is a chaste man. Indeed, the central plot involves a scheme to bring shame down upon him by staging a scene in which he appears to be involved in an illicit liaison.

Aubusson is a rather insipid hero. In her prose preface to the folio Finch admitted that she had originally thought to call the play *The Queen of Cyprus*, claiming that it could have "as aptly apply'd" as the title she ultimately settled on (12). Apparently, then, the poet/playwright herself thought the queen of essential importance to her theme. It is, in fact, the women in *Triumphs* who are responsible for moving along the action of the play; they are more resourceful and more interesting than the men, and they are willing to take risks to bring about the ascendancy of love and innocence. The exiled queen of Cyprus, given asylum at Rhodes, through her own cleverness and perseverance is finally united with Lauredan, the man she loves. And Marina, the other heroine of the play, disguises herself as a man, mingles with soldiers, endangers herself with the lustful advances of the powerful villain Rivalto, and endures poverty and ignominy, all for her beloved fiancé Blanford.

Finch's preoccupation with comedy and songwriting was cut short as the country moved toward revolution. The Finches must have followed with grave concern the events of 1688. Since coming to the throne in 1685, James II had repeatedly tried to promote the Roman Catholic church in England. In 1687 he issued a Declaration of Indulgence that suspended the Test Act (which aimed to restrict both Catholics and Dissenters), insisting that he had the right to set aside laws and over-rule Parliament. With the birth of his son in the summer of 1688 and the threat of a continued royal line of Roman Catholics, the country reached a state of crisis. A coalition of Tory and Whig parliamentary leaders began secret negotiations with William of Orange, the Dutch husband of James's Protestant daughter, Mary, and a widely recognized champion of Protestantism, to invite him to England.[2]

After William of Orange arrived on the southwest coast of England at Torbay in November 1688, the situation confronting James II and his followers became desperate. Early in December, fearing for the safety of his heir, he secretly sent Queen Mary and the infant Prince of Wales to France. That action, as his biographer, Maurice Ashley, remarks, "merely underlined William's impression—wrong though it was—that he was Louis XIV's obedient ally" (*James II* 262).

The king now faced several options: to negotiate with William, to fight it out, or to go into temporary exile in France until the political storm subsided.[3] It is not difficult to imagine the anxiety that Finch must have felt for her country, her king, and, especially, her husband, because Heneage, in addition to being one of James II's personal attendants, was also now a colonel in his army—and a number of officers and soldiers had already deserted James (Carswell 198).

James decided upon temporary exile, but his first attempt to flee was a failure. On December 12, as his boat lay stranded waiting for the tide, the king, in disguise, was seized by an angry mob of fishermen at Faversham and, along with his party, taken prisoner. After his identity became known, he was able to send a message to Heneage Finch's father, Lord Winchilsea, who had been the lord lieutenant of Kent until James dismissed him and a number of other lieutenants the previous year. Winchilsea placed James under his protection until he could be returned safely to London in the company of several lords from Whitehall.[4]

James's act of flight was viewed by many members of the peerage as "desertion," and Winchilsea himself later cast his vote in favor of offering the crown to William of Orange—a vote that must have been exceedingly painful news to his Jacobite son. William dispatched his troops to Whitehall, where James now took refuge, and James was ordered by the provisional government to leave England. The next day, unhindered, he departed for France, arriving there on December 14, 1688.[5]

Anne and Heneage Finch spent their own first days following their monarch's exile at Kirby Hall in Northamptonshire as guests of Christopher, Viscount Hatton, and his third wife, Elizabeth Haslewood. The Hattons were not only friends and sympathetic followers of the Stuart cause but also relatives of the Finches. Viscountess Hatton was the daughter of Anne Finch's former guardian, William Haslewood, and thus the cousins had spent a good part of their childhood together. Furthermore, Anne Hatton, Lord Hatton's daughter by his first wife, Cecilia Tufton, was married to Daniel Finch, second earl of Nottingham (*DNB*; Hatton 2: 60).

Letters from the manuscripts of the Hatton family correspondence for this period reveal something of the mood of the times.[6] At one point during the Finches' stay at Kirby Hall, the earl of Nottingham wrote to his father-in-law, Viscount Hatton, warning of possible violence in the area. Followers of William of Orange were to pass by on their way to Northampton, and Nottingham gave unheeded advice that the Kirby household might be safer if they temporarily removed to Kensington (Hatton 2: iii).

During the revolution Anne Finch also suffered the pain of separation from her half-sister, Dorothy Ogle, whom she affectionately addressed in her poems as "Teresa." Sometime prior to March of 1687, Ogle had also joined the court of James II, as a maid of honor for Princess Anne, younger daughter of James and wife of Prince George of Denmark (Hatton 2: 66). By the end of November Anne and her husband had deserted to her father's enemies, and Ogle remained behind, probably still in London (Ashley, *James II* 255). While at Kirby Hall on New Year's Eve, 1688, Finch addressed a poem to her half-sister that suggests the turbulence many families experienced during the revolution as individual members were uprooted. The poet asks:

> When dear Teresa, shall I be
> By Heaven, again restor'd to you?
> ("To My Sister Ogle" 38)

Ogle was later to retire to Maidwell in Northamptonshire, where she died unmarried in 1692 (Reynolds, introduction to *Poems* xxi).

The revolution ran its bloodless but turbulent course during 1689. William and Mary were offered the crown in February, and oaths of allegiance to the new monarchs were soon required of clergy and lay persons alike (Clark 146). The clergy of the Church of England were given until September 1, 1689, to take the oath, or they were to be suspended and deprived of their positions by February of the following year. Eight bishops and about four hundred clergy refused (Ashley, *Glorious Revolution* 189). Among the lay people who refused to take the oath was Heneage Finch, who thus became, with his wife, part of the group known as Nonjurors.[7]

During 1689 the Finches continued to seek refuge with friends and relatives around the countryside. Lord Hatton, their host at Kirby Hall, had his position of custos rotulorum of Northamptonshire taken away in February, though William restored him to his office by September (*DNB*; Cokayne, vol. 6). And between May and August of 1689 Hatton was at Tunbridge Wells in Kent, where he was taking the waters for his health (Hatton 2: 134–37). Sometime during the first part of that year, Anne and Heneage Finch left Northamptonshire for the family seat in Kent, for her poem "Upon Ardelia's Return Home," an account of a walk in Eastwell Park, is dated July 1689. Perhaps they quit Kirby around the time that Hatton was deprived of his office. It is also possible that the couple were called to Eastwell because of the failing health of Heneage's father, the second earl of Winchilsea.

In August the earl died, and Charles Finch, the sixteen-year-old posthumous son of Heneage Finch's older brother, Lord Maidstone, became the third earl of Winchilsea.[8]

The poems Finch wrote during this period are strongly political in nature and suggest the tremendous unrest and upheaval experienced by those loyal to James II. Her elegy "On the Lord Dundee," for example, shows her sympathy with the Jacobite struggle. James Graham of Claverhouse, Viscount Dundee, was an officer who had led Scottish dragoons and cavalry south on behalf of James (*DNB* "Graham"; Clark 276–77). He was slain at the battle of Killiecrankie in Scotland in July 1689, and Finch commemorates his death while also acknowledging the blow to the Jacobite cause:

> Fame, shall the gloomy Tyrant disposess,
> And bear you, on her golden wings,
> You, that have borne the cause of Kings. . . .
>
> (82)

Other poems from 1689 include "Caesar and Brutus," which is constructed around the theme of betrayal. Also containing heavy political overtones is "The Change," which anachronistically portrays an idyllic Arcadia that has been spoiled by contemporary political events. It contains the following bitter lines:

No Love, sown in thy prosp'rous Days,
Can Fruit in this cold Season raise:
No Benefit, by thee conferr'd,
Can in this time of Storms be heard.

(85)

Despite the settling of relations in 1689 between the new monarchy and Parliament, when William III gave royal assent to the Bill of Rights, Finch's life continued to be anything but settled. On April 29, 1690, her husband was arrested on charges of Jacobitism.

Heneage Finch and five other people, whose identities will probably never be known, gathered secretly at the coastal town of Hythe. Their hope was to sail to France in order to join James II, who had set up an exiled Stuart court at St. Germain, just outside Paris. As they were preparing to board a small vessel, they were suddenly discovered. All six men attempted to make their escape on horseback, but in the ensuing chase, Finch's horse threw him and he was taken prisoner.[9] Many years later he was to refer to the incident cryptically (and perhaps ironically) in his diary as his "great Escape" (F-H ms. 282, 28).

A notation in Luttrell's *Brief Historical Relation of State Affairs* (2: 38) indicates only that on April 29, 1690, Colonel Heneage Finch was captured at Hythe, Kent, by four men who took him to London. The *Calendar of State Papers, Domestic, May 1690–October 1691*, contains the following additional information under an entry from Whitehall for May 2, 1690: "The Earl of Shrewsbury to the Lord Chief Justice. Col. Heneage Finch who was lately taken in Kent as he was going to France, having been brought to me at my office, I have directed the person in whose custody he is to attend you with him, and I have herewith sent the letter and examinations which I received at the same time" (4).

There is no additional information about the specific charges filed against Finch. No record exists in the Public Record Office list of warrants issued for April and May of 1690. Occasionally during tense or traumatic times, as in those early months following the revolution and settlement, a secretary of state might issue a warrant directly, rather than through the usual means by which charges were brought against someone suspected of a serious crime. That Finch's name does not appear on the Controllment Roll for that Easter term indicates the seriousness of the situation, for it suggests that more direct, forceful means were used to bring charges against him.[10]

In light of the political climate of the early 1690s, one can make an informed supposition about Finch's motives in trying to reach France, and about the new government's reasons for suspecting that his actions were treasonous.

The events of the preceding months had probably convinced the Finches that the situation was desperate: the Jacobite cause had met with repeated failures, William had brought England into the Grand Alliance in his growing war against France, and the deprivation of Nonjurors meant that those who refused to swear allegiance to William were now subject to persecution, including fines and imprisonment (Ashley, *England* 178–82). Having sought asylum in France, the deposed James hoped to organize the resistance against William and Mary. The English Parliament had declared war on France the previous year—partly for economic reasons, since France was England's greatest commercial and colonial competitor, and partly for religious/political reasons, since Louis XIV's continued recognition of James as the legitimate king greatly inflamed English fears of a Catholic despotism.[11] In March 1690, five regiments from France landed at Cork (Ashley, *James II* 269–73). James, moreover, was optimistic about receiving help for his cause from Ireland, particularly since the English navy had had little success in cutting off Ireland from France. By April, when Heneage Finch decided to sail to France, William III was already preparing to go to Ireland himself. It was, therefore, a crucial time for the Jacobite cause. And Finch knew that. He was an officer and a courtier who, along with his wife, had loyally served the Stuart monarchy. He was also a deeply committed Anglican, and in the previous few weeks he had witnessed what seemed to him egregious acts as Church of England clergy and bishops were systematically deprived of their positions and their incomes (Rupp 24). He must have thought it imperative that April that he attempt to join James in France and actively participate in the resistance movement. The town of Hythe, which was not too far from the family seat of Eastwell, would be a convenient place for departure for France. Moreover, since he had recently served in Parliament as the king's nominee from Hythe, he might have hoped for local loyalty toward James II and toward himself that would give him a degree of security in his dangerous Jacobite activity.

The day following Finch's appearance in custody before the earl of Shrewsbury, instructions were given regarding payment of a reward to those who had captured him. The *Calendar of State Papers* May 3 entry is as follows: "The Earl of Shrewsbury to Mr. Jephson. Thomas Mount, Nicholas Ingham, Ralph Hatton, Thomas Tournay and James Foldred, the persons who took Col. Finch, having been at charges in bringing him to town, I desire you will recommend them to the Lords of the Treasury for a gratuity. Mr. Brockman, a member of Parliament for Hythe, the place where the action happened, will attend you with this and give a more particular account of the matter" (4). The Mr. Jephson to whom the earl made his request was William Jephson, secretary for England, and most likely the person who issued a direct warrant against Finch. Jephson, a Whig and professional soldier, had been among the first to join William of Orange at Exeter and was appointed secretary the previous year as part of William's provisional government (Carswell 123, 189–90, 218).

Sometime following Finch's arrest and arraignment he was released on his own recognizance, as several entries in Luttrell indicate. On June 2 he appeared before the Court of King's Bench "pursuant to a recognizance," but the case was carried over until the following term (Luttrell 2: 50). Again on July 9 his case was heard before the King's Bench, and again it was continued over (Luttrell 2: 73). On November 28, 1690, seven months after his arrest, the case against Finch was finally discharged from the court, probably for insufficient evidence (Luttrell 2: 133).

Entries in both Luttrell and the *Calendar of State Papers*, with the numerous charges of treason and the frequent severe sentences imposed during this period, are sufficient to suggest the extreme anguish that Anne Finch must have endured for months. The June that Heneage's trial began, for instance, Captain Charles Hatton, whose family had ties both to Anne's family and to her husband's, was sentenced. Hatton, brother of Lord Christopher Hatton, her Kirby host, was committed to the Tower "for handing to the presse a treasonable paper against the government" (Luttrell 2: 84).

The judicial process in England in the seventeenth century was slow and tedious, with cases frequently being continued for years. (The first custody case involving the infant Anne Kingsmill, which lasted over a year, is a case in point.) One can imagine Anne Finch's suffering during this period as she waited for the outcome of the case. The titles of most of the poems she wrote during that year are in themselves a testimony to her state of mind: "On Absence," "The Losse," "To Death," "A Song on Greife," "The Consolation," "Ardelia to Melancholy," "A Preparation to Prayer," "Gold Is Try'd in the Fire," and "On Affliction."

For much of that year Finch stayed at Godmersham in Kent while Heneage was in London preparing his defense. Godmersham was a large priory house located in the village of Godmersham, a mile or so northeast of Eastwell. It was originally built as a residence house for the prior of Christ Church, Canterbury, but after the dissolution of the monasteries under Henry VIII it passed to the dean and chapter of Canterbury Cathedral, who leased it.[12]

While at Godmersham she wrote another play, *Aristomenes: Or, The Royal Shepherd*, and as one might expect, given the circumstances, it is a tragedy. It is from the epilogue to *Aristomenes* that we know of her whereabouts at that time, for she asks that the play's many faults be excused because of the somber circumstances under which it was written:

> And since the Play so many ways does fail,
> For her own sake, the Author thought itt fitt
> To lett the Audience know when this was writt,
> 'Twas not for praise, or with pretense to witt:
> But lonely Godmersham th' attempt excuses,
> Not sure to be endur'd, without the Muses. . . .
>
> (411)

The play was written only as a diversion, she here implies, for it was composed at "lonely Godmersham," that "shade" where no poetic Muses could survive.

Aristomenes is set in ancient Greece and based upon the historical character who was prince of the Messenians and Arcadians.[13] In her prose preface to the folio Finch explains that she wanted to portray the leader, Aristomenes, as good rather than great, so that he would be "the best of Men." He, presumably like her own deposed monarch, James II, is caught up in the vicissitudes of war and politics. He is a good human being, but not an idealized leader of heroic stature. The tragedy that befalls him is not his own death but, rather, the death of his beloved son. Aristomenes is ultimately victorious in battle, but his is a hollow triumph, for he loses that which he values above all—his son Aristor. Aristomenes comes to the realization at the end of the play that good is tainted with evil, victory with defeat, and as he stands over the body of his slain son, he sees also that

> Defeated Armies, slaughter'd Friends are here;
> Disgraceful Bonds, and Cities laid in Ashes.
>
> (V.i.417–18)

There is none of the active evil in this play that one encounters in *The Triumphs of Love and Innocence.* The tragedy that ensues is not due to villainous action; the characters are trapped by circumstances that offer no clear, unequivocal answers. Aristomenes is captured by the Lacedemonian king Anaxander because their countries are at war. Anaxander offers Aristomenes freedom if he will but pledge not to wage war any longer upon the Lacedemonians. In Aristomenes' code, however, such a pledge would be dishonorable, so he chooses instead to remain a prisoner. When he tries to escape, he is aided by Amalinthia, Anaxander's daughter, who betrays her own father in helping his enemy. She, however, is also caught in a double bind, for she loves Aristor and therefore cannot refuse aid to Aristor's father. When she is eventually killed by Clarinthus, a Spartan lord and chief counselor to her father, it is because Clarinthus sees her as a traitor.

Rather than portraying villainy, Finch makes the virtue of Aristomenes and the love of two couples the play's true focal points. One pair of lovers survives: Demagetus, son of the prince of Rhodes, and Herminia, Aristomenes' daughter. But in this fallen world, things do not always work out as we hope they will, even for the best of rulers. Thus Amalinthia and Aristor die in each other's arms, and the play closes with these words of Aristomenes':

> Since Man, by swift returns of Good and Ill,
> In all the Course of Life's uncertain still;

By Fortune favoured none, and now opprestt,
And not, 'till Death, secure of Fame, or Rest.
(V.i.426–29)

In the prose preface Finch discusses her motivation and intention in
writing this play. Her comments here provide one of the few instances
in which she refers directly to her personal life, and because they reveal
much about her suffering during this difficult period, her remarks are
significant enough to be quoted at length:

> . . . I must acknowledge that the giving some interruption to those
> melancholy thoughts, which possesst me, not only for my own,
> but much more for the misfortunes of those to whom I owe all im-
> maginable duty, and gratitude, was so great a benefitt; that I have
> reason to be satisfy'd with the undertaking, be the performance
> never so inconsiderable. And indeed, an absolute solitude (which
> often was my lott) under such dejection of mind, cou'd not have
> been supported, had I indulg'd myself (as was too natural to me)
> only in the contemplation of present and real afflictions, which I
> hope will plead my excuse, for turning them for releif, upon such
> as were immaginary, & relating to Persons no more in being. I had
> my end in the writing, and if they please not those who will take
> the pains to peruse them, itt will be a just accusation to my weak-
> nesse, for letting them escape out of their concealment. . . . (12)

In addition to their obvious biographical relevance, Finch's remarks
also suggest the extent to which her writing had become for her a
means of objectifying that inner world of the imagination and freeing
her from the helplessness and passivity that were her lot as a woman.
Finch's private life was inextricably involved in the life of the state. The
world about her was being turned upside down and the threat of cata-
clysmic consequences was real. The times called for action, but only
for the action of men. The life of the body politic was controlled by
men's deeds; even the very life of her own husband stood in jeopardy,
for he, too, had responded with action, had attempted to influence the
course of English history. But Finch was learning something crucial
about the way in which the process of writing works for a woman.
Though concealment and passiveness and submission were all traits

that her culture admired in women and imposed upon them, there was liberation in the subversive act of writing. And if she had to stand by powerlessly and grieve for her country, her monarch, and her husband, she could at least break out of that inner prison—the despondency of her own mind—and liberate herself through words.

Close to the end of the ordeal of Heneage Finch's prosecution for Jacobitism, Anne Finch returned to Eastwell, for her poem "A Letter to Daphnis at London" is dated from there on October 21, 1690.[14] It was probably around that time that Heneage Finch's nephew Charles, the current earl of Winchilsea, invited the couple to reside with him at Eastwell. By the end of 1690, then, Anne Finch, reunited with her husband and at last settled securely in a home, entered into a new period in her life.

FIVE

Settling Down

The effect of the Bloodless (or Glorious) Revolution on Finch was enormous, for she and her husband remained loyal to the Stuart house. For Heneage Finch's refusal to take the oath of allegiance, he was exiled from court, cut off from a promising career, and forced to face, with his wife, the prospect of a future of persecution and financial hardship. Settling down at Eastwell in the countryside of Kent marked an end for Anne Finch to the trauma of the years immediately following the revolution. Secluded from public life and from the turbulent world of politics, she and her husband adapted to country living and moved into a period of apparent calm and stability.

Just before the Finches settled at Eastwell there had been dissension between Lady Maidstone, mother of the new earl of Winchilsea, and the dowager countess, widow of the deceased earl.[1] There are many indications, however, that life at Eastwell was most pleasant by the time Anne Finch and her husband were invited to reside there permanently. For much of the time during the remaining thirty years of her life, Eastwell was to be her home.

This beautiful Elizabethan mansion had belonged to Sir Moyle Finch, who received permission from Queen Elizabeth to embattle the thousand-acre Eastwell estate in 1589. It was his widow, Elizabeth Finch, who became the first countess of Winchilsea in 1629. Remodeled in the eighteenth century and completely rebuilt in the nineteenth century and again in 1926, from much of the original stone, Eastwell Manor is now a majestic hotel in imitation Tudor style. The elegantly simple building of much smaller proportions that is depicted in a 1790 drawing of Eastwell, however, is probably closer to what the original manor looked like.[2]

Eastwell Park is rich in history. The current Lake House, on the banks of the lake near Eastwell Church, is a restored building dating back to Norman times (see Parkins). The estate, which did not come into the Finch family until the sixteenth century, at one time belonged to the earl of Northumberland, grandson of the Hotspur immortalized in Shakespeare's *King Henry the Fourth* plays.[3]

The most mysterious and fascinating tale associated with Eastwell has to do with a man reputed to be Richard Plantaganet, illegitimate son of Richard III and the last of the Plantaganet line. The story was familiar to Finch, and her husband, who undoubtedly had learned it from his father, was fond of repeating it to others.[4] Heneage Finch's ancestor Sir Thomas Moyle supposedly discovered, in the process of building a house on his newly acquired Eastwell property, that one of the masons was reading a book in Latin. Startled to find such literacy in a common laborer, Moyle questioned him and, when he had gained his confidence, learned his story.

The man, known as Richard, claimed to have been raised by a schoolmaster and been well cared for. One day while he was in his early teens he was visited, he said, by a well-dressed stranger who brought him to a camp where soldiers were preparing for battle. He was taken to a man clad in a rich suit of armor, who told him that he was King Richard III and that he, the boy, was his natural son. The king then explained that the next day a battle would be fought there at Bosworth Field, a battle that would decide the future for both of them. If he was victorious, the king added, his natural son would one day inherit the crown. He warned the boy, however, to reveal his identity to no one, for if he was defeated in battle, then the earl of Richmond would surely seek out the lad, were he known to be a Plantaganet, and kill him.

Once King Richard was slain, the boy fled, keeping his identity secret as the reign of the Tudors began. From that time on, he explained to Moyle, he had lived a simple life as a poor laborer. And Moyle, moved by the story of the elderly man, built a cottage for him on the Eastwell grounds and provided for his needs for the remainder of Richard's life.

Though Richard III is known to have had two illegitimate children prior to his marriage to Anne Neville (John of Gloucester and Katharine Plantaganet), the legend of this additional offspring, Richard Planta-

66

ganet, has never been satisfactorily proved, though it has tantalized scholars from time to time. In the ruins of the church on the Eastwell estate one can still see the reputed tomb of Richard Plantaganet. And the parish register for Eastwell records his burial: "Richard Plantaganet was buryed the 22nd daye of December anno ut supra ex registro de Eastwell sub anno 1550."[5]

The grounds at Eastwell are spectacular; even today one can see the beautiful landscapes that Finch celebrated in such poems as "From the Muses, at Parnassus," "Upon Ardelia's Return Home," and "Upon My Lord Winchilsea's Converting the Mount in His Garden to a Terras." The terraces and formal gardens that surround the mansion are probably not very different from what they were after her husband's nephew, Charles, undertook to landscape the area. The groves of ancient oak and beech, the rolling hills and lush valleys, and the rich fields dotted with grazing sheep are still a part of the estate. On a clear day the distant prospect of the sea is visible from the highest point of the land (undoubtedly the hill Finch identified in "From the Muses, at Parnassus" as Mount Parnassus). In another poem not in the Reynolds edition, "An Invocation to the southern Winds," Finch offers a particularly lovely description of the grounds. Written in 1703 to welcome Charles Finch on his arrival in London after a dangerous voyage back from Holland, she asks that he soon be reunited with his homeland in the peaceful setting of Eastwell:

> Whilst *Eastwell* park does each soft gale invite,
> There let them meet and revel in delight,
> Amidst the silver beeches spread their wings,
> Where ev'ry bird as in *Arcadia* sings.
> Where the tall stag in the descending boughs,
> May brush the beamy product of his brows.
> Where lesser deer o're run th' extended lawns,
> And does are follow'd by unnumber'd fawns.
> The even plains invite the racer's feet,
> As valour steady and as fancy fleet.
> Whilst fragrant turf the Rider's heart revives,
> And paradise surrounds him while he strives.
> Where two fair heads the true *Parnassus* grace,
> And Poetry's a native of the place.

Those *Eastwell* hills let ev'ry breeze renew,
Which from adjoining seats kind neighbours view;
Pleas'd in the artful gardens which they boast,
With such a prospect rais'd at nature's cost.
                    (*Pope's Own Miscellany* 121–22)

Not far from the house is Eastwell Church, which, Edward Hasted records, "was always esteemed an appendage to the manor" (3: 202). It is on the bank of a lake created in the middle of the nineteenth century; in the early eighteenth century that lake was the brook from which water was drawn for the manor house. The church, made of flint with ashlar around the windows, was built in about 1380, with additions made in the fifteenth century. It consisted of two aisles and two chancels, with a square embattled tower at the west end. In Finch's day it contained the magnificent marble effigies of the first countess of Winchilsea and her husband that are now on display, with other Finch family monuments, at the Victoria and Albert Museum.[6] Its medieval stained glass has also been preserved and may be seen at Kings College, Cambridge, and Kings School, Canterbury, as well as at nearby Wye College (Councer). Eastwell Church now lies in ruins, the victim of a combination of war, neglect, and vandalism.[7]

THIS, THEN, WAS THE SETTING in which Finch composed much of her mature work, and at Eastwell as in London she was consistently nurtured in her writing by her husband, who functioned as her editor and amanuensis. One of the first things that Heneage Finch did after his case was dismissed from the Court of King's Bench was to take up the task of compiling his wife's poems in a manuscript volume.

She had probably begun this volume, an octavo manuscript with a gilt-edged morocco binding, very shortly before he was discharged by the court. Most likely a relative or close friend advised collecting the poems as a distraction for the anxious wife. The neat, precise handwriting of the first part of the manuscript is unidentified; it is definitely not Anne Finch's, for it bears no resemblance whatever to the four known letters that are in her hand.[8] Her handwriting, incidentally, is nearly illegible, a fact she herself must have been well aware of and which undoubtedly caused her to seek the aid of others in transcribing her poems.

The octavo manuscript opens with "The Introduction," which declares the right of women to write poetry and to develop their minds. Then follows a number of her most recent poems, all with a common theme of loss and suffering—poems such as "To Death," "The Losse," "A Song on Griefe," and "On Affliction." After thirty-six poems were transcribed, Heneage took over, beginning in the middle of page 87. Among the first poems he transcribed is "A Letter to Daphnis at London," the date of which October 21, 1690, gives further support to the supposition that the octavo was begun just before his return from London and that he took over compiling the poems almost immediately thereafter.[9]

Fifty-six poems had been transcribed in the octavo, with about thirty blank pages remaining, when the manuscript was abandoned as a means for preserving her poems. Most likely the octavo was seen as inadequate because of its limited length, for it would not have been large enough to contain her two plays, which she included in her second and larger manuscript—a folio. It may also be that Finch decided upon a manuscript meant for more public circulation. This is particularly likely since she published her first poem in 1691 and must have grown increasingly aware of the possibility of a wider audience for her poetry. This would also explain why the very personal poem "On Myself" was not retranscribed from the octavo, and why the prose preface, addressed to the readers of her poems, was written specifically for the folio manuscript and affixed to the beginning of it.

The octavo was still kept for private purposes, however, and it shows evidence of editing. Two poems in it were obliterated by scribbling out each line, and the pages containing two other poems were torn out of the volume. In one instance the octavo was used for drafting a poem. Following the great storm of November 27, 1703, Finch wrote the rough draft of an ode, "On the Hurricane," which her husband copied down in a hurried, careless hand on pages 143–54 of the octavo.[10] A number of corrections were made at different times, with whole revised passages pasted over their original versions. At the end of the transcription, following several explanatory notes, appears the following notation: "This poem was written at Wye College and finished Feb. 9th 1703/4."

At some point after Heneage Finch had finished transcribing his wife's poems in the octavo, she decided to drop her original pen name of Areta and adopt a new one, Ardelia. He then went through and erased all the Aretas, substituting her new pseudonym, except for the one Areta he missed on page 70.

Around 1694 or 1695 Heneage Finch began to compile the folio manuscript, which is entirely in his hand save for an occasional correction or title that she supplied.[11] Whatever occupations he took up when he retired to the country, one he took seriously was that of editor, transcriber, and muse for his wife's poetry. The role that Heneage Finch played in his wife's development as a writer is enormous. First, he provided the love and tranquility that she found essential to her writing. But beyond that he was in a very real sense her literary helpmate and greatly encouraged her in her writing, as poem after poem attests. "To Mr. F. Now Earl of W.," for example, is addressed to Heneage, who, as the subtitle tells us, "going abroad, had desired Ardelia to write some Verses upon whatever Subject she thought fit, against his Return in the Evening" (20). Moreover, his commitment to editing her works was lifelong. From the earliest manuscript of her poems to the manuscript prepared thirty years later around the time of her death (the Wellesley manuscript), Heneage Finch's hand is evident, both literally and figuratively.

Anne Finch's earliest publications were songs—and all appeared anonymously. The song beginning " 'Tis strange this Heart" was set to music by R. Courteville and published in *Vinculum Societatis*, a songbook that appeared in 1691. Two years later another song ("Love, thou art best of Human Joys") saw publication as part of *The Female Vertuoso's, A Comedy*, written by T. Wright and dedicated to the Finches' host at Eastwell, Charles, fourth earl of Winchilsea. (The dedication of this play to Charles, who was barely twenty-one years old at the time, and the playwright's inclusion of this poem by Charles's aunt, are further evidence that his reputation as a strong supporter of the arts was well deserved.) That same year, in a special issue of the *Gentleman's Journal* entitled the *Lady's Journal*, the song appeared again.[12]

Henry Purcell set that same song to music, and it was included in the fifth book of the 1694 *Comes Amoris: or The Companion of Love. Being a Choice Collection of the Newest Songs now in Use*. It must have been a particularly popular song, for it was reprinted in a collection of Purcell's "choicest songs" entitled *Orpheus Britannicus*, in both the 1698 edition and the second one of 1706.

The next poems Finch had published were religious ones. Six were included in volume 1 of the 1696 *Miscellanea Sacra*, which apparently sold well enough to go into a second edition two years later. These poems, again all "by an unknown hand," were "On Easter-Day," "A Preparation to Prayer," "Gold Is Try'd in the Fire," "On Affliction," "Psalm the 137th, Paraphras'd," and "The Second Chapter of the Wisdom of Solomon, Paraphras'd."

That first decade of retirement at Eastwell, then, was most beneficial for Finch's poetry. Her poetic output was at least double what it had been the previous decade, and around the time of her thirtieth birthday (in 1691) she began to develop enough confidence to allow some of her poems to be published—albeit anonymously. This was due in part to her husband's encouragement. But much of the impetus for the flowering of her poetic genius must also be traced to her life at Eastwell.

In the prose preface she credits "the solitude, & security of the Country" at Eastwell, as well as the gracious support of her sensitive and learned host, for her serious commitment to writing (8). She even goes so far as to claim that had not the new earl invited her and her husband to settle at Eastwell, she might well have ceased writing altogether and allowed those few compositions she had already written "to have sunk into . . . oblivion." Explaining precisely why she has now dedicated herself to "the service of the Muses," she continues:

> But when I came to Eastwell, and cou'd fix my eyes only upon objects naturally inspiring soft and Poeticall immaginations, and found the Owner of itt, so indulgent to that Art, so knowing in all the rules of itt, and att his pleasure, so capable of putting them in practice; and also most obligingly favorable to some lines of mine, that had fall'n under his Lordship's perusal, I cou'd no longer keep within the limmitts I had prescrib'd myself, nor be wisely reserv'd, in spite of inclination, and such powerfull temptations to the contrary. (8)

Charles Finch, the posthumous son of Heneage's older brother, had been raised at Eastwell by his widowed mother, Lady Elizabeth Maidstone, with an assortment of Finch aunts, uncles, and siblings (I'Anson

56; *Burke's Peerage*). He was educated at All Souls College, Oxford, of which his uncle, Leopold William Finch, was the warden.[13] Even as a young man he began to develop a number of literary friendships, most notably with Joseph Addison and Jonathan Swift, and occasionally he himself wrote poetry.

Around the time of his eighteenth birthday, in September of 1690, Anne Finch wrote "From the Muses, at Parnassus," a poem extolling his already evident virtues and abilities. Addressed to Lady Maidstone, the poem compliments her son, the young Lord Winchilsea, as a worthy descendant of a noble line.[14] After his marriage in 1692 to Sarah Nourse of Woodlands, Wiltshire, and his coming of age a year later, Charles began to assume the responsibilities of lord of the Eastwell manor (Luttrell 2: 584).

Not only was the young Lord Winchilsea an enthusiastic reader of poetry, but he also enjoyed having literary performances at Eastwell. In the prologue to *Aristomenes*, written probably some months after that tense period when the tragedy itself was composed, Anne Finch addresses her host upon the occasion of first reading her play to him. The scene she evokes is of a cozy gathering around a warm winter's fire, and the mood is decidedly relaxed. But her host's judgment of the play, she tells him, is worth more than "if whole troops, of vulgar Critticks swarm'd" (337).

Another domestic literary scene is documented in "A Prologue to Don Carlos," which, the subtitle indicates, was acted by young ladies of the Eastwell household in the year 1696. In introducing the performance of Thomas Otway's drama to the Eastwell gathering, Finch humorously addresses her audience and describes the young beauties who will be acting the play. The young thespians would presumably have included some of her husband's sisters, half-sisters, and nieces, as well as Charles's wife, Lady Sarah, any other available female relatives or friends, and possibly Finch herself.

DURING HER RETIREMENT in the country, while Finch occupied herself with her writing, she also spent much time with friends and family, as well as with excursions about the Kent countryside. And she developed an interest in history and local lore. "The Circuit of Appollo," for example, has a learned note on Wye and the birthplace of Aphra Behn; "From the Muses, at Parnassus" has genealogical information;

and poems such as "Upon the Death of King James the Second," "All Is Vanity," and "Fanscomb Barn" contain scholarly footnotes that go beyond simple identification. In "An Invitation to Dafnis," discussed elsewhere, Finch documents her husband's varied artistic and scholarly interests. And as poems such as "An Invitation to Dafnis" and "A Ballad to Mrs. Catherine Fleming at Lord Digby's" suggest, she kept informed of her husband's antiquarian studies.

Heneage Finch himself, in a letter to William Charlton in February 1701, describes his rural occupations: "But indeed, Sir, my confinement to a country life, and having given over the usual exercises propper to itt,[15] has made me take delight in the study of Antiquity, which I ever loved, but, which I never had the leasure whilst I lived in the Town, to apply my self to. And now my Books, and a small collection of Medals, help to fill up those vacancys of my Time, which wou'd lye upon my hand" (BL Sloane ms. 3962, 284–87).

Other evidence of Heneage Finch's continued involvement in antiquarian studies may be found in Thomas Hearne's frequent inclusion of his name among the list of book subscribers (especially volumes 3–5) and Heneage's own journal, which records anecdotes of historical note (F-H ms. 282, 54). In 1703 he became involved in research on a neolithic long barrow near Childham known as Julaber's Grave (Piggott 57). He later became a member of the Society of Antiquaries, and his letters to the noted scholar Dr. William Stukeley, printed in Nichols's *Illustrations* (769–82), are both learned and playful. (Members of the society were given Druidical names; Finch signs himself "Cyngetorix" and addresses Stukeley as "Chyndonax.") Finch also shared an interest with his brother-in-law, Lord Weymouth, in antique medals.[16] In short, Finch's reputation in later years as an antiquarian scholar appears to have been well deserved.

But despite their varied activities and interests, life must at times have been very quiet for the couple, and perhaps somewhat dull after the excitement of those years in London. Something about their life in Kent can be learned from Heneage Finch's letters, a number of which have been preserved among the manuscripts of the Thynne Papers in the library of the marquess of Bath at Longleat in Wiltshire. One letter of special interest, dated February 8, 1697, is addressed to his brother-in-law, Lord Weymouth.

He begins with thanks for his brother-in-law's most recent gift. "I can never enough," he writes, "expresse my sence of my obligations to your Lords^P. So great a share of the comforts I enjoy, in these times of hardship, proceeding from your Lordships generosity" (245). Since Heneage Finch lost his position following the revolution, it is possible that the couple had no income beyond what money might have been left from the modest inheritance Anne Finch received from her father. The financial situation of the Finches must have been strained, and apparently Lord Weymouth was a kind benefactor, for other letters contain expressions of deep gratitude to him from both of them.

Heneage Finch continues his letter with complaints of a lameness in one of his knees, which the doctors have just diagnosed as gout. It must have been around this time that Anne Finch wrote her playful fable "The Goute and Spider." In the poem, addressed to her husband "After his first Fitt of that Distemper," she offers her suffering spouse a moral lesson of patience, then playfully observes that he is not wealthy enough "to sooth the bad disease / By large expenses to engage his stay," nor yet poor enough "to fright the Gout away" (31–32, lines 52–55). (Gout, a painful inflammation of the joints caused by a uric acid imbalance in the metabolism, was known even in the late seventeenth century to be aggravated by the consumption of certain rich foods.) [17] She concludes her poem with these comforting words, suggestive of the intimate relationship they still shared thirteen years into their marriage:

> May you but some unfrequent Visits find
> To prove you patient, your Ardelia kind
> Who by a tender and officious care
> Will ease that Grief or her proportion bear
> Since Heaven does in the Nuptial state admitt
> Such cares but new endearments to begett
> And to allay the hard fatigues of life
> Gave the first Maid a Husband, Him a Wife.
> (32, lines 55–62)

Heneage Finch's letter continues to describe in a subdued tone the bleak, lonely existence of their life at Eastwell that winter: "This is a lonely Winter to us, having no Neighbours within reach of a visite (this hard weather) now the best of them my good Ld: Thanet, and his Family, are out of the country. And indeed, this wou'd be an uncomfortable Place did not my Ld. Winchilsea's good humour, and good Principles, make any place agreable." Winters in Kent, when most people departed for the city, must have been particularly difficult. A similar mood of depression is evident in another letter to Lord Weymouth the following December. After referring to the ill health that both he and his wife were suffering, Heneage Finch writes that there is "seldom anything worth informing" his lordship about, and he tells of their strong desire to be in London to see Lord Weymouth and friends (Longleat Thynne Papers 250–51).

For several years, probably from 1700 until 1704 or longer, Anne and Heneage Finch took up residence at Wye College, just about two miles from Eastwell. Possibly the couple desired more privacy than the full household at Eastwell could provide, or they might have wished to impose less on the young earl's hospitality. There is, in any case, no indication that their relationship with Lord Winchilsea and his family was any less cordial than previously. In his letters to his brother-in-law during this period, Heneage Finch alludes to events at Eastwell and passes on greetings from Lord and Lady Winchilsea. Anne and Heneage Finch must therefore have been in frequent communication with the Eastwell household and must have retained close ties with Heneage's nephew and his family.

The first mention of Wye College in Anne Finch's poetry occurs in the poem known simply as "Fragment." In it she refers to her present situation as one of

> Retirement, which the World *Moroseness* calls,
> Abandon'd Pleasures in Monastic Walls,
> (13, lines 22–23)

and in a note she identifies the monastic walls as "Wye College in Kent, formerly a Priory."

Wye College was founded in the fifteenth century by Cardinal Thomas Kempe, who appropriated the Royal Manor of Wye as part of his new College of Saint Gregory and Saint Martin. It was later converted into a free school for educating local children. The manor of the original religious house, however, was in the possession of the Finch family for decades, and various family members lived there from time to time.[18]

Some of Finch's poems reflect her interest in local color. "The Lawrell," for example, contains allusions to people such as Dick Halks and Holbourn Harry who live in or around the village of Wye. "Fanscomb Barn," a burlesque of Milton, is named for a place that the poet tells us is a well-known haunt for local beggars: a "Place of sweet Repose to Wand'rers poor" (210, line 8). The poem relates the exploits of two of these beggars—the delightful Strolepedon and Budgeta. Some of the more humorous lines in the poem describe in mock-elevated language the young students from Wye College who frolic along the stream of nearby Pickersdane:

> Thus sung the Bard, whom potent Liquor rais'd,
> Nor so contented, wish'd sublimer Aid.
> Ye Wits! (he cry'd) ye Poets! (Loiterers vain,
> Who like to us, in Idleness and Want
> Consume fantastick Hours)....
>
> . . . .
>
> To *Helicon* you might the *Spring* compare,
> That flows near *Pickersdane* renowned Stream,
> Which, for Disport and Play, the Youths frequent,
> Who, train'd in Learned School of ancient *Wye*,
> First at this Fount suck in the Muses Lore,
> When mixt with Product of the *Indian* Cane,
> They drink delicious Draughts, and part inspir'd,
> Fit for the Banks of *Isis*, or of *Cham*,
> (For *Cham* and *Isis* to the *Bard* were known,
> A *Servitor*, when young in *College-Hall*,
> Tho' vagrant Liberty he early chose,
> Who yet, when Drunk, retain'd Poetick Phrase.)
> (Lines 90–94, 99–110)

Another poem from Finch's days at Wye College, and one that demonstrates her good humor, is "An Apology for my fearfull temper in a letter in Burlesque upon the firing of my chimney At Wye College March 25th 1702" (see app. A). Poking fun at herself, she writes of an incident one night when the chimney of her bedroom fireplace began sputtering loudly. Alarmed, she ran throughout the house in her nightgown, awakening everyone with screams of "Fire" and demanding that all get out their of beds and out of the house. As everyone stood barefoot and scantily clothed in the cold March air, it was discovered that the troublesome chimney was, indeed, no threat whatever to anyone's safety, and the skittish night summoner herself became the object of everyone's mirth.

The humor of "An Apology for my fearfull temper" is typical of the tone in many poems that Finch wrote in her thirties and forties. After she was settled securely in Kent, the despair and grief evident in her poetry of those first years following the revolution soon gave way to the playfulness of the seduction poem to her husband, "An Invitation to Dafnis," or the charming song for her brother-in-law, "For my Br. Les: Finch. Upon a Punch Bowl." Moreover, one can see in some poems from this period, such as "Ardelia's Answer to Ephelia," the strong satirical strain that became more evident in her later poetry. And also present in the poetry from those first years of her retirement to the country is an impulse to contemplate nature.

SIX

"Nature Unconcern'd":
Nature Poems and
Humanistic Sensibilities

*A*fter her move to Kent, Finch had the leisure to take long walks in the lovely park at Eastwell and to wander about the countryside, garnering the rich images that found expression in such poems as "A Nocturnal Reverie" and "The Petition for an Absolute Retreat." Of the more than 230 poems she wrote, however, only about half a dozen are devoted primarily to descriptions of external nature, and these, with the exception of the two just named, are not among her better poems.[1] Yet invariably these have been the poems included in standard anthologies. A few recent anthologies of women's literature have offered a more representative selection of her work, as have the small collections of her poetry that Denys Thompson and Katharine Rogers have edited.[2] The popular image of Finch that still exists today, however, is that of a nature poet.

The reason for this continued misrepresentation of her work is that until recently her reputation has rested almost entirely upon Wordsworth's celebrated remark in his 1815 supplementary essay to the preface of the *Lyrical Ballads* that

> excepting the 'Nocturnal Reverie' of Lady Winchilsea, and a passage or two in the 'Windsor Forest' of Pope, the poetry intervening between the publication of the 'Paradise Lost' and 'The

Seasons' does not contain a single new image of external nature, and scarcely presents a familiar one from which it can be inferred that the eye of the Poet had been steadily fixed upon his object, much less that his feelings had urged him to work upon it in the spirit of genuine imagination. (*Prose* 3: 73)

Wordsworth's praise has been a mixed blessing. It resurrected Finch's name from the obscurity that befell any pre-nineteenth-century English woman writer. But for nearly two hundred years it has distorted the general perception of her as a poet and thwarted recognition of the depth, the quality, and the diversity of her work. It is therefore essential that her few nature poems be placed within a proper literary context.

Wordsworth's remark has set the tone for critics, anthologists, and literary historians throughout the nineteenth and much of the twentieth century. It has caused Finch to be analyzed, anthologized, and categorized almost exclusively as a nature poet and precursor of Wordsworthian Romanticism. Edmund Gosse, for example, who discovered the folio manuscript of her poems in 1884, heralds her as a misplaced poet whose "temper was . . . foreign to the taste of her own age" and who was possibly "the first of the new romantic school" (*History* 35–36). Reynolds declares in *The Learned Lady in England, 1650–1760*, that Finch "delicately foreshadowed tastes that ruled in the romanticism of a century later" (152), and in the lengthy introduction to the still-standard edition of her poems, Reynolds makes repeated comparisons between Finch and Wordsworth, declaring some of her verses to be "exactly Wordsworthian in substance and mood" and maintaining that "Wordsworth's strong interest in Lady Winchilsea is justified by the law of affinities" (cxxxii).

The misjudgment in representing such a richly diverse poet as a nature poet and Romantic precursor is doubly ironic, for under close examination even those few poems that deal with external nature are less Romantic and far more a product of her age than Wordsworth's comments might lead one to suppose. "A Nocturnal Reverie," her most widely anthologized poem since the eighteenth century, is a case in point.[3]

There is much in "A Nocturnal Reverie" to recommend it as Romantic. The setting is rustic, dark, and secluded, and when the persona begins to speak of her serenity in the midst of nature, one senses all the proper movements for some Wordsworthian recollected tranquility. The poem recalls the opening scene in act V of Shakespeare's *Merchant of Venice*, in which Lorenzo and Jessica exchange a series of imaginative musings on the beauty of nature, each beginning with the phrase "In such a night." Finch's poem, however, is something of a tour de force, its entire fifty lines a single sentence constructed around clauses that begin, "In such a night . . . when. . . ." The descriptions are specific and contain numerous visual, auditory, and olfactory images of nature. Moreover, the scene is a nocturnal one, with night transforming the appearance of everything, so that the imagination of the reader is fully engaged. All is thinly veiled, clouded, and hidden in shadows, suggesting an air of Gothic mystery that would appeal to the Romantic sensibility:

> In such a *Night*, when passing Clouds give place,
> Or thinly vail the Heav'ns mysterious Face;
> When in some River, overhung with Green,
> The waving Moon and trembling Leaves are seen;
>
> . . . .
>
> When darken'd Groves their softest Shadows wear,
> And falling Waters we distinctly hear;
> When thro' the Gloom more venerable shows
> Some ancient Fabrick, awful in Repose. . . .
>
> (268–69, lines 7–10, 23–26)

There are other suggestions of Wordsworthian Romanticism in the poem as well. The mood is reflective. Nature, the poet tells us, can renew the weary spirit, can calm the confusion and rage that torment the human soul. Furthermore, the dichotomy between the social world and the natural world is emphasized. Nature's serenity is marred by man: the kine are able to feed contentedly only because they are temporarily "unmolested," and all of nature's creatures enjoy their "shortliv'd Jubilee" only "whilst Tyrant-*Man* do's sleep" (line 38). Lastly, there is even the suggestion that nature possesses transcendental attributes:

> But silent Musings urge the Mind to seek
> Something, too high for Syllables to speak.
>
> (Lines 41–42)

But these very lines, when taken in the context of what follows them, demonstrate the essential difference between Finch and Wordsworth:

> Till the free Soul to a compos'dness charm'd,
> Finding the Elements of Rage disarm'd,
> O'er all below a solemn Quiet grown,
> Joys in th' inferiour World, and thinks it like her Own. . . .
>
> (270, lines 43–46)

A comparison of these lines with the conclusion of Wordsworth's "Ode: Intimations of Immortality from Recollections of Early Childhood" is revealing. While the "meanest flower that blows" may cause Wordsworth to have "Thoughts that do often lie too deep for tears," Finch's response to nature is quite different. Wordsworth is inspired to "thoughts" that turn inward and seeks meaning within himself, whereas Finch, as a devout Anglican, is inspired to seek beyond herself, to look to heaven for meaning. Moreover, she is dealing not with nature in a generalized sense but with nature at a specific time and place. It is not *any* grove, any meanest flower, that can bring relief from life's pressures and a chance to refresh oneself: it is this particular time and place— a night such as this in this very setting. And the poet is well aware that such retreats from life's cares are temporary at best ("Till Morning breaks, and All's confus'd again" [line 48]). In such moments of respite, the poet tells us, she seeks to speak "Syllables" that will articulate her sense of a divinity beyond herself, but such musings cannot be expressed. Hers is a thoroughly orthodox and rational approach. One may be seduced into a false illusion that man and nature are one; one even, "in such a Night," occasionally "Joys in th' inferiour World, and thinks it like her Own." But the soul's source is elsewhere, and Finch knows ultimately that the world of nature is but an "inferiour" world.

It is notable that in his supplement to the preface, what Wordsworth specifically notes in his praise of Finch is, in addition to her fresh images of external nature, her "feelings" and "genuine imagination," though of course the concept of these terms, as Wordsworth understood them, would have been foreign to her. Wordsworth, like Finch, is concerned with the process of perceiving nature, as well as the ability of nature to infuse one with a transcendent spirit. For him it is not simply that nature is invested with value. In Finch's poetry there are moral implications to nature as well, as can be seen in some of her pastoral poems, such as "The Change." The difference is that for her there is an irreconcilable dualism that exists between man and nature, so that nature and the human soul remain two separate realities. The dualism that Ann Messenger finds inherent in the argument of "To the Nightingale" is present in all of Finch's nature poems, including "A Nocturnal Reverie."[4]

There are other characteristics of "A Nocturnal Reverie" that mark it as decidedly not Romantic in a Wordsworthian or Shaftesburian sense. As with all Finch's nature and pastoral verse, it is men and women, not nature in the abstract, who are the focus of the scene. At the center of the poem is a lovely, brief tribute to her friend Lady Salisbury, whose beauty and virtue withstand "the Test of every Light" (line 20). Moreover, the careful control and sense of containment that the heroic couplets supply are another reminder that here are rational, moralistic reflections, not the ecstatic soarings of a free Romantic spirit. There is also humor in the poem, and even social satire. The glowworms are likened to "trivial Beauties" who similarly wait for twilight to appear, realizing that it is their most favorable hour to shine. Even the quasi-Gothic description quoted above is immediately undercut by a touch of whimsy and mild self-irony. An unidentified figure, "Whose stealing Pace, and lengthen'd Shade we fear," appears upon the darkened pasture, but reality checks the rampant and foolish imagination of the frightened sojourners, for they recognize that the threatening intruder is but a harmless grazing horse, noisily chewing forage.

All nature can do, Finch believes, is provide a temporary retreat from the world so that the spirit can renew itself. Moreover, the poem's conclusion is a reminder that daylight brings a return to everyday activities and a renewed pursuit of those often illusive but nevertheless attainable joys of life:

> Our Cares, our Toils, our Clamours are renew'd,
> Or Pleasures seldom reach'd, again pursu'd.

Wordsworth, incidentally, deleted four lines from the poem when he prepared for Lady Mary Lowther in 1818 a manuscript of works by women poets, including sixteen Finch poems.[5] Two of the lines are the only mildly satirical ones in the entire poem:

When scatter'd Glow-worms, but in Twilight fine,
Shew trivial Beauties watch their Hour to shine.
(Lines 17–18)

The other two lines Wordsworth deleted are the tribute to Lady Salisbury. Neither satire nor poetic compliments to female friends appear to have pleased him.

The ideal retreat is the subject of another of Finch's well-known nature poems, "The Petition for an Absolute Retreat." It contains many instances of what Wordsworth referred to as the poet's eye being "steadily fixed upon his object." In its celebration of simplicity and naturalness, as well as in its style, it bears similarities to Robert Herrick's verse. (Such similarities have been noted elsewhere in this study.) Finch's debt to Herrick is especially evident in the following passage:

Cloath me, Fate, tho' not so Gay;
Cloath me light, and fresh as *May:*
In the Fountains let me view
All my Habit cheap and new;
Such as, when sweet *Zephyrs* fly,
With their Motions may comply;
Gently waving, to express
Unaffected Carelessness:
No Perfumes have there a Part,
Borrow'd from the *Chymists* Art. . . .
(70–71, lines 64–73)

When placed alongside the final lines of Herrick's "Delight in Disorder," the resemblance is striking:

A winning wave, deserving note,
In the tempestuous petticoat;
A careless shoestring, in whose tie
I see a wild civility;
Do more bewitch me than when art
Is too precise in every part.
(41)

Both poems convey a similar idea: Finch would have her garments yield to the breezes in much the way that Herrick would have his lady's

83

clothing yield to the movement of her body, and both poets scorn the cosmetic arts in preference for naturalness. Both poems also contain a tone that is distinctively light and charming and that reflects simplicity in style. The meter and rhyme of the last four lines in the Finch passage recall the closing lines of "Delight in Disorder," with four words in those lines echoing key words in the Herrick passage: "waving," "carelessness," "part," and "art."

"The Petition for an Absolute Retreat" also bears some similarity to Andrew Marvell's "Garden," as Reuben Brower has already noted (71–75). But while both poems are reflective, Finch's, unlike Marvell's, describes a real retreat that is truly a part of the natural world, rather than an abstract meditative state. For her, moreover, nature provides an object lesson, an understanding of reality that Marvell's poem lacks. Thus a withered oak becomes for her a *memento mori,* and the temporary retreat, as in "A Nocturnal Reverie," provides the means for renewing her spiritual self and for viewing both "the Height, from whence she came," and the paradise that awaits her (line 277). But the principal way in which her poem differs from Marvell's is in her sense of society. Finch's poem is thoroughly peopled. In lines 8–21, for instance, she describes what she is retreating from and what sort of people she wants to join her, and lines 164–201 contain a lengthy passage in praise of friendship and a tribute to her friend Arminda, whom she would have join her. Furthermore, in lines 104–05 Finch appears to be directly answering Marvell, who, in the eighth stanza of "Garden," rounds off his description of paradise with this startling assertion:

> But 'twas beyond a mortal's share
> To wander solitary there:
> Two paradises 'twere in one
> To live in paradise alone.
>
> (60–63)

In her description of her retreat, Finch also evokes the Garden of Eden, but her paradise is incomplete without a mate:

> Give me there (since Heaven has shown
> It was not Good to be alone)
> A *Partner* suited to my Mind,
> Solitary, pleas'd and kind;

Who, partially, may something see
Preferr'd to all the World in me;
Slighting, by my humble Side,
Fame and Splendor, Wealth and Pride.

(Lines 104–11)

Finally, she devotes the conclusion of this section to praise of human love as the gift heaven has given to bring people closer to God.

For Finch, then, it is human beings that provide the spiritual continuity and depth to life, even in a rustic retreat. For this reason, the men and women in her poems seem always to be set against a temporary background of nature, rather than within it.

A similar focus upon people is evident in her poems on nature as it is manifested in the English garden. Much has been written about the early eighteenth-century movement in gardening.[6] Relevant here is Maynard Mack's reminder that what the eighteenth century meant by "natural," which implied "not oppressively trammeled or corseted by man, yet always conspicuously responding . . . to human pleasure and human need," was different from the later Romantic sense of the word (*Garden* 56).

Finch frequently expresses the belief that redemptive value lies not with nature but with the artistic creations of men and women. Those poems of hers that deal with gardening ultimately praise not so much the gardens as the gardeners. In "Upon My Lord Winchilsea's Converting the Mount in His Garden to a Terras," for example, Finch honors her husband's nephew, whose new landscaping of Eastwell both refined nature and corrected the aesthetic errors of his ancestors. In his wisdom, the young Charles "Removes a Mountain, to remove a fault," a mountain that long had stood "concealing all the beautys of the Plaine" (34, lines 8, 10). Lord Winchilsea's innovations are bold, and as Finch describes them, they reveal the sense of vast design that was to become the hallmark of such renowned eighteenth-century landscape artists as Capability Brown:

So lies this Hill, hew'n from itts rugged height,
Now levell'd to a Scene of smooth delight,
Where on a Terras of itts spoyles we walk,
And of the Task, and the performer talk;
From whose unwearied Genius Men expect

All that can farther Pollish or Protect;
To see a sheltring grove the Prospect bound,
Just rising from the same proliffick ground,
Where late itt stood. . . .

(Lines 17–25)

In designing the gardens and remodeling the house, Charles has employed Augustan principles of design, so that "gracefull simetry, without is seen, / And Use, with Beauty are improv'd within" (lines 53–54). Yet throughout the poem, and again in its conclusion, the poet stresses that her intent is primarily to honor the lord of this estate. It is he, after all, whose art has controlled nature and brought it into harmony with Augustan aesthetic principles, using form and reason to impose order upon his world.

"To the Honorable the Lady Worsley at Longleat" is another honorific poem whose praise of an estate's gardens similarly becomes a tribute to the gardener who designed them. And here, again, it is not the mansion that is singled out for description but the grounds of the estate, for it is they that most fully reflect the lord of this estate as an artist/creator. The poem is addressed to Lady Worsley, Finch's friend and the niece of her husband, and it contains much hyperbolic praise of her. But the laudatory verses to her father, the Viscount Weymouth, are the true nexus of the poem. Weymouth has laid out the gardens in Dutch fashion, and the descriptive passages of the flowered labyrinths, terraced landscapes, and Italian-style fountains and cascades are a tribute to his genius. He has "th' original improv'd," and by doing so, has made of this lovely setting a Garden of Eden (54, line 72). But, the poet writes, paradise did not get its name from the beauty and fruitfulness of external nature, but from Adam and Eve, "th' accomplish'd Pair / That gave the Title and that made itt fair" (lines 107–08). Thus, what makes a garden a paradise, what gives meaning to nature, is not the physical beauty or lushness of the place but the moral and spiritual attributes of the men and women who inhabit it. And that is why, whether in the gardens of Longleat or the gardens of Eden,

'Twas Paradice in some expanded Walk
To see Her motions, and attend his Talk.

(Lines 110–11)

But if human beings remain at the heart of Finch's poetry, one must yet be careful to avoid too loosely applying such terms as "Augustan" to her, as if there were a single, monolithic world view or eighteenth-century humanistic tradition.[7] Finch is a woman, and while the intent of this chapter has been to differentiate her nature poems from a Romantic framework and to define specific ways in which her conceptualization of nature differs from Wordsworth's, something must be added. For once such distinctions have been made, one is still left with an impression that there is a feminine quality about her descriptions of nature that makes them, if not compatible with a Romantic sensibility, at least inconsistent with the values of order, cohesiveness, systematic structure, and light that are traditionally associated with the Enlightenment.

In their sense of rustic retirement as displacement, in their concern with shade and darkness, and in their recurrent images of circuitous wandering and straying in lonely haunts, Finch's nature poems display traits that several feminist critics have identified as characteristic of a feminine poetics. Ruth Salvaggio, for example, who argues in *Enlightened Absence: Neoclassical Configurations of the Feminine* that England's Enlightenment was formed and sustained by suppressing feminine phenomena, writes that in poems such as "Petition for an Absolute Retreat," "it was not only Finch's description of herself and her retreat that betrayed her 'writing as a woman.' It was also her very configuration of shade and wandering and wavering as feminine, as that elusive substance of a 'woman-thing'" (112).

"The Petition for an Absolute Retreat" contains many images suggestive of the plight of the displaced female poet and her efforts to construct what Nancy K. Miller calls "a feminocentric protest" ("Arachnologies" 273). In the opening stanza, for instance, Finch longs for a place where she might find freedom:

> Give me O indulgent Fate!
> Give me yet, before I Dye,
> A sweet, but absolute Retreat,
> 'Mongst Paths so lost, and Trees so high,
> That the World may ne'er invade,
> Through such Windings and such Shade,
> My unshaken Liberty.
>
> (68–69, lines 1–7)

It is, notably, only through the "windings" and lost paths that the poet can claim unshaken Liberty—and retain it. Similarly, the bird in her poem "The Bird," emblematic of the poet/singer, earns its own "wild freedom" by being "a wand'rer" in shady groves (265–66).

Most perceptive is Salvaggio's analysis of the weaving metaphors Finch uses and the process of writing as weaving—or, in Salvaggio's words, the way in which the poet may be said to be " 'weaving' herself through her own poetic imagination."[8] Sandra M. Gilbert and Susan Gubar, who first noted in *The Madwoman in the Attic* the significance of weaving imagery in the writings of several women, see in such mythological weavers as Ariadne, Penelope, and Arachne a metaphor for the female artist (525–28, 641–42). And in alluding briefly to Finch's use of the Arachne tale in her poem "A Description of One of the Pieces of Tapestry at Long-leat," they relate that myth to "the female fall from authority" (525). More recently, Miller has analyzed what she terms "Arachnologies," recognizing these narratives of the spider artist "both as a figuration of woman's relation of production to the dominant culture, and as a possible parable (or critical modeling) of a feminist poetics."[9]

It is, however, not only Finch's imagery that defines her "feminist poetics" and her self-identity as a poet. Later chapters take up a discussion of her melancholic poetry, her pastoral poetry, and, in particular, the way in which she links the long pastoral tradition of retreat poems to her sense of the necessity for female companionship. Finch's poetic identity and her development of a poetics were also influenced in part by her religious sensibilities, by her political commitments, and by the important literary relationships she formed after she returned to London.

SEVEN

London and Its Literary Life

espite her initial welcoming of rural tranquility, Finch occasionally longed for the city. Heneage Finch's letters indicate that as
early as 1697 he and his wife periodically experienced loneliness
and isolation in the country. In the early 1700s Anne Finch, now in
her forties, began to travel more often and to pay frequent visits to
friends and relatives. In the year 1704, for example, while still living
at Wye College, the Finches spent time at Longleat in Wiltshire with
Heneage's sister and brother-in-law, Lord and Lady Weymouth; visited
Leweston in Dorsetshire, the family home of Grace Strode, wife of
Henry Thynne (and hence the daughter-in-law of Lord and Lady Weymouth); and then spent the winter with Lord and Lady Hatton at Kirby
in Kent.[1] In addition to visits to friends and family members, Finch also
occasionally spent time at Tunbridge Wells, the famous health resort
(her poem "The Prodigy" grew out of her 1706 stay at that fashionable
spa). But her apparent restlessness and need for the stimulation of city
life continued.

Another indication of the Finches' readiness to abandon country retirement is that Heneage tried three times during the first decade of the
new century to return to Parliament, beginning in 1701 when he stood
unsuccessfully for Rochester in the county of Kent (Henning 2: 324).
The political climate of 1701 would have made the time seem propi-
tious for a seasoned Jacobite to contemplate a public career once again.
William III was extremely unpopular with many of his British subjects.
His accession to the throne had marked the beginning of England's
involvement in the long and costly Nine Years' War or King William's

War against France. The general antiwar sentiments expressed in the following lines from Finch's "All is Vanity," a Pindaric ode written probably around 1694 or 1695, were shared by most English citizens at the turn of the century:

> Trail all your Pikes, dispirit every Drum,
> March in a slow Procession from afar,
> Ye silent, ye dejected Men of War!
> Be still the Hautboys, and the Flute be dumb!
> Display no more, in vain, the lofty Banner;
> For see! where on the Bier before ye lies
> The pale, the fall'n, th' untimely Sacrifice
> To your mistaken Shrine, to your false Idol Honour!
>
> (241, lines 103–08)

The Second Partition Treaty, which William had negotiated without the consent of the English ministers and which Louis XIV soon violated, angered many citizens, who first learned of its terms in the summer of 1700 (Haley 44–46). Dissension between William's ministers and the members of Parliament seemed irreconcilable, his foreign policy appeared to be in shambles, and there were such deep divisions between the Tories and the more anti-French Whigs that Parliament ended with prorogation in June of 1701 (C. Hill, *Century* 259). So great was William's frustration that he even spoke of abdication (Haley 46).

As the problem of Spanish succession developed, public opinion became sharply polarized about the advisability of entering into another war with France. William was ailing (he was to die the following spring), and there were numerous reports in the press of delegations to James II's exiled court in St. Germain.[2] The immensity of the political divisions in England during 1701 is highlighted by a celebrated incident involving a petition that a grand jury and justices of the peace of Kent, joined by some Whig freeholders, presented to the House of Commons on May 8. Their request that funds be approved for military supplies to protect England, though well within their rights as British citizens, was termed "Scandalous, Insolent, and Seditious." The five men who presented the petition were taken into custody and subsequently, on the order of Tory Speaker Robert Harley, transferred to the Gate House Prison, where they remained until the prorogation of Parliament (Oldmixon 235; C. Hill, *Century* 259).

Perhaps the final contributing factor in Heneage Finch's decision to run for Parliament was the death on September 5 of James II, the monarch to whom his allegiance had remained steadfast during the years following the Bloodless Revolution. James Francis Edward, James II's son (known as the "Old Pretender"), was immediately recognized as the rightful king of Great Britain by France's Louis XIV, the pope, and the king of Spain.[3] For the first time since the revolution the Finches must have had a real hope that the Stuart monarchy might soon be restored. And it was important that men sympathetic to the Stuart cause be elected to Parliament.

But Heneage Finch was unsuccessful in his bid for the Commons. In the final months of 1701 William was able to rally support and gain increased acceptance for his Grand Alliance, which was signed in The Hague just two days after James's death. The election swung toward the Whigs, and when the new Parliament convened on December 31, it was once more anti-French and unified in its commitment to war (Haley 48).

During the reign of Queen Anne, Heneage Finch twice again tried to run for Parliament. As the daughter of James II and a known sympathizer with the Tories, Anne was more acceptable to the Finches than William and Mary were. In 1705, and again in 1710 when the Tory ministry returned to power with Robert Harley as its head, Heneage Finch stood for Maidstone in Kent (Henning 2: 324). Both times he was unsuccessful, though in 1710 a Tory majority was elected to the House of Commons.

By 1708 the Finches had apparently taken up residence in London, for in August of that year, Lady Morrow wrote to her daughter that after calling on the vice-chamberlain, she paid a visit to her friend Mrs. Finch.[4] From that point on, Finch spent large portions of time in London, though she and her husband often returned to Eastwell for extended periods. The Finches may at first have stayed with relatives or temporarily rented a place in London, but at some time, quite likely by 1710 or 1711, they acquired a townhouse in Cleveland Row, a short street, two blocks in length, that today still bears its original name.[5] It runs directly along St. James's Palace, where Anne and Heneage Finch first met in the service of the future king and queen of England, and it faces the Chapel Royal, where they were married in 1684. Thus Finch, now in her fifties, returned to a place that must have held some cherished memories, as well as some bitter ones, for it was twenty years since they had fled London and gone into exile following the revolution.

The nostalgic implications of her return to London are touched upon in her poem "A Tale of the Miser and the Poet," whose subtitle indicates that it was written "about the Year 1709." The poem consists in part of a dialogue between Mammon, representative of the Whig mercantile and political concerns, and a Poet, who speaks for art and the Royalist sensibility. Mammon tells the Poet:

> . . . Brave Sir, your Time is ended,
> And *Poetry* no more befriended.
> I hid this Coin, when *Charles* was swaying;
> When all was Riot, Masking, Playing;
> When witty Beggars were in fashion,
> And Learning had o'er-run the Nation. . . .
>
> (191, lines 29–34)

And the Poet, harking back to the days when wit and letters reigned, hopes that "New *Augustean* Days revive / When *Wit* shall please, and *Poets* thrive" (lines 98–99).

Another poem reflective of her move from the country to London is "The puggs a dialogue between an old & young dutch Mastiff" (see app. A). Probably written shortly after her move to London, this poem is sportive on the surface but contains a cynical parable about adjustment to the ways of the court. The dialogue is between a young Dutch mastiff who lives in Cleveland Row with his mistress (Finch) and an old pug who lives in Leicester Fields with his owner, a knight (Sir Andrew Fountaine). The young dog complains of losing his favored position with his mistress since the arrival of a small jet-black pug named Yanica. The knight's dog, wise in the ways of the world, coaches the younger dog, who had been living in the country but has recently been transported to the city. He warns him that since he has now "removed to the court" (i.e., the vicinity of the court, where Cleveland Row is located), he

> Must swallow wrongs for which by nature
> Your mouth seems a convenient feature.
>
> (W ms. 54)

Indeed, he is told, given the injustices he must learn to accept, he should count himself fortunate if his mistress has so long held him in such favor. Clearly Finch was aware that many of the wrongs she and her husband had endured years ago had now to be forgotten or "swallowed" if they were to adapt to their more public life in London.

But there were many benefits for Finch in her move to the city and her new involvement in its literary life. The year 1709 saw some significant publications for her, as well as the beginning of an important literary relationship. Her pindaric ode "The Spleen," which had been published anonymously in Charles Gildon's miscellany eight years earlier, was brought out in a pirated edition in 1709 by the notorious Henry Hills (known frequently as "Pirate Hills"), along with John Pomfret's "Prospect of Death." While she had cause to be upset with the appearance of this unauthorized pamphlet, she was perhaps pleased at the poem's growing popularity.[6] "The Spleen" would become her best-known poem during her lifetime and her most frequently anthologized poem throughout the eighteenth century.

That year also saw the printing of two of her poems in Delariviere Manley's two-volume edition of *The New Atalantis* (to be discussed in the next chapter), and though these poems were published anonymously, the accompanying narrative contained enough biographical information about the poet's previous attachment to the court and her subsequent move to the country so that Finch's identity was probably generally known.

Of more importance, however, was the appearance that year of three of her pastoral poems in Jacob Tonson's sixty *Poetical Miscellanies*. Finch's "Pastoral Dialogue Between Two Shepherdesses," "Adam Pos'd," and "Alcidor" were sandwiched between two anonymous poems by Jonathan Swift ("Baucis and Philemon" and "To Mrs. Biddy Floyd") and Alexander Pope's "Pastorals." Not only did that collection mark Pope's first publication, but the inclusion of his "Pastorals" along with the "Pastorals" of Ambrose Philips started one of the most celebrated literary debates of the eighteenth century. And the significance of this miscellany was almost immediately recognized; Richard Steele, in the May 3, 1709, issue of the *Tatler* (no. 10), called it "a collection of the best pastorals that have hitherto appeared in England."

Finch most likely came to be included in such a prestigious miscellany through her friendship with Swift, who must have been the intermediary between her and Tonson.[7]

Swift was a friend of Charles, third earl of Winchilsea, who is mentioned several times in his *Journal to Stella*, and it was probably through Charles that Finch and Swift first became acquainted. In any event, from his account books it is known that by December 29, 1708, he was playing piquet with her—and winning (60). But the relationship must have consisted of more than simple chitchat over an occasional game of cards, for two weeks later he wrote to Robert Hunter, "I amuse myself sometimes with writing verses to Mrs Finch" (*Correspondence* 1: 121). Swift obviously became acquainted with her poetry and, admiring it, undertook the task of encouraging her to publish. One result of his efforts is "Apollo Outwitted. To the Hon. Mrs. Finch, (since Countess of Winchilsea,) under the Name of Ardelia" (see app. B). This sixty-four-line homage, probably the verses Swift referred to in his letter to Hunter, is much more than the conventionally elaborate tribute that Nicholas Rowe's poem is, and its humorously argued thesis most likely had a strong influence on Finch's literary future.

In his poem Swift portrays Apollo as enchanted with the lovely young Ardelia (again, the name Finch took for herself), and he attempts to seduce her. Ardelia, however, is not to be outwitted, and she coyly asks that he bestow a gift upon her by putting the Muses at her disposal. This granted, she quickly calls upon Thalia, the Prude, to aid her, thus thwarting Apollo's advances. Unable to take back what he has already granted, Apollo takes his revenge by inflicting upon her such modesty and pride that she will not make her verses public:

> Then full of Rage *Apollo* spoke,
> Deceitful Nymph! I see thy Art;
> And though I can't my Gift revoke,
> I'll disappoint its nobler Part.
>
> Let stubborn Pride possess thee long,
> And be thou negligent of Fame;
> With ev'ry Muse to grace thy Song,
> May'st thou despise a Poet's Name.
>
> Of modest Poets thou be first,
> To silent Shades repeat thy Verse,

Till *Fame* and *Eccho* almost burst,
Yet hardly dare one Line rehearse.
(*Collected Poems* 1:77–78, lines 49–60)

Apollo's final vengeful curse is that Ardelia may at last know fame, but only by yielding ultimately to the plea of one whose political leanings she despises:

May you descend to take Renown,
Prevail'd on by the Thing you hate,
A Whig, and one that wears a Gown.
(Lines 62–64)

(Swift, an Anglican clergyman, may have been twitted by Finch for his Whig propensities; he became a Tory shortly after this poem was written.)

The wit and gentle affection of these lines is unmistakable, and it is not difficult to imagine the effect such a persuasive argument might have had upon the hesitant Finch. Having one of the foremost writers of the age write a highly complimentary poem urging her to publish must have done much to help her overcome her reluctance; within two years of the appearance of Swift's poem in print (1711) she published her own volume of verse.

There is, moreover, other evidence that Swift encouraged her to seek publication and aided in furthering her literary career. When Finch did bring out her volume of poems, it was published by Swift's own publisher and friend, John Barber. Barber, who was a royal printer during the last four years of Queen Anne's reign, spent many hours working with Swift on the *Examiner*, and Swift's biographer, Irvin Ehrenpreis, describes Barber as growing "from a trusted colleague into a close, highly confidential friend."[8] Furthermore, Swift shared both a literary and social relationship with Barber's reputed mistress, Delariviere Manley. They were partners on the *Examiner* and were on very friendly terms (Morgan 18, 174; Ehrenpreis 2: 471, 644, 680). Swift may have introduced Finch to Manley; he almost certainly was responsible for giving manuscript copies of her poems to Manley, who, as noted, printed them in *The New Atalantis* in 1709 and 1711 (see the next chapter).

Another of Swift's poems from 1709 that makes mention of Finch is the somewhat enigmatic "'In pity to the empty'ng Town.'" Swift, or the persona of the poem, satirically depicts Mayfair as having been created to compensate city folk for loss of the benefits and delights of the country. Having declined an invitation to visit in the country, the poem's persona offers the following explanation:

> Howe'er such Verse as yours, I grant
>   Would be but too inviting
> Were fair Ardelia not my Aunt,
>   Or were it Worsly's writing.
>
> [Then pray] think this a lucky Hitt,
>   Nor e'er expect another
> For honest Harry is no Witt,
>   Tho he's a younger Brother.
>
> (*Collected Poems* 1: 455,
>   lines 17–24)

Finch was the aunt of Frances Thynne, daughter of Thomas Thynne, first viscount of Weymouth, and Frances Finch, Heneage's sister. In 1690 Frances Thynne married Robert Worsley, brother of Swift's friend Henry Worsley. However, as Pat Rogers concludes in his edition of Swift's poetry, this poem remains obscure.

There is yet another indication of the friendship between Finch and Swift. In the Wellesley manuscript is a curious poem that contains obvious references to Swift. On the basis of internal evidence (particularly the final stanza), the poem appears to have been written some time around 1714, following Swift's retirement—one might almost say exile—to Dublin. With the return of the Tories to power in 1710, Swift had finally abandoned the Whig party that he had become increasingly disillusioned with and had devoted his energies over the next four years to political journalism on behalf of Tory causes. Bitter and frustrated at not gaining the bishopric he had so long hoped for, he had been dealt a cruel drubbing by his appointment in 1713 as dean of St. Patrick's Cathedral in Dublin, and the fall of the Tories from power in 1714 was the coup de grace. When Swift left London on May 31, 1714, it would be twelve long years before he again saw the capital. The poem, quoted in its entirety, contributes further to an understanding of the friendship of these two writers:

The misantrope

Life at best
Is but a jest
A face a glass a fiddle
A shew a noise
Makes all it's joys
Till worn beyond the middle

Age is worse
The doatards curse
Consumed in endless story
In tales of tubs
Intreagues and drubs
Retold by Grandsires hoary

Who wou'd then
Converse with men
More then his needs enforce him
Since tedious fools
Or boys from Schools
Are most that do discourse him

These to fly
Retired I lye
Unknown and all unknowing
And think't enough
Not nonsense proof
My own I am not shewing.

(W ms. 96)

Though "tales of tubs" was a common proverbial phrase, it may well here be an allusion to *The Tale of a Tub*, a work for which Swift had come to be known as a blasphemer and apostate, but also as a misanthrope (long before the publication of *Gulliver's Travels*). The references to "intreagues" and "drubs" are possible references to the political battles and disappointments Swift had recently endured. The concern with retirement in the final stanza is also pertinent to Swift's situation, particularly since Finch's treatment of it here is so unlike her treatment of the subject in poems such as "The Petition for an Absolute Retreat," where it is portrayed as an idyllic respite, a temporary retreat to a pastoral setting.

Of primary interest in this poem is the persona Finch adopts. The speaker's voice is that of a man, one who by retiring from society in middle age has escaped the fate that all aged men are threatened with: becoming hoary grandsires whose only companions for conversation are "tedious fools" and schoolboys. In other words, the persona is very like Swift, if not Swift himself, and in her subtle and sympathetic identification with him, Finch is at once both honest and compassionate. It is likely that she felt a special kinship with a fellow writer who, like herself, experienced exile for political reasons. Furthermore, through her clever handling of the rhythm, she achieves in these sportive sestet stanzas an additional softening of the charge of misanthropy that might be leveled against the poem's speaker. How sadly ironic that her description of aged dotards was prophetic of what would become of Swift years later in the throes of Ménière's Syndrome.

ON AUGUST 4, 1712, Charles Finch died unexpectedly (F-H ms. 282, 44). Because he left no male heir, his uncle, Heneage Finch, acceded to the title as fourth earl of Winchilsea, and Anne Finch became a countess.[9]

In writing of the death of his friend Charles in a letter to Stella, Swift observed: "Poor Lord Winchilsea is dead, to my great grief. He was an worthy, honest gentleman, and particular friend of mine; and what is yet worse, my old acquaintance, Mrs. Finch, is now Countess of Winchilsea, the title being fallen to her husband but without much estate" (*Correspondence* 1: 55). Though Swift's grief for the loss of his longtime friend was genuine, so, too, was his expression of compassion and concern for Anne Finch, and with good cause. Charles Finch, though sympathetic with the cause of the Nonjurors, had been willing to compromise with the government sufficiently to be given public appointments of some value by both King William and, later, Queen Anne. As Swift observed of Charles, "Being very poor he complied too much with the party he hated" (*Correspondence* 1: 138). Heneage Finch, however, would not compromise. On succeeding to the peerage he refused the oaths and consequently could not be seated in the House of Lords (Henning 2: 324; Cokayne 12: 781).

Moreover, the new earl and countess of Winchilsea did, indeed, face great financial difficulties, for the Eastwell estate was involved in complex litigation that the former earl had not been able to settle before his death. The subsequent court cases and land sales, reported in *Journals of the House of Lords* (19: 659, 668) and *English Reports* (1: 475–77), as well as in Heneage Finch's journal (F-H ms. 282, 108), give some indication of the entangled financial problems and the extended legal battles that Heneage and Anne Finch inherited.

Briefly, the difficulties began when Charles Finch borrowed money on the estate in 1700 to pay some debts. After convincing the dowager countess of Winchilsea, his stepmother, to mortgage her jointure to help him, he thought he had effectively altered the original agreement so as to protect her interests, but in fact, he had not. Following his death, his only daughter, Marianne, and her husband, Philip Herbert, filed suit and then tried to have the Court of Chancery decree reversed so that they, rather than the new earl of Winchilsea, could inherit the full estate.

Heneage Finch's ordeal began with a Chancery trial on July 9, 1713. He was awarded the estate but could not receive it until an appeal filed by Marianne and Philip Herbert was heard. On April 24, 1714, the House of Lords dismissed the appeal and confirmed the allotment of the estate to Heneage Finch. There was more litigation involving creditors, however, and a second Chancery trial began on August 5, 1715. On November 8, 1716, a receiver was ordered onto the estate, and Eastwell remained in receivership until July 15, 1718. On October 17, 1719, Heneage Finch later recorded, Justice Parker "confirm'd Sr Tho: Gevys Report concerning my accounts and allowance &c." And, finally, on February 19, 1720, what Heneage Finch refers to as "[t]he simple contract Creditors cause" was heard before Justice Parker, with the creditors being "excluded" (F-H ms. 282, 110). It took, then, almost eight years for the legal squabbles that involved the Eastwell estate to be settled.

In 1713, just a year after Finch became the countess of Winchilsea, a small octavo volume of her verse was published by John Barber in a single edition under the title *Miscellany Poems, on Several Occasions*. It contained eighty-six poems and her play *Aristomenes*. The title page at first indicated only that the poems were "Written by a Lady," though three subsequent title pages printed that year did bear the name "Lady Winchilsea" (I. A. Williams, *Points* 73). Apparently she agreed to drop her anonymity, perhaps in hopes that sales of the book might be increased.

It is tempting to speculate on the possible relationship between Finch's becoming a countess and her finally seeking or allowing publication of a book of her poems. Ann Messenger notes in her article "Publishing Without Perishing: Lady Winchilsea's *Miscellany Poems* of 1713" that "[a] countess had less to fear from a largely hostile public than a plain 'Mrs.'" (28). However, while her title undoubtedly offered a new source of privilege, it may not have been the only motive for her decision to publish, for she had always been an intimate of aristocratic circles. What may have been highly significant was her new involvement in London literary society and, in particular, the influence and encouragement of some of the most prominent writers of the time.

In addition to her friendship with Swift, Finch also had at least a slight acquaintance with both Nicholas Rowe and Matthew Prior. Rowe had been familiar with her poetry since the 1690s when she was living in Kent (see her "A Poem, Occasion'd by the Sight of the 4th Epistle Lib. Epist: 1. of Horace"). Unlike Swift, however, he did not encourage her to publish, and his poem "An epistle to Flavia, on the sight of two Pindaric Odes on the Spleen and Vanity," in fact approves of her reluctance to see her poetry in print (Chalmers 9: 468). Years later, after the opening of his play *The Tragedy of Jane Shore* at London's Theatre Royal in 1714, Finch wrote a verse epilogue for it that most likely was part of one public performance (see ch. 3).

Even less is known about her acquaintance with Prior. Reynolds includes "To Mr. Prior from a Lady Unknown" among Finch's collected works but suggests that the poem is of doubtful authenticity.[10] Though not particularly distinguished, it is competent in its conventional tribute to Prior, and stylistically and thematically it bears enough resemblance to other laudatory poems of hers so that its attribution need not be called into serious doubt. The inclusion of the trimeter lines in the poem's conclusion, and the general use of prosody, as well as the humble stance of the female speaker in the poem, are all typical of Finch.

In several other poems she makes reference to Prior. In "A Tale of the Miser and the Poet, Written about the Year 1709," both he and Rowe are singled out as examples of English poets whose talents have not yet received proper recognition. In the Wellesley manuscript "The agreeable" mentions Prior by name as a poet whom all aspire to imitate in verse (57), and "A Letter to Mrs Arrabella Marow" refers to his confinement in prison (83). Moreover, "The last chapter of Eclesiastes Paraphras'd" in that manuscript contains a handwritten note at the bottom of the page identifying Solomon as Mr. Prior (61).

The only evidence of a personal acquaintance between the two poets is found in a poem with the lengthy title "To a Lady who having desired me to compose somthing upon the foregoing Subject prevail'd with me to speak the four first lines extempore and wou'd have had me so proceeded in the rest with the following verses." This poem, which is immediately preceded in the Wellesley manuscript by a poem entitled "To the Lord March upon the death of his sparrow," makes reference to "Prior, who that day I met" (103). Both the tone of the poem and the fact that March, with whom Finch is commiserating on the death of his pet, is addressed as a youth, help date the poem's composition as sometime between 1706 and 1711.[11]

Prior, like Swift, became involved in political conflicts during the reign of Queen Anne. Under Robert Harley's government he was chief negotiator for the Treaty of Utrecht in 1713, which ended the War of the Spanish Succession. When the Whigs were reinstated in power, however, he was called back from Paris and placed under house arrest for just over a year. When he was finally released (some months after he finally took the oath of allegiance to the government), he was left poverty-stricken and at the mercy of friends for support (Eves 357–63).

Prior's biographer, Charles Kenneth Eves, assumes that Finch met Prior through her husband's relative Daniel Finch, earl of Nottingham (181), but there is no indication that that branch of the family had much contact at all with Heneage Finch and his immediate family. It is likely that Swift was the means by which the two became acquainted, for

Prior developed a friendship with Swift, whom he met in the autumn of 1710 and with whom he liked to take long walks around St. James's Park (Ehrenpreis 2: 447).

Although Finch was on amiable terms with Swift, as well as with Rowe and Prior, her most substantive literary friendship was with Alexander Pope. That friendship has been misunderstood and misrepresented by virtually all critics who have written about her. Relying on Reynolds as their source, they have perpetuated the erroneous notion that at various times Pope's relationship with Finch was anywhere from ambiguous to downright antagonistic. The facts, however, are that Pope admired her poetry, encouraged her in her writing, and published her; that she wrote several poems to him; that he himself wrote and published a poem in tribute to her; that he was an intimate, personal friend of the Finches and frequently called upon them in their London townhouse; and that the friendship was sustained for perhaps a decade, until the time of her death.

It is not known how or when they first met. It is possible that they could have been introduced to each other when they both appeared in Tonson's 1709 *Poetical Miscellanies*. Or the painter Charles Jervas may have been the source of their first meeting. Jervas, who was a good friend of Pope's, lived just around the corner from the Finches' house on Cleveland Row, and Finch already knew Jervas by 1712 or early 1713 when she wrote "To Mr. Jervas, Occasion'd by the Sight of Mrs. Chetwind's Picture."[12] In December 1713, "To Mr. Jervas" appeared in Richard Steele's *Poetical Miscellanies*, along with another poem of hers, ascribed to "the Countess of W——.[13] The miscellany opened with one of Pope's contributions and included additional poems by him, as well as by Steele, Ambrose Philips, John Gay, and others. It is possible that Pope gave her poems to Steele, for there is no evidence that she knew Steele or any of the other people connected with the project. That Pope owned a copy of "To Mr. Jervas" in an untitled earlier version of the poem, written in Heneage Finch's hand, goes further to suggest that he saw it before its revised published version and may have given a copy to Steele. Pope's copy of the poem was discovered, incidentally, because he used the back of the page to transcribe part of the eleventh book of *The Iliad* (BL Add. ms. 4807). An inveterate paper saver, he frequently used the backs of letters and other manuscripts for drafts of his poems.

There is, in any case, irrefutable evidence that Finch and Pope were acquainted around the time that Steele brought out his *Miscellany*, for Pope was a guest at the Finches' London townhouse for dinner that December.

Reynolds's distortion of the Pope/Finch relationship began with a sentence that she took out of context from one of his letters and that she also misquoted just enough to make its meaning more compatible with her interpretation. In the letter, dated December 15 [1713], Pope is explaining to his friend John Caryll why it is that on Caryll's last day in London, though he had heard Caryll was "so kind as to stay at Common Garden Coffeehouse a considerable time" expecting him, Pope was unable to meet him. Pope writes: "The truth was this: I was invited that day to dinner with my Lady Winchelsea, and after dinner to hear a play read, at both which I sat in great disorder with sickness at my head and stomach. As soon as I got home which was about the hour I should have met you, I was obliged to goe directly to bed" (*Correspondence* 1: 203–04). Reynolds misquotes the first of these sentences, deleting the emphatic "that day" as well as making other minor changes. More serious, however, is that she leaves off the second sentence altogether, undercutting Pope's obvious intent to explain his apparent neglect of his friend, rather than to criticize Lady Winchilsea (introduction to *Poems* lvi). Furthermore, she concludes, with no more evidence than this letter, that it was one of her own plays that Finch read (*Love and Innocence*), that Pope was an unwilling listener, and that the play was the direct cause of his illness—all of which are most spurious conclusions.

One additional piece of evidence that Reynolds offers for what she calls in Pope "certain serious lapses from this attitude of friendship" (xvii) is the play *Three Hours After Marriage*, which he anonymously co-authored with Gay and Arbuthnot in 1717. She assumes that a minor character from the play, Phoebe Clinket, is a satirical portrait of Finch, even though Phoebe is spoofed for her eagerness to have her play performed (Finch never sought performance for either of her two plays) and in general bears almost no resemblance to Finch.

The basis for the identification of Phoebe Clinket with Finch is the E. Parker Key to the play, also published in 1717. There is strong evidence, however, that Parker and other enemies of Pope acted from malice in wrongly identifying some of his friends with satirical portraits in the play. Richard Morton and William M. Peterson, editors of the 1961 edition of *Three Hours After Marriage*, claim that the Parker Key incorporated his "sedulous findings" in order to make the false claim that the Scriblerus triumvirate (Pope, Gay, and Arbuthnot) had personally attacked their known friends, such as Lady Winchilsea (i–iii). Pope's biographer, George Sherburn, reaches a similar conclusion. Claiming that there is no evidence, either external or internal, for the identification of the ludicrous and egotistical Phoebe Clinket with Finch, Sherburn writes that "[i]n making their identification with Lady Winchilsea, Pope's enemies, with obvious malice, picked an authoress of position, known to be intimate with Pope" (195). Similarly, when the play first appeared the character Mrs. Townley was falsely identified as the wife of Dr. Mead, widely recognized as a friend of the three authors (193–95).

There are other indications that Pope and Finch were on the best of terms during 1717, the year *Three Hours After Marriage* was staged. In a letter to John Caryll written August 6, 1717, just six months after the Drury Lane performance of the play, Pope mentions that he has recently been at Lord Winchilsea's, as well as at the homes of several other friends, and he comments: "All these have indispensable claims to me, under penalty of the imputation of direct rudeness, living within 2 hours sail of Chiswick" (*Correspondence* 1: 417–18). It is most unlikely that Pope and Heneage Finch would have such ties of friendship if Pope had just insulted his wife publicly in a satirical play.

The year 1717 also marked the publication of Pope's *Works*, and he included Finch's poem "To Mr. Pope" as one of the commendatory poems customarily included in such volumes. Its heroic couplets offer praise for the younger poet, as well as advice on how to deal with envious and malicious criticism. Finch assumes here the role of an older, worldly-wise aunt who is both supportive and protective of her brilliant young protégé.

That same year Pope published eight of her poems in a miscellany he edited entitled *Poems on Several Occasions*.[14] Only the duke of Buckingham is more generously represented in the collection, save for Pope himself, whose poems all appear anonymously. Finch's poems, however, are given proper attribution, and her name appears in a prominent position on the title page.

One of her poems in that miscellany is "To Mr. Pope, in answer to a Copy of Verses, occasion'd by a little Dispute upon four Lines in the Rape of the Lock" (printed in the Reynolds edition of her poems as "The Answer [To Pope's Impromptu]"). As the poem indicates, Pope apparently showed Finch the manuscript of *The Rape of the Lock*, which he was busy revising, and a friendly dispute developed, most likely over the lines for the invocation of the goddess Spleen in canto iv:

> Parents of Vapors and of Female Wit,
> Who give th' *Hysteric* or *Poetic* Fit,
> On various Tempers act by various ways,
> Make some take Physick, others scribble Plays.
> (*Rape* 189, lines 59–62)

Being herself splenetic and noted for her poem "The Spleen," Finch appears to have taken up the quarrel on behalf of women writers in general, justifying them by citing "Poetick Dames of yore." Pope was inspired by the good-natured dispute to compose "IMPROMPTU, *to Lady* WINCHELSEA," a lovely poetic tribute to Finch:

> In vain you boast Poetick Dames of yore,
> And cite those Sapphoes wee admire no more;
> Fate doom'd the fall of ev'ry female Wit,
> But doom'd it then when first Ardelia writ.
> Of all examples by the world confest,
> I knew Ardelia could not quote the best,
> Who, like her Mistresse on Britannia's Throne,
> Fights and subdues in quarrells not her own.
>
> To write their praise you but in vain essay,
> Ev'n while you write, you take that praise away,
> Light to the Stars the Sun does thus restore,
> But shines himselfe till they are seen no more.
> (*Minor Poems* 120)

Finch responded with her own poem, "The Answer [to Pope's Impromptu]," in which she gently admonished him to "sooth the Ladies" (103). The tone of her poem, including her affectionate address to him as "Alexander," speaks to the cordial, if gently bantering, nature of their friendship. And, incidentally, Pope's poem to her and her "Answer" are the only two poems in the Wellesley manuscript that had previously appeared in print. Their inclusion in a manuscript begun close to the time of her death and meant to preserve her unpublished work suggests the great degree of pride and pleasure that she must have taken in their friendship.

Another poem included in Pope's 1717 miscellany tells us even more about the mutual affection between this aging poet, already well into her fifties, and the widely acclaimed young star of the literary scene, still in his twenties. In "The Mastif and Curs, A Fable inscrib'd to Mr. Pope," Finch depicts Pope as the strong English "masty" who is attacked by petty enemies:

> The little dogs by ladies kept
> Who snarl or flatter for reward.
>
> (131)

None, she writes,

> . . . durst fasten on his skin.
> So well his greater strength they knew,
> Who dirt and scandal on him threw.

When asked by a well-meaning man why he endures these spiteful attacks, the mastiff (Pope) replies:

> Tis fit that some account I yield,
> Why I'm so slow to take the field;
> Or to employ my well known pow'r,
> Such carping vermin to devour.
> But whilst I keep them all in awe,
> From their assaults this good I draw;
> To make you men the diff'rence see,
> Between this bawling troop, and me.

Comparison your observation stirs,
I were no masty if there were no curs.

(132–33)

Finch's sympathy for the falsely maligned Pope is unmistakable. Behind the satirical tone of this poem is the voice of an intimate, steadfast friend. She undoubtedly recognized in Pope, as she did in Swift, a writer who, like herself, was in many ways a displaced figure. She must have felt a natural empathy with the hunchback whose deformity gave him a physical difference perhaps even greater than her gender difference in the primarily masculine literary society of eighteenth-century England. Moreover, both were afflicted for much of their lives with nervous disorders, and probably they identified with aspects of each other's temperament. Furthermore, both poets, though accepted in many aristocratic circles, were nevertheless marginal people because of their political and religious ideologies. Beyond their shared Tory allegiances, both endured persecution for their religion. Indeed, the restrictions imposed upon Pope for his Roman Catholicism were even greater than those suffered by the Nonjuring Finches. As a Catholic, Pope could not hold public office, vote, attend a public school or university, or live within ten miles of London.[15]

One final poetic tribute to the lasting friendship of these two writers comes from the pen of John Gay. In 1720, the year of Finch's death, Gay wrote a poem to celebrate Pope's completion of his translation of *The Iliad*, the monumental project he had been working on for years. "Mr. Pope's Welcome from Greece," subtitled "A copy of verses written by Mr. Gay upon Mr. Pope's having finished his translation of Homer's 'Iliad,'" describes the friends who appear to welcome Pope back from his lengthy metaphoric journey to Greece. There, waiting on the quay, Gay writes,

See next the decent Scudamore advance
With Winchilsea, still meditating song.[16]

EIGHT

Female Friendships
and Women Writers

*T*he extraordinary value that Finch placed upon female friendship is attested by the frequency with which friends figure prominently in her poetry, from her earliest poems to those written in the last months of her life. In addition to a number of occasional poems, there are thirty-five or so verse epistles, many of which are in the pastoral mode, as well as numerous other poems containing passages that honor friends or celebrate female friendship. These poems give evidence of an informal community of friends who were a powerful intellectual and social force in Finch's life and who played a vital role in her development as a writer.

The women who figure significantly in Finch's writing can be grouped into two general categories. First, there were those friends and relatives who were a part of her daily life and who helped her function satisfactorily within the limited social structure that the vicissitudes of state affairs and a chronic mental illness imposed upon her. And then there were the female literary acquaintances who supported and sustained her in her writing, sometimes forming a network with the literary world at large.

The semiseclusion of Anne and Heneage Finch from public life and their retirement to the country after the 1688 revolution brought its disappointing moments. Years later she was to look back fondly on those exciting days at court,

When all was Riot, Masking, Playing;
When witty Beggars were in fashion.[1]

Friendships, then, undoubtedly provided an antidote to possible lone-liness or boredom following the Finches' exile from court and from London, that center of political and cultural activity. Female friends, moreover, offered sympathy and support during those times when Finch feared reprisals against her Nonjuring husband. A number of her poems written during the period subsequent to his arrest and trial re-veal a despondency that she repeatedly suggests can find partial relief only in the comfort of friends. Finally, in the last eight years of her life, once Heneage Finch had succeeded to his peerage and the couple was plagued by new adversities, there was a renewed emphasis in her poetry on the importance of friendship.

Finch's frequent anxiety, however, was not all related to the politi-cal conditions of the early eighteenth century. Janet Todd, analyzing the phenomenon of female friendships in eighteenth-century fiction, remarks that the friendship of women is often a solace, "the last but-tress against the irrationality always implied in the female condition" (*Friendship* 409). For Finch, who struggled repeatedly against that pecu-liarly female malady of melancholy, with its symptoms of physical and mental impotence and the threat of possible madness, the fear of loss of control over her own life must have been great. (Her response to her illness is discussed more fully in chapter 11.) In a very real sense, friendships were for Finch a vital, empowering, and nurturing source in her private life.

The women who people the domestic scenes in Finch's poetry are primarily aristocratic friends and family members with whom she shared common political, cultural, and religious sensibilities. The verses addressed to them are often warm and intimate, frequently suggest-ing strong family ties as well. One such family with whom her life was closely linked was the Thanets. In 1684, within months follow-ing the marriage of Anne and Heneage Finch, Catherine Cavendish married Thomas Tufton, sixth earl of Thanet (*DNB* "Tufton"). Lord Thanet, like Heneage Finch, was a gentleman of the bedchamber to the duke of York (Reresby 432), so it is likely that the lifelong friendship between these two families began during those court days. When the Finches were first married they lived in Westminster, near Great Russell Square, where Thanet House was located. One can assume that the newly married couples, who shared common court ties, exchanged frequent visits.

Shortly after the Bloodless Revolution, when the Finches fled London, they took shelter with various friends and relatives, including Lord and Lady Thanet, whose estate of Hothfield lay in Kent. Though he ultimately took the oath of allegiance for William and Mary and retained his seat in the House of Lords, Thanet was well known as a sympathizer with Jacobites and Nonjurors (*DNB* "Tufton"; Luttrell 2: 22, 183). In one of her most frequently anthologized poems, "The Petition for an Absolute Retreat, Inscribed to the Right Honble Catharine Countess of Thanet, mention'd in the Poem under the Name of Arminda," Finch remembers those days when

> . . . sad *Ardelia* lay;
> Blasted by a Storm of Fate,
> Felt, thro' all the *British* State;
> Fall'n, neglected, lost, forgot,
> Dark Oblivion all her Lot;
> Faded till *Arminda's* Love,
> (Guided by the Pow'rs above)
> Warm'd anew her drooping heart,
> And Life diffus'd thro' every Part.
> (73, lines 159–67)

Though the poet here celebrates the delights of friendship in general, she also expresses deep gratitude in particular for her loyal friend and concludes that she must have Arminda in her pastoral retreat. The ardor of her gratitude, in this poem and in others, suggests how important she found the support of such friends during those most difficult times of her life when she had to deal with political upheavals, displacement, and serious bouts of illness from a nervous disorder diagnosed as a splenic condition.

Finch also maintained a close relationship with the children of Lady Thanet, especially her two oldest daughters, Catharine and Anne Tufton. Quite possibly her involvement in the children's lives helped her compensate for her own childless marriage. In any case, her relationship with the young Catharine Tufton (born in 1692, a year earlier than Anne) produced two poems. In "A Poem for the Birth-Day of the Right Honble The Lady Catharine Tufton," Finch commemorates the birthday of the youngster (given the poetic name of Serena) and pays tribute to her illustrious family lineage. The other poem, "To the R^t Honble the Lady C. Tufton," is a verse epistle that marked the occasion of the poet's receiving the first letter Catharine ever wrote to anyone. Praising Serena's skillful prose style, Finch proclaims that she is the inheritor of her mother's grace in both talent and physical beauty, and she pledges lasting friendship to Serena and to the entire Tufton family.

Finch's affection for Catharine's younger sister, Anne, developed into a more mature friendship between the two women following Anne Tufton's marriage in 1709 to James Cecil, earl of Salisbury. Anne Tufton is undoubtedly the Salisbury praised in "A Nocturnal Reverie" as standing "the Test of every Light, / In perfect Charms, and perfect Virtue bright" (269, lines 19–20). A greater testimony to the intimacy of their relationship than these lines of stylized praise, however, is a delightful poem found in the Wellesley manuscript, "The white mouses petition to Lamira the Right Hon:^ble the Lady Ann Tufton now Countess of Salisbury" (see app. A). The tone of this poem, cast entirely in nine-syllable couplets of feminine rhymes, is unselfconsciously playful; the mouse will gladly surrender its freedom if it can be Lamira's "first captive," an ambition "To which so many hearts are growing":

> With all respect and humble duty
> And passing every mouse in Beauty
> With far more white than garden lillies
> And eyes as bright as any Phillis
> I sue to wear Lamira's fetters
> And live the envy of my betters.
>
> (92)

And finally, suggestive of the full range of emotional experiences the two women shared, we have another poem from the Wellesley manuscript, the solemn elegy "On the Death of the Queen" (97). The poem, discussed elsewhere, contains expressions of Jacobite sympathies but also, in part, nostalgic recollections of the poet's former happy days at court. The death of Mary of Modena is therefore depicted both as a personal loss for the poet and as a symbol of the sad passing of a way of life for the entire country. In the poem Anne Tufton appears as Lamira, the friend who comforts Ardelia as the poet mourns for a loss that is at once both private and public, both personal and political.

Another family whose women figure prominently in Finch's poetry is the Thynnes. Indeed, three generations of Thynnes were her friends, beginning with Frances Thynne, who was her sister-in-law and the wife of Thomas, Viscount Weymouth and master of Longleat. Anne and Heneage Finch were frequent visitors at Longleat, whose mansion and formal gardens she celebrates in such poems as "A Description of One of the Pieces of Tapistry at Long-Leat" and "To the Honorable the Lady Worsley at Longleate."[2] The extent and duration of the friendship between the Finches and the Thynnes are marked by numerous poems pertaining to the Longleat household and to significant family events. These include "On the Death of Hon. James Thynne" (a eulogy for the death of Lady Weymouth's younger son) and "The Following Lines occasion'd by the Marriage of Edward Herbert *Esquire*, and Mrs. Elizabet Herbert" (Lady Weymouth's granddaughter). There are also some lovely verses in the Wellesley manuscript that were inserted in a letter to Lady Weymouth "written from Lewston the next day after my parting with her at Long Leat." In these lines the poet declares that the effect of separation upon those who love each other is dependent upon the degree of their love, just

> As wind opposed to fire
> Extinguishes a feeble flame
> But blows a great one higher.

Hence, she maintains,

> In friendship too the like we find
> If tender and sincere
> And separation to the mind
> Does more the friend endear.
> (100)

Another female of the Longleat household with whom Finch was on very close terms was the daughter-in-law of Lord and Lady Weymouth, Grace Strode. In 1695 she married Henry Thynne, known in several poems as "Theonore" and admired by Finch for his knowledge of the fine arts (see "A Description of One of the Pieces of Tapistry at Long-Leat"). It was possibly around the time of their wedding that she wrote "To the Painter of an Ill-Drawn Picture of Cleone, The Honorable Mrs. Thynne," a poem that praises Grace Thynne's extraordinary beauty, wit, and "enliv'ning Air" while remarking on the artist's inability to capture these on canvas (59). Grace Thynne was about the same age as Finch, and the poem's reference to the "sympathizing Joy we share" suggests that the friendship between the two women was based upon more than familial ties alone.

Following the death of her husband on December 20, 1708, Grace Thynne moved with her two daughters to the Strode family home of Leweston (Luttrell 6: 386). Letters among the Percy family manuscripts in the library of the duke of Northumberland at Alnwick Castle indicate that Finch was among the visitors who occasionally came from Longleat.[3] A playful poem in the Wellesley manuscript entitled "After drawing a twelf cake at the Honble Mrs. Thynne's" suggests that this warmhearted relationship between the two friends was a lasting one. Written on January 6, 1716, the day after Finch and her husband had celebrated Twelfth Night at the home of Grace Thynne, the poem humorously records the festivities. In the traditional game that accompanied the serving of the large, elaborately decorated cake, cards were drawn, each representing members of a court.[4] This particular evening, however, inappropriateness marked every drawing and was evidently the source of much frivolity and good-natured joking. Finch drew the queen, a choice ill suited, she declares, to her "retiring mind" (91). Her husband drew the knave's card, yet with the financial problems that still plagued him, sweeping "his patience and his pence away," she observes that for a knave he would be but "poorly made / And wou'd disgrace the beneficial trade." Mrs. Higgons, a family friend, was designated the king, though with her generous heart, the poet declares, she would surely give away the entire state treasury and bankrupt the nation.[5] Mary, the innocent, youthful daughter of Grace Thynne, drew the card that the poet, in sportive slang, terms "the slut." And the hostess for this festivity, Grace herself, drew the fool, which prompted her friends to remark:

> She cou'd have found no title so unfit
> Or such a foil to her establish't wit.

One of the most important friendships of Finch's last years was with a daughter of Grace and Henry Thynne, Frances, who in 1715, at the age of sixteen, married Algernon Seymour, earl of Hertford.[6] It is evident that the relationship went through a transformation as the young girl matured, so that despite the disparity in their ages, they became close friends. As a child Frances Thynne must have known Finch, her great-aunt by marriage, primarily as the woman who wrote whimsical and tender poems to the children of relatives and friends about pet mice and birthdays and first attempts at letter writing. Perhaps the poet early encouraged her great-niece in literary interests. A curiously prophetic poem, one of the uncollected poems that appears neither in the Reynolds edition nor in the Wellesley manuscript, is "Epistle to Mrs. Thynne."[7] In this poem Finch avers that though a statue should be made to capture the beauty of Mary, Grace Thynne's younger daughter, it is poets and writers who will honor the older and equally beautiful Frances. The reference to Frances as being "two lustres short of female prime" would indicate, if one recalls that a lustrum is five years and assumes that twenty-one is the age of female prime, that she was eleven when the poem was written (and hence places its date at around 1710). It is noteworthy that the future countess of Hertford, remembered today as a patron of such writers as Richard Savage, William Shenstone, and James Thomson (whose "Spring" from *The Seasons* is dedicated to her), should have so early evidenced this propensity to support the literati.

In any event, sometime around the marriage of Frances Thynne to Lord Hertford, the relationship between the two women appears almost to have reversed, with the older woman now dependent upon the sensitive, intellectual young Hertford for support and encouragement in her writing. In her declining years Finch faced serious health problems, including in 1715 a life-threatening illness, and that, as well as the literary precociousness of Lady Hertford, probably contributed to the change.

It was perhaps during that year of 1715 that Finch sent to her great-niece a volume of her poems (most certainly the 1713 volume) with some verses addressed "To the Right Honourable, The Countess of

Hartford, with her volume of Poems." In six heroic couplets the poet requests that the gentle Lady Hertford "look with favour on Ardelia's muse," as had her father, Henry Thynne, before her (61). And in the few remaining years of Finch's life, Lady Hertford was to do just that.

Following their wedding, Lord and Lady Hertford took a house in London in Albemarle Street (Hughes, *Hertford* 18). Its proximity to Cleveland Row, where the Finches had a townhouse, made it convenient for the exchange of visits between the two women. In a letter to his mother-in-law, written possibly in 1717, Lord Hertford explains that his wife "is very well & gone to the Park with Ldy Winchilsea" (Hughes, "Lady Winchilsea" 633). We may assume that such shared outings were frequent.

Sometime shortly after Lady Hertford's marriage, Finch wrote "To the Countess of Hertford on her Lord's Birthday." This poem, another of the still-uncollected poems found in scattered manuscripts, praises Lady Hertford as well as her husband and pays tribute to their marriage as an ideal union (BL Add. ms. 4457). Of greater interest, however, is a poem from the Wellesley manuscript containing the lengthy title "To the Right Honourable Frances Countess of Hartford who engaged Mr Eusden to write upon a wood enjoining him to mention no tree but the Aspin & no flower but the King-cup" (72). The poem can easily be dated, for it contains a direct reference to a whimpering infant Eliza who is old enough to smile and therefore would have to be at least a month or two of age. The aspen tree is nature's "Rattle to some peevish wind," the poet writes,

> As your Eliza when her griefs she tells
> In little whimperings you appease with bells
> Till thousand tender smiles her face adorn
> And yours a thousand tender smiles return.

Since Lady Hertford's baby, Betty or "Eliza" Seymour, was born November 24, 1716, the poem was undoubtedly written early in 1717. The date is of some significance, for the poem recounts an incident from what must have been one of Lady Hertford's earliest literary gatherings, held either at Marlborough Castle in Wiltshire or at Lady Hertford's favorite "Hermitage," St. Leonard's Hill in Windsor Forest, some miles from London (Hughes, *Hertford* 97). Lady Hertford was later to become well known for these gatherings; Thomson's "Spring" is reputed to have been written in part during his visit to one at Marlborough in 1727. If the jocular tone of Finch's poem is any indication of the mood at these literary affairs, one can understand their popularity. The poet uses her poem as an occasion to chide Lady Hertford lightheartedly for demanding the composition of some verses from Lawrence Eusden and then so restricting him in subject matter that no poetic inspiration was possible.[8] After enumerating the sights on the country estate that Eusden *could* have described poetically had he not been limited to one type of tree and a single variety of flower, Finch then jokingly scolds her friend for "misus'd influence and Poetick force." The poem concludes, however, with indirect compliments to Lady Hertford as a patron of the arts and a promise that if she becomes less rigid in her requests, she shall be rewarded for her kindness by "The happier muse."

As final testimony to the depth of friendship between Finch and her great-niece, we have the moving words of Heneage Finch in a letter written to Lady Hertford in 1725, five years following his wife's death:

Dearest Madam:

I am so sensible of your Ladyship's goodness to me in communicating your most excellent poem, and so charmed with the beauty (for I think it very fine) and piety through it, that I would express what I feel, but I cannot in the terms it deserves. I cannot but think how my dear wife (who truly knew your value) would have been delighted if she could have seen this and others of your Ladyship's performances in this kind. She would have wished you (as I must in her stead) to proceed. Of all my relations, you alone knew how to distinguish her by a friendship which she had the most grateful sense of as long as she lived. You and your Lord showed it at all other times, so more particularly at the time when comfort of friends was most wanted. She had many in her health; but in her decline and sickness, none but Lord and Lady Hertford exerted themselves in being more kind than (if possible) at other times; and this she was very sensible of, and your Ladyship will believe it has ever laid a greater obligation upon me than all the effects of your goodness to me, which I feel as I ought, and which I beseech God may ever be returned upon you and yours.

I must repeat that I think with pleasure my poor wife would have read everything from your hand, and especially that last piece, the poetry of which is extremely good, and the piety very great and moving. I wish it may teach others of your sex (and ours too) if not to write so well, yet to live as that teaches and you practice. It should be more seen (though not shown by me without your permission). I have but room to tell you that I am, Madam,

Your most affectionate obedient servant,
Winchilsea.[9]

A friend and frequent correspondent of both Grace Thynne and her daughter, Lady Hertford, was Mrs. Arabella Marrow, daughter of Sir Samuel Marrow, baronet of Berkswell, Warwickshire. It was undoubtedly through the Thynne circle that Finch first met Mrs. Marrow and her mother, Lady Marrow. In a letter to Arabella Marrow's sister, Lady Kay, dated August 1708, their mother writes briefly of visiting Finch. The letter is of interest because it further documents Finch's chronic melancholy, but, more important, it gives additional testimony about the personality of the poet: "Friday last I went to town. . . . From the Vice Chamberlain I went to see Mrs. Finch, she ill of the spleen. Lady Worsley has painted a pretty fire-screen and presented her with; and notwithstanding her ill-natured distemper, she was very diverting— Mrs. Finch I mean."[10] We have much internal evidence from Finch's poems that she was herself a charming, good-natured woman who enjoyed a hearty laugh, even at her own expense, and who could be a personable companion. Lady Marrow's firsthand account of a visit to her during one of her confinements with an attack of melancholy indicates that even when suffering under physical and emotional impairment, she could still be good company and a lively, witty conversationalist.

In "A letter to Mrs. Arrabella Marow," a prose and verse epistle dated October 18, 1715, Finch refers to a well-known poet of the time, Elizabeth Rowe (née Singer), who published under the pseudonym of Philomela:

> Sad Philomela hasted down
> Her spouse's fate to grieve
> As now dispairing in the Town
> Of ought that cou'd relieve.
>   (W ms. 84)

Married in 1710 to Thomas Rowe, Elizabeth Rowe (1674–1737) was widowed on May 13, 1715, and as Finch's lines indicate, the widow thereafter left London to retire to Frome. Elizabeth Rowe was the eldest daughter of Walter Singer, a Dissenting preacher (Todd, *British Women Writers* "Rowe"). Following the death of her mother, her father moved the family to Frome, less than five miles from Longleat, and it was at Longleat that Finch and Rowe probably became acquainted. The reference in "A letter to Mrs Arrabella Marow," occurring within the context of information about mutual friends, strongly suggests a personal acquaintance. Moreover, a close relationship existed between the Thynnes and the Singers, with Henry Thynne even undertaking to instruct Elizabeth Singer Rowe in French and Italian. It seems most likely, then, that during one of Finch's frequent extended visits to Longleat the Thynnes would have introduced her to their neighbor, particularly since both women were poets.

There are other indications of a connection between the two poets. In a reference to Philomela in "A Tale of the Miser and the Poet," written, according to the subtitle, "about the Year 1709," Finch decries the present state of poetry. The best poets, she complains, are "Slighted, or Discarded," and, she rhetorically asks,

> Meets PHILOMELA, in the Town
> Her due Proportion of Renown?
> (192)

Moreover, in a letter written to Lady Hertford in 1720, Elizabeth Rowe comforts her friend on the death of "My Lady ———," who can only be Lady Winchilsea, for no other friend of Lady Hertford's is known to have died around that time. In the letter Rowe reminds Lady Hertford of "the extraordinary character she [this unnamed lady] left behind her" (qtd. in Reynolds, introduction to *Poems* xxxix).

With the appearance in 1696 of *Poems on Several Occasions*, Elizabeth Rowe gained immediate fame, becoming widely known as "the Heavenly Singer." By 1704 she and Finch had had some form of contact with each other, for the well-known Rowe was reading Finch's poems in manuscript and encouraging her in her writing. This is evident from a letter Rowe wrote from her home at Frome to Grace Thynne at Longleat, which asked, in a postscript, that thanks be extended to

Finch, who was obviously at the time still visiting the Thynnes: "p.s. my service to Mrs. Finch I thank her for letting me have the Copy of the Storm 'twas impossible for her to have obliged me more I have sent to beg the favour of Milton" (Hughes, "Lady Winchilsea" 633). In a verse and prose epistle entitled "A Letter to the Hon[ble] Lady Worseley at Long-Leat" and dated from Leweston, August 10, 1704, Finch thanks her hostess for the recent "few happy days which I passed at Long-Leat" (W ms. 88). Most likely, then, during that visit Rowe was also at Longleat and either heard about or was shown a copy of "A Pindarick Poem Upon the Hurricane," a description of a devastating storm that occurred the previous year. Since Rowe does not write to Finch directly but asks her friend to convey a message, we can assume that she received a copy of the poem from Finch in person while both were at Longleat, and that she thanked her then for obliging her. "A Pindarick Poem Upon the Hurricane" is a lengthy ode (373 lines, including the accompanying hymn), and to have copied it by hand would have been a task that a sister poet would have acknowledged in more than a simple postscript in a letter to a third party. The wording of the postscript, moreover, which offers no comment on the poem itself but simply commends the poet for her kindness in honoring the request for a copy, suggests that praise of the poem had already been offered. Rowe must have read the poem or heard it read aloud while she was at Longleat and admired it enough to request her own copy of it. The obscure reference to Milton is apparently an allusion to a conversation between the two poets and Mrs. Thynne.

While there is no evidence of a true friendship between Finch and Rowe, there was, apparently, mutual artistic respect and the sort of sustaining, nurturing support that has historically been essential in order for women to gain public acceptance for their writing.

Those such as Elizabeth Rowe, Catherine Fleming,[11] and the countess of Hertford, who were all part of a circle of friends and personal acquaintances, were not the only women to aid and encourage Finch in her development as a writer. Other literary women who quite possibly had never met her in person nevertheless circulated manuscripts of her poetry and wrote exhortative verses to her. There were certainly male authors who played important roles in shaping her literary career; the influence of such towering figures as Pope and Swift was, as noted earlier, highly significant. But the sustaining, empowering source of Finch's drive for poetic achievement was to a great extent the consistent support of female friends, both private and literary.

Long before Finch became known publicly as a poet, she enjoyed recognition and encouragement from other female writers in what appears to have been an informal, loosely structured type of network. Rowe's connection with her is just one example. Another involves Delariviere Manley, whose scandalous narratives of court life and aristocratic society earned her immense popularity—and notoriety.[12] Though there is no hard evidence that the two authors ever met, circulated manuscripts of Finch's poetry obviously reached Manley, quite possibly through their mutual friend Jonathan Swift (see chapter 7). Three of Finch's poems, none of which had previously been printed, were included, one each, in three of Manley's early books.[13]

"Life's Progress" appears in the first volume of Manley's *Secret Memoirs and Manners of Several Persons of Quality, of Both Sexes. From the New Atalantis, A Island in the Mediteranean,* which was published in May 1709. Bearing the title "The Progress of Life," the poem differs slightly from the version published in Finch's 1713 *Miscellany Poems,* primarily in the use of classical allusions instead of biblical ones (e.g., "Parnassus to the Poet's eyes" in the earlier version was later changed to "Not Canaan to the Prophet's eyes"). Manley introduces the poem by a brief portrait of a woman whose virtuous character she contrasts with that of the three other people she has just been describing satirically. The description accurately applies to Finch and indicates several points of interest. First, whoever passed on copies of these poems to Manley had some familiarity with Finch's personal life: "The Lady once belong'd to the Court, but marrying into the Country, she made it her business to devote herself to the Muses, and has writ a great many pretty things: These Verses of the Progress of Life, have met with abundance of Applause, and therefore I recommend 'em to your Excellencies perusal" (168). Second, this intermediary between the two women authors spoke highly of Finch; hence Manley's remark, after having just described an obnoxiously proud woman, that there was nothing about her "so commendable, as her value for that fourth Person which was with them in the Coach [i.e., Finch]." And finally, the assurance that the verses of this lady "have met with abundance of Applause" suggests that the network responsible for the circulation of Finch's manuscripts must have been rather extensive.

On two other occasions Manley's printing of a Finch poem marked its first appearance in print. The second volume of *The New Atalantis*, published in October 1709, includes "The Hymn," and "The Sigh" appears in letter XI of Manley's *Court Intrigues, in a Collection of Original Letters, from the Island of the New Atalantis*, published in 1711. Like "Life's Progress," both these poems appear in Manley's texts in earlier versions than the ones printed in Finch's 1713 *Miscellany Poems*.

"The Hymn" affords particular opportunity for analysis of its later emendations, since, unlike the other two poems, it is dated (February 9, 1704) and appears in the octavo manuscript. The hymn concludes "A Pindarick Poem Upon the Hurricane," the poem that Elizabeth Singer Rowe admired and requested a copy of. Since the octavo manuscript was begun in the latter half of 1690 and completed in 1691, this poem must have been added to it at a much later date.[14]

The version of "The Hymn" that Manley printed was earlier than the one found in the octavo. The few emendations in the octavo version essentially involve the substitution of Hebraic or Christian references for classical ones: for example, Jove is replaced by "the Almighty." In Manley's introduction to "The Hymn" she has Lady Intelligence indicate to Lady Virtue that it is part of a longer poem on the recent hurricane, so she was familiar with the entire ode. Before Heneage Finch transcribed the ode and hymn in the octavo, then, the poem in an earlier draft was shown to Manley.

Another instance of sympathetic cooperation and communication between contemporary women authors involves an obscure poet known only as Mrs. Randolph.[15] Sometime in the 1680s she saw a manuscript copy of Finch's "A Pastoral Between Menalcus and Damon" and responded with a poem eulogizing her as heir to Orinda (Katherine Philips). This poem delighted Finch enough for her to have it included at the beginning of the folio manuscript of her poems that Heneage Finch began to compile around 1694 or 1695.[16] More important, it elicited from Finch a poem that is of relevance here, for in it she expresses awareness that both she and Randolph have a link with women writers of the past. In "An Epistle From Ardelia To Mrs. Randolph in answer to her Poem upon Her Verses," Finch thanks her sister poet for her generous praise and responds with her own laudatory comments on Randolph's talent. What is significant, however, is that she evokes the memory of Sappho, compares Randolph to Philips in her role as poet/friend, and vaguely suggests the awareness of a continuum in the female literary experience—a continuum that could not be realized fully by women writers until at least two centuries later.

In this epistle Finch claims that women will no longer yield to men the sole right to claim the title of poet; remembering Sappho and the literary heritage of women, Ardelia proclaims,

> Then we'll no more submitt, but (in your name)
> To Poetry renew our Ancient Claime.
>
> (95, lines 13–14)

Randolph has honored Ardelia by declaring her the rightful heir of Orinda's fame. And Ardelia, recalling the intimate friendships celebrated in Philips's poetry, suggests that she proudly stands in a relationship to Randolph that parallels that of Orinda's "glorious friend" to Orinda:[17]

> Thus, have you Madam, by your lines enhanc'd
> My humble worth, and so, my fame advanc'd,
> That where-so-ere that Panigerick's shown,
> It stands inferiour only to your own;
> And whilst Orinda's part you far transcend,
> I proudly bear that of her glorious Friend,
> Who though not equaling her lofty Witt,
> Th' occasion was, of what so well she writt.
> Might I the paralell yett more improve,
> And gain as high a Station in your Love. . . .
>
> (Lines 27–36)

Only Randolph's love can inspire Ardelia to write, she declares, and she concludes her poem with an avowal that poet and friend are inextricably linked:

> Since upon you, itt does alone depend
> To make a Poet, when you make a Friend.

Finch's sense of a relationship between female friendship and poetry might well owe its origin in part to her high regard for two of her most famous literary predecessors, Katherine Philips and Aphra Behn. Both these women, who lived just a generation earlier, wrote pastoral poems that extolled female friendship. While it would be erroneous to claim that a tradition of female pastoral friendship poetry existed in her day, Finch was aware that both Philips and Behn offered a means by which she might modify some of the more patriarchal elements inherent in pastoral poetic conventions, particularly by introducing the theme of female friendship.

Philips, known as "The Matchless Orinda," wrote numerous poems to women celebrating the love of friends. Some of these lyrics elevate female friendships to metaphysical and religious heights. There has been speculation that the "Society of Friendship" mentioned in her verse was a formal artistic salon over which she presided; it is more likely, however, that this "Society" was a metaphor for the spiritual bond between friends, especially those with shared literary interests.

In several lines inserted in the prose preface, lines that Finch claims are "some of the first lines I ever writ," she tells of her invocation to Apollo and his response to her:

> I grant thee no pretence to Bays,
>   Nor in bold print do thou appear;
> Nor shalt thou reatch Orinda's prayse,
>   Tho' all thy aim, be fixt on Her.
>
> (7)

Her admiration of Philips was readily acknowledged in the many allusions to Orinda scattered throughout her verse. It is certain that Philips's poems were well known to her, and in fact, she quite possibly chose her pen name from Philips's "A retir'd friendship to Ardelia. 23rd Augt. 1651." Finch adopted this pseudonym in the early 1690s, shortly after her settlement at Eastwell. "A retir'd friendship to Ardelia," which is the only instance in which the name appears in Philips's work, is a retirement poem. It urges Ardelia to leave the world, with all its "quarreling for Crowns," "treachery," and "changes in our fate" (27). For Finch, recently uprooted in the aftermath of the revolution, this poem must have touched some poignant personal emotions.

In many of her pastoral poems celebrating platonic love, Philips addresses her friends under pseudonyms, as Finch was also to do. (See, for example, "Friendships Mystery, to my dearest Lucasia," or "To

Mrs. M.A. at parting.") In these poems there is a strong relationship between female friendship and the incipient pastoral theme of desire for escape from the world. This is evident in a poem such as "Invitation to the Country," where the poet writes to Rosania of a rural retreat:

> When no distractions doth the soule arrest:
> There heav'n and earth open to our view,
> There we search nature, and its author too;
> Possessed with freedome and a reall state
> Look down on vice, on vanity, and fate.
>   There (my Rosania) will we, mingling souls,
> Pitty the folly which the world controuls
> And all these Grandeurs which ye most do prize
>   We either can enjoy or will despise.
>
> (103–04)

In 1684, less than a decade before Finch left London and settled in the country in Kent, Aphra Behn published her *Poems Upon Several Occasions*, which included a number of poems in the pastoral vein. Among the best of these is "The Golden Age." It begins with a conventional longing for that "Blest age" when nature and humanity lived in harmony. In Arcadia, the poet tells us, there was eternal spring and the earth was forever fruitful. The contrast between the Golden Age of the past and the current world is then extended to the political and social realm. Arcadia was uncorrupted by the "rough sound of war's alarm," and there were no civil laws or religious injunctions to restrict and control human behavior. Nature and her creatures were benevolent. Even the snake in that prelapsarian Eden lacked "spiteful Venom," so the nymphs, unlike poor Eve, could play in unmolested innocence (6:139, st. 4, line 1; st. 3, line 17).

For the first five stanzas, then, Aphra Behn does not deviate much from traditional treatment of standard pastoral themes. The idyllic past is contrasted with the barbarous present, and all the familiar differences are noted.

In the last five stanzas, however, all the themes introduced in the first half of the poem converge in what becomes the poet's ultimate concern: the politics of gender in the contemporary age as revealed through an understanding of the Golden Age. If the current world is tainted and corrupt, its effects are felt most by women. What above all marks the Golden Age as distinct from the poet's contemporary world, she writes, is that pleasure reigned supreme there. Women, Behn implies, were then as free as men now are to give and receive love without inhibitions and restraints:

> The Nymphs were free, no nice, no coy disdain
> Deny'd their Joyes, or gave the Lover pain;
> The yielding Maid but kind Resistance makes;
> Trembling and blushing are not marks of shame,
>   But the Effect of kindling Flame:
> Which from the sighing burning Swain she takes,
> While she with tears all soft, and down-cast-eyes,
> Permits the Charming Conqueror to win the prize.
>   (St. 6, lines 97–104)

In stanza 8 the poet begins a strong invective against "cursed Honour" who "first didst damn, / A Woman to the Sin of shame." The poet/persona now reveals her own sex as she identifies with womankind, vehemently proclaiming that honor "rob'st *us* of our Gust" (line 119 [emphasis mine]). By being forced to bind up their tresses and contain their beauty, as well as their passion, women are cast into roles as temptresses but denied their natural inclination to satisfy the desires they arouse:

> Now drest to Tempt, not gratify the World:
> Thou, Miser Honour, hord'st the sacred store,
> And starv'st thy self to keep thy Votaries poor.
>   (Lines 135–37)

Women are portrayed by Behn as the victims of ecclesiastical and civil institutions that enslave their very sexual natures. Hence they are caught in a double bind: they awaken desire, but they are also the ones who are supposed to deny its fulfillment. Thus there are only two possible roles available for a woman: the tease or the harlot. And Behn, who had been maliciously typed in public as the latter in her personal life, had cause to know what a price women paid for heeding their own sexuality.

In the final stanza she directly addresses the young maid Sylvia as she employs the familiar *carpe diem* convention—but with a new twist. It is not an ardent male lover who concludes the poem's argument by urging Sylvia to seize the day; it is the amorous poet/persona who once again includes herself among the nymphs of this new Arcadia, this liberated world she would call forth:

> Then let us, Sylvia, yet be wise,
> And the Gay hasty minutes prize.

Finch knew and admired Behn's poems, even if she could not emulate her frankness in her treatment of love and female sexuality. Finch's close involvement with aristocratic circles and her early connections with the court, as well as her lifelong devotion to the Church of England, made her extremely conscious of the necessity for maintaining propriety, particularly since the very act of writing was itself highly suspect for a woman. We know, for instance, that she was sensitive to the criticism that Behn had endured for writing too freely of passion.

In "The Circuit of Appollo," a lighthearted account of a literary contest in which a Paris-like Apollo is asked to choose the best female poet, Finch offers superlative praise for Behn. But although she claims that there "was not on the earth / Her superiour in fancy, in language, or witt," Finch nevertheless feels it necessary to acknowledge that "A little too loosly she writt" (92). And in her prose preface she justifies her own poetic treatment of love. Her remarks in the preface are worth quoting, for they suggest the pressure she must have felt as a woman author:

> For the subjects, I hope they are att least innofensive; tho' sometimes of Love; for keeping within those limmitts which I have observ'd, I know not why itt shou'd be more faulty, to treat of that passion, then of any other violent excursion, or transport of the mind. Tho' I must confesse, the great reservednesse of Mrs. Philips in this particular, and the prayses I have heard given her upon that account, together with my desire not to give scandal to the most severe, has often discourag'd me from making use of itt, and given me some regrett for what I had writt of that kind. . . . (10)

Finch's response to Behn's poetry demonstrates the complexities involved in the issue of gender difference. The category "women" in this case is reticulated with issues of class, political and religious ideology, and sexual orientation. Finch's privileged position as a member of the aristocracy, her high church Anglicanism, and her general ideological commitments caused her to shy away from the frank sexuality that the middle-class Behn embraced in her poetry. Much of Finch's love poetry is conservative, even reactionary, when placed beside Behn's.

Yet despite the multiplicity of differences reflected in the concern Finch expressed about Behn's lack of reserve, it is obvious that Finch learned much from her, as well as from Philips.[18] Both taught her that the pastoral tradition could be molded to the needs of a woman writer and that love was a fit topic for a female poet—though being too open about passion could, as Behn showed, lead to public censure. And both also suggested to her the possibility of a link with woman writers/friends of the past and the present.

A number of early English authors place a similar high value upon female friendships. The theme of friendship is recurrent in seventeenth- and eighteenth-century women's writings and is found in diverse types of literature. In addition to Behn and Philips, Jane Barker and Mary Lee, Lady Chudleigh, wrote poems in tribute to friendship. The theme of female companionship and love is also central to the plays of Margaret Cavendish, duchess of Newcastle, especially *The Convent of Pleasure* (1669). And much of the polemical prose of Mary Astell justifies female communities and friendships as the best means for women to develop Christian morality and sustain virtuous lives.[19]

Finch was not, then, the only early woman writer to acknowledge the value of female friendship, but none praised it more highly and more consistently than she did. In her life as well as her poetry, female friendships figured prominently. Women friends were a mainstay of her social and domestic world and an essential part of her commitment to poetry. Her female literary predecessors, moreover, offered her a post-humous friendship that reached across time, encouraging her in her own literary pursuits and giving her, however tenuously, the sense of a female literary and spiritual continuum.

NINE

Arcadian Anachronisms:
Place and Time in
the Pastorals

*I*n the chapter on Finch's love poems it was suggested that she frequently uses generic traditions and literary conventions in a manner that affords her more freedom of expression than would otherwise have been available to a woman author. In "The Unequal Fetters," for example, she evokes *carpe diem* imagery only to subvert the reader's expectations, ultimately reversing the *carpe diem* theme and creating within the poem a bitter feminist statement about the falseness inherent in traditional seduction arguments. Similarly, in "The Cautious Lovers" the conventions of such pastoral dialogues between lovers are overturned as the poem develops its ironic statement about love in early eighteenth-century English society.

This chapter and the next will examine more closely Finch's use of one particular generic tradition, the pastoral. Though she experimented with some genres only briefly (the song, for example, she virtually abandoned after her early poetry), she remained fond of the pastoral throughout her life. It was a genre that she found adaptable to a wide range of themes and styles, so that by focusing on it, we are able to gain a sense of the richness and diversity of her art. Moreover, she is at her most innovative in her pastoral poems. Though many women later in the eighteenth century and throughout the nineteenth wrote pastorals, Finch was one of the first to use this mode in a radical way.

By situating herself within the conventions of pastoral poetry, Finch could usurp male poetic prerogative. In a number of her poems the stance of the pastoral poet provides her with a freedom from gender restrictions. In some of her pastorals she deconstructs gender and sexuality in order to re-create an ungendered space. The pastoral genre offered her a vehicle for reconstructing this "free space," because its tradition of playing around with gender was already established in Renaissance English literature. In Shakespeare's *Tempest*, for example, there is the ambiguous gender of Ariel (a role, incidentally, that has frequently been the object of cross-gender casting). Then there is Rosalind in *As You Like it*, whose wanderings through the Forest of Eden dressed in shepherd's clothes represent a woman's appropriation of masculine power. And in *Venus and Adonis* there is a reversal of customary courtship roles as an aggressive Venus pursues the reluctant youth who would rather hunt than dally with her in the fields. As Dorothy Mermin observes in her splendid article "Women Becoming Poets," the experiences of Finch and other women poets of the last half of the seventeenth century could begin to "fit existing poetic conventions, although not the dominant social ones."[1]

Most definitions of the pastoral are so abstract and inclusive as to be of little value.[2] It seems most useful, therefore, to understand the pastoral genre in its historical context as a philosophical concept, which is how Finch seems to have understood it, and to realize that the tradition she found so appealing was multifarious, with roots dating back to early classical poetry but with a rich variety of sources reaching her from both European and English Renaissance literature as well.[3]

Pastoral can refer loosely to any literature that treats of rustic life but also embodies philosophical concepts. And at the center of pastoral poetry is this paradox: the pastoral presents an ideal life of rustic simplicity and ease, the re-creation of an Arcadia or a Garden of Eden, but this ideal can only be realized through art, which is a product of a sophisticated and therefore tainted urban society. Thus the pastoral concept is frequently realized through the juxtaposing of disparate values to create a tension between such opposite elements as art and nature, the town and the country, courtly sophistication and rural simplicity, heroic action and contemplative retirement, responsibility and freedom, the troubling present and a Golden Age of the past, and so on.

One of Finch's most successful uses of the pastoral mode is in "An Invitation to Dafnis," a poem that relies heavily upon contrasts and employs a number of pastoral conventions. Here the genre provides an opportunity for her to create that "free space" and to reverse gender roles. The persona of this poem, Ardelia herself, is charmingly seductive in her feminine flaunting, and ultimate subverting, of the *carpe diem* convention. The invitation to her husband, known here as Dafnis, is, as we are told in the subtitle, "To leave his study and usual Employments,—Mathematicks, Paintings, etc. and to take the Pleasures of the feilds with Ardelia." Thus, the first of the poem's several antitheses is introduced immediately: the intellectual pursuits of scholarly confinement versus the sensuous pleasures of rural abandonment.

The poem opens with a recounting of Arcadian delights, but it is not set in Arcadia, nor does it lose its sense of contemporaneity. Rather than casting her seduction poem in an artificial Golden Age, Finch retains a sense of the real while calling to mind for her Dafnis, and for the reader, what Arcadian pleasures *were* like. "When such a day, blesst the Arcadian plaine," she begins, thereby infusing the present with images of an idyllic past to create a simultaneous vision of two ages, while creating an art/nature antithesis as well:

> When such a day, blesst the Arcadian plaine,
> Warm without Sun, and shady without rain,
> Fann'd by an air, that scarsly bent the flowers,
> Or wav'd the woodbines, on the summer bowers,
> The Nymphs disorder'd beauty cou'd not fear,
> Nor ruffling winds uncurl'd the Shepheards hair,
> On the fresh grasse, they trod their measures light,
> And a long Evening made, from noon, to night.
> Come then my Dafnis, from those cares descend
> Which better may the winter season spend.
> Come, and the pleasures of the feilds, survey,
> And throo' the groves, with your Ardelia stray.
>
> (28, st. 1)

Dafnis is indeed being asked to sport with Amaryllis in the shade, but his Amaryllis is a real woman, and her "invitation" to her husband blends a touch of naughtiness with the reality of their domestic relationship. Throughout the poem Finch maintains this dual vision, which is ultimately a tension between art and nature.

The poem's title, with its use of the familiar classical name Dafnis and its announcement of the poem's intent to entice Dafnis "to take the Pleasures of the feilds with Ardelia," is alone sufficient to set the reader up for certain *carpe diem* expectations. The suggestion that "An Invitation to Dafnis" is to be part of a well-known generic tradition elicits from the reader the anticipation of a variety of pastoral themes and images, and it is this anticipation that the poet can now play against. Because Finch is using a decidedly masculine seduction convention but converting it to a vehicle for feminine response, the reader simultaneously experiences both traditional expectations for this genre and amused surprise at the poet's deviation from these expectations. This is, after all, not Marlowe's passionate shepherd pleading to his love, nor Sidney's lusty shepherd conniving for the favors of his chosen nymph. It is the slightly coy Ardelia, who lures her husband with a gently enticing "invitation." If we forget the role of a classical nymph and of her shepherd/suitor, and the stock responses that Finch's Augustan contemporaries would have had even to the title of this poem, we are missing much of the poem's charm and its subtle artistry. Finch does not here burlesque the pastoral conventions, as Swift was to do a decade later in "A Description of the Morning" and "A Description of a City Shower." The sensibility with which we should approach "An Invitation to Dafnis," however, is similar to the one that is required for Swift's urban pastorals. As Roger Savage advised in his article "Swift's Fallen City: 'A Description of the Morning,'" our understanding of such a poem depends, in part, upon our recognizing that the poem owes "some sort of allegiance to a *genre* with rules and hereditary images . . ." (183).

In the opening stanza of "An Invitation to Dafnis" the poet evokes Arcadia. It is a pleasant summer's day, Ardelia tells Dafnis, and they, like the nymphs and shepherds of old, ought to take advantage of it. The intellectual studies that now consume his time, she says, are more appropriate to the winter season. So "Come," he is urged, "and the pleasures of the feilds survey / And throo' the groves with your Ardelia stray" (28).

The present day suggests for Ardelia an idyllic Golden Age, and if we recall that shepherds and their nymphs spent such a day sporting on the grass, the invitation to Dafnis to "stray" with her through the groves takes on tantalizing sexual overtones. In this poem, however, it is not the use of the persona alone that gives Finch freedom to write about love and sexuality—topics that would otherwise have been considered improper for a woman to deal with. It is the genre itself that is the primary source of her creative freedom. One of the specific advantages for her in using the pastoral is that it supplies a license, enabling her through the weight of its traditions, through its "hereditary images" and its anticipatory themes, to achieve an artistic emancipation.

In the second and third stanzas, the art/nature motif hinted at earlier is more fully developed. As each studious occupation of Dafnis is enumerated, it is juxtaposed with its counterpart in nature. His intellectual concerns are thus weighed singly and collectively in balance against the natural world, the pastoral world. Rather than read poetry, he is admonished, he should view "the subjects of each rural muse"; the geometric problems he is working with a compass should be forsaken for the opportunity to be where fairy circles have marked the ground; and his painstaking task of putting illuminations on vellum should be abandoned for a vision of far brighter colors in the fields of poppy and corn. The geography book he is consulting may describe entire kingdoms in a single page, but, he is chided, not even the description of the entire world is equal to the experience of this single temperate day in the English countryside.[4]

In the first stanzas of the poem, then, the poet has introduced, through a series of juxtaposed opposites, the art/nature conflict that is at the center of much pastoral poetry. Her treatment of the theme thus far has been, if witty, nonetheless somewhat superficial. But in the fourth stanza, through development of a brilliant extended metaphor, Finch probes the very heart of the paradox. As the stanza opens, that alluring temptress Ardelia offers one final item in the catalog of her beloved's interests. Shut away in his study, he has been tracing in detail the war campaigns on behalf of his deposed monarch, James II. Do not, she playfully teases him, plead "That mighty Bastions keep you from the feild," or think that "tho' lodg'd in Mons, or in Namur, / You're from my dangerous attacks secure." Not only has Ardelia become more aggressive, but she has now made his studies into a metaphoric fortress that she vows to storm with her own troops. These personal martial forces that she shall gather to challenge Louis and to steal away her Dafnis are none other than Apollo and the Muses. With their help, her poetry will be victorious, enabling her to storm every fort and take every town to win Dafnis. Her poems, she says, like the songs of Orpheus on his magic lute, will make everyone defenseless against her attack, for her "strong, confederate Syllables" are the strongest weapons one can muster.

Several of the senses are focused upon singly, with a separate stanza devoted to each of these senses. The images of the first stanza all suggest the sense of touch and kinetic sensation: Arcadia is warm yet shaded; the climate is temperate, so that no rains blast the plains; a gentle breeze stirs through the summer bowers, yet it disturbs neither dress nor curly hair of the young shepherds and nymphs. In the second stanza it is the visual senses that are portrayed: the beauty of nature exceeds man's geometric designs, and the brilliance of flower and sea surpasses the colors of paintings. (But, significantly, the poetry that Dafnis is reading is not declared inferior to the rural subjects that have inspired it; Dafnis is simply admonished not to neglect to view these subjects in nature.)

After the short third stanza, which praises nature, and the fourth, which celebrates the superiority of poetry, the fifth stanza is devoted to yet another of the senses, that of sound. And this stanza also introduces yet another pair of conventional conflicting elements, that of town and country. The town-and-country conflict is pervasive in the history of pastoral poetry, for, as Frank Kermode has noted, it is "the social aspect of the great Art-Nature antithesis which is philosophically the basis of pastoral literature" (37). In this stanza, then, images of various auditory pleasures in the natural world are juxtaposed with a satiric portrait of the world of the city. The songs of birds and the murmurs of springs and rivers are contrasted with the false and grating speech of courtiers, disgruntled unpaid sailors, and brawling townspeople.

"An Invitation to Dafnis" begins with love, with a wife's playfully luring her husband to partake of country pleasures. It is fitting, therefore, that the poem should conclude with an image of faithful conjugal love and its rewards:

> As Baucis and Philemon spent their lives,
> Of husbands he, the happyest she, of wives,
> When throo' the painted meads, their way they sought,

Harmlesse in act, and unperplext in thought,
Lett us my Dafnis, rural joys persue,
And Courts, or Camps, not ev'n in fancy view.
  So, lett us throo' the Groves, my Dafnis stray,
  And so, the pleasures of the feilds, survey.

                                                    (30)

The story of Baucis and Philemon (Ovid's *Metamorphoses* 8: 611–724)
recounts the fate of an aged Phyrgian couple noted for their enduring
love. For their generous hospitality to the disguised Jupiter and his son
Mercury, the couple was richly rewarded. Their modest cottage was
transformed into a splendid temple in which they presided as priest
and priestess, living out their last days as they had their first, in harmony with nature and with the gods. Furthermore, in fulfillment of
their request that they not be separated by death, both were one day
simultaneously changed into trees, so that they remain an oak and a
linden, intertwined as one.

  In addition to the domestic sentiments of affection and fidelity that it
imparts, the myth is also appropriate to Finch's pastoral themes. Baucis
and Philemon, like Dafnis and Ardelia themselves, are not the eter-
nally youthful shepherd and nymph of an Arcadia, yet their love and
their closeness to nature bring them lasting peace and contentment.
They exemplify, moreover, at least a partial reconciliation in the conflict
of art and nature that the poem has centered around. It is, paradoxi-
cally, through the sophistication of art that the poet can reclaim for us
the simplicity of Arcadia. The legend of Baucis and Philomen has, as
Donne would put it, made them "fit for verse," and that verse, whether
Ovid's or Finch's, is the only means by which Arcadia can be re-created
for us. That is why Finch opens her poem with Arcadian images, and
why Ardelia's final plea to Dafnis to come "stray" with her takes on
the force of a philosophical imperative.

  One further aspect of this poem deserves comment. As noted, Finch
is here consciously writing in the mainstream of the seventeenth-
century *carpe diem* tradition, yet in her poetics she is very contemporary;
one senses more kinship with such eighteenth-century writers as Pope
and Swift than with earlier writers such as Dryden. This is particularly
true in "An Invitation to Dafnis" in her sense of a dual vision expressed
through use of such rhetorical techniques as polemic imagery and the

grammatical structure of the heroic couplet itself. Though the overall structure of the poem and the development of its thought are stanzaic, with recurrent concluding refrains, it is the Augustan sense of order and balance in the couplets which moves the stanzas along, energizing the whole, as can be seen in the following passage:

> Come, and attend, how as we walk along,
> Each chearfull bird, shall treat us with a song,
> Nott such as Fopps compose, where witt, nor art,
> Nor plainer Nature, ever bear a part;
> The Cristall springs, shall murmure as we passe,
> But not like Courtiers, sinking to disgrace;
> Nor, shall the louder Rivers, in their fall,
> Like unpaid Saylers, or hoarse Pleaders brawle;
> But all shall form a concert to delight,
> And all to peace, and all to love envite.
> Come then, my Dafnis, and the feilds survey,
> And throo' the Groves, with your Ardelia stray.
>
> (St. 5)

"An Invitation to Dafnis" demonstrates Finch's maturity in handling her craft. The poem is structured around a series of contrasting values pitted in opposition to each other, just as its heroic couplets are themselves structured on principles of syntactic balance. Her ear for the poetic line is strong and sure. The rhythmic awkwardness that occurs occasionally in some of her early songs or in such lyrics as "An Invocation to Sleep" is missing here, as is the singsong effect of tetrameter couplets with frequent feminine rhymes that is found in such poems as the 1689 "Upon Ardelia's Return Home." Instead, one finds here a unity between symmetry of line and development of idea. Similarly, Finch's earlier tendency to mix iambic tetrameter and pentameter couplets, to intersperse them at random with triplets or substitute an Alexandrine for one line of the couplet, or to use midline full stops that work against the sense of the couplet as a self-contained unit, all give way here to a rhythmically and thematically satisfying verse form.[5]

A brief comparison of Finch's poem and its closest literary ancestor, Herrick's well-known "Corinna's Going A-Maying," may help demonstrate some of the ways in which she adopted literary traditions and adapted them to her own use. A comparison may also reveal something about the politics of gender in the Golden Age. Both poems are steeped in the *carpe diem* tradition, both are centered around an art/nature dichotomy, and both open with a plea to a loved one to seize the rural pleasures of the day. Furthermore, in both poems the person addressed is confined within a room and is being gently berated—Corinna for her sluggishness and Dafnis for his bookishness. Even the stanzaic structure of each is similar, with its frequent use of juxtaposed opposites to reinforce thematic elements. And Herrick's refrain, with its variations on "Come, my Corinna, come," is echoed in Finch's "Come then, my Dafnis," refrain. But the primary similarity between the poems is, as we have seen elsewhere in noting Herrick's influence on Finch, a matter of tone. Unlike the persistent, passionate seducer one encounters in many *carpe diem* poems, Corinna's lover and Ardelia are gently teasing in manner, and their sexual aims are only mildly suggested. It is the wit and genial humor of these two personae that make both poems so thoroughly charming.

But there are differences between the two poems. Herrick's lovers reside in Arcadia, whereas for Finch's couple, Arcadia can only be temporarily achieved through poetry (i.e., the beauty of the day merely *suggests* Arcadia to Ardelia, and the rural retreat that she proposes is not meant to last beyond a few brief hours). Consequently, Finch's treatment of the paradoxical nature of art seems more suggestive than Herrick's.

The most obvious way in which Finch departs from the model of Herrick's poem, and from the entire generic tradition of the pastoral, is that she reverses conventional roles of swain and nymph. By establishing herself as a female speaking subject in a love poem, she creates a revisionary pastoral. Her poet is not a shepherd, piping his tunes to win the affections of some reluctant nymph, some "slug-a-bed" Corinna. Instead, we are faced with something unusual in English literary history, a pastoral poet/persona who is the nymph as well as the aggressor in the amorous pursuit. Moreover, the carefree Arcadian swain has been transformed into a scholarly, diligent husband. And for this scene of domestic love Finch has brought to bear the whole tradition of pastoral poetry and given it the freshness of her individual talent.

ANOTHER ADVANTAGE FOR FINCH in using the pastoral mode, in addition to its allowing her to write of love and passion as she would not otherwise have been able to do with propriety, is that it gave her a vehicle for criticizing her own age and for speaking as a public poet. While personal lyrics and letters do form a substantial portion of the body of her poetry, in many of her most significant poems her poetic stance is clearly that of a moral spokesperson addressing the ills of her society. The conventions of pastoral poetry, especially when combined with her satiric eye, supplied her with an authority normally denied to a female author. Consequently, the generic tradition of the pastoral helped her to legitimize her "public" voice and became for her an enabling device for artistic liberation.

It is probably no coincidence that "Ardelia's Answer to Ephelia," Finch's most sustained effort at satire, contains a pastoral framework. The tradition of using the pastoral poem for satiric commentary is an old one, dating back at least to Juvenal's sixth satire, but for antecedents of this particular poem one could turn to more contemporary sources. Donne's "Satyre 6," with its devastating portrait of a fop and its vision of a visit to court as a descent into hell, is a distant relative of Finch's poem. The nearest relative, surprisingly, seems to be Rochester's "A Letter from Artemisia in the Town to Chloe in the Country."

A comparison of "Ardelia's Answer to Ephelia" with Rochester's satire offers an excellent opportunity for focus on gender differences, particularly since there are no significant distinctions of class or political ideology between these two poets that might blur gender differences. Both Rochester and Finch were Royalists from aristocratic families, and both began writing while in the literary environment of the Court Wits. Indeed, Rochester's residence at court preceded hers by only two years; until his death in 1680, he served Charles II, and as we have seen, she maintained close ties with the Stuart monarchy until its ouster.

By the time Finch joined the court, Rochester was generally recognized as a major poet of his day (Farley-Hills 7). His influence upon her early work is evident, though as noted earlier, she did keep her writing secret while at court, not wanting, as she later confessed, to be ridiculed as a "Versifying Maid of Honour" (preface 8).

Rochester's "Letter from Artemisia in the Town to Chloe in the Country," regarded by some as his finest piece of social satire, was twice published in broadside in 1679 and appeared again in the volume of his poems published just weeks after his death.[6] "Ardelia's Answer to

Ephelia," written in the early 1690s, bears much similarity to his poem in thematic detail and in use of narrative and dramatic techniques.

The disparate values that form the basis of satirical commentary in Finch's poem are precisely those traditionally associated with pastoral verse—country versus city, rural simplicity and innocence versus court sophistication and corruption, and natural female beauty and behavior versus the artificiality in manner and appearance of court nymphs. These antitheses are also found in Rochester's poem, though they are less prominent and exist primarily by implication. Both poems also have a complex narrative structure that involves several speaking characters, so that sometimes there are narratives contained within narratives. The form both poets adopt is that of a verse epistle from one female friend to another, and the persona of each poem is a female poet whose sharp wit and piercing eye provide a lively account of city life. Finch's persona is Ardelia, the poetic name she repeatedly used for herself, but only, with few exceptions, in her most personal poems or in those with possibly inflammatory political or social implications that she withheld from publication. "Ardelia," then, often appears to be closely identified with the real-life poet.

In responding to her friend's invitation to visit her in town, Ardelia recounts her previous visit to London, and her recollections become, as the poem's subtitle indicates, an occasion for "reflecting on the Coquetterie and distracting humor of the Age." Rochester's Artemisia, on the other hand, resides in the town and writes to bring her country friend Chloe up to date on London's social life and the latest gossip. Thus both epistles are filled with anecdotes that demonstrate the corruption and degradation of London aristocratic society, though the perspectives of the two personae differ greatly.

At the center of both poems is a satirical portrait of a court nymph who embodies the decadence of her society. The literary evolution of the nymph is part of a long tradition in both the pastoral and satire, and the traditions frequently overlap. In satires against feminine use of cosmetic arts, for example, the town nymph, with all her paint and artificial mannerisms, is generally contrasted with her innocent country cousin.[7] In the Rochester poem (*Poems* 104–12) the nymph, identified ironically only as "a fine lady," is an affected, loquacious coquette who flits about, assuming "fifty antic postures" (line 94). She is sycophantic with an old acquaintance they meet by chance, a fop whom Artemisia describes as a "dirty, chattering monster." Though well read and possessing a discerning wit, the "fine lady" is utterly devoid of self-knowledge: "to her was known / Everyone's fault and merit, but her own" (lines 164–65). Finch's Almeria is a similarly loud and ostentatious flirt who fawns all over Ardelia. Furthermore, she is described, in words that echo Rochester's description of his coquette, as one who "discerns all failings, but her own" (39, line 27). Like Rochester's "fine lady," she also assumes a variety of antic poses and indulges in grand but hypocritical displays of affection for the fop she encounters by chance. Almeria, moreover, "flies round the Coach" (line 46), showing herself at the windows for public admiration, just as Rochester's fine lady "flies upstairs" to meet Artemisia and commences to show herself at the window.

However, despite similarities in some narrative sequences and in descriptions of the nymph and the fop, Finch's poem deviates markedly from Rochester's. In his persona's report on the amorous escapades and intrigues of London's high society, women do not fare well. Theirs is, Artemisia tells Chloe, a "silly sex" (line 56), and throughout her sardonic narration there is no portrait of a woman that one can hold up in contrast to that of the "fine lady." Indeed, Artemisia's epistle closes with her grim story of Corinna, the courtesan who seduces a foolish squire so that he

> Believes, then falls in love, and then in debt;
> Mortgages all, ev'n to the ancient seat,
> To buy this mistress a new house for life;
> To give her plate and jewels, robs his wife.
> And when t' th' height of fondness he is grown,
> 'Tis time to poison him, and all's her own.
>
> (Lines 242–47)

Rochester offers the reader nothing to counteract that image of women as manipulative, conniving hypocrites who perpetuate a corrupt social system. Though not much of a participant in the predatory world that the poem depicts, Artemisia neither does nor says anything to present a more balanced view. Ultimately, then, Rochester's use of a female persona does not impart any sympathy with women. On the contrary, it allows him to present an even harsher condemnation of women than would have been possible with a male persona. Criticism from one's own kind, after all, is always the most devastating.

One further point: the men who are portrayed in Rochester's poem are *victims* of their town nymphs. The husband of the "fine lady" is a drunken, cuckolded fool whose wife prevails upon him, "though much against his will" (line 76), to bring her repeatedly to London to pursue her social adventures. Her lengthy explanation to Artemisia of why fops make better lovers than do men of wit (who are less easily deceived and manipulated) intensifies the poem's sexually biased psychological milieu. The message of the poem is clear: women are in control, and if the city is evil and its inhabitants all debauched, then it is women who are most to blame.

The satirist often offers us, either directly or indirectly, a concept of what constitutes a healthy body politic so that we can recognize and accept the validity of his diagnosis of an unhealthy one. Rochester scoffs and sneers contemptuously at the world his Artemisia describes, but he is as aloof as is his persona, and the satiric view he offers is finally a nihilistic one. One senses in "A Letter from Artemisia in the Town to Chloe in the Country" that the diseased world Rochester describes suffers an incurable illness. This illness, in the poet's view, is endemic in society, and it is passed on through the female sex.

Finch's concept of satire is quite different. In her prose preface, written ten years later, she defends her use of satire and carefully defines her purpose in writing "Ardelia's Answer to Ephelia," declaring that "the whole intention of itt, was in general to expose the Censorious humour, foppishnesse and coquetterie that then prevail'd. And I am so far from thinking there is any ill in this, that I wish itt oftener done, by such hands as might sufficiently ridicule, and wean us from those mistakes in our manners, and conversation" (11).

The overt corrective intent of Finch's satire, as well as her concept of the poet as moral advocate, differentiates her poem from Rochester's. The values she contrasts throughout "Ardelia's Answer to Ephelia" are clearly defined; she supplies ethical touchstones and examples of health (to continue the metaphor begun earlier). Because of her simplicity and goodness, Ephelia, to whom Ardelia is writing, brings her love and spiritual freedom. And in direct contrast to the decadent Almeria is the young Alinda, whose reputation Almeria tries to destroy with malicious gossip, but whom Ardelia defends as

> Discreet, and witty, civil and refin'd,
> Nor, in her person fairer than her mind.
>
> (Lines 176–77)

But it is the narrator who is of primary importance. In his essay "The Muse of Satire," Maynard Mack notes the importance of determining for the reader the moral character of the persona. "For the satirist especially," writes Mack, "the establishment of an authoritative *ethos* is imperative" (195). Finch takes great care to develop for the reader an understanding of the sensibilities of her narrator, thereby providing a moral basis for her persona's censorious eye. Almeria's catty remarks to the fop about Ardelia offer further opportunity for defining the poem's conflicting values: Ardelia is criticized for her intellectual pursuits, her preference for the rustic to the fashionable and opulent, her sense of religious devotion, her eschewing of literary fads, her disdain of courtly vice, and her refusal to engage in gossip. These attributes, which are all positive, assert the norms that Ardelia stands for. And since Finch has frequently identified herself in the body of her work as Ardelia, they also, to some degree, define her. For though she uses a variety of personae, speaking sometimes in male voices (as in "Ralph's Reflections" and "A Pastoral Between Menalcus and Damon"), in working-class voices (as in "A Pastoral Dialogue Between Two Shepherdesses" and "An Epilogue to the Tragedy of Jane Shore"), or in a configuration of several voices (as in her verse plays), it is with the persona of Ardelia that she most closely identifies herself. In her love lyrics to her husband, in her personal verse epistles to female friends, and in those poems of a more politicized or autobiographical nature, it is frequently Ardelia who speaks.

By contrast, the structure of Rochester's poem, as David Vieth notes, "resembles a room full of mirrors endlessly reflecting one another," so that no "true" perception is offered by its characters, either singly or collectively, and certainly not by Artemisia herself (introd. to *Poems* xl). In point of view, Rochester's Artemisia is more a passive observer than a moralist. Finch's Ardelia, however, is a participant who interacts with other characters, often engaging in dialogue with them, and her actions are as important to the poem's satirical statement as are her words.

Each persona views herself as a poet, but they view the role of women authors in general very differently. Artemisia begins her epistle to Chloe somewhat reluctantly, disclaiming any responsibility for attempting verse, since it is by Chloe's command that she writes. She, like Ardelia, recognizes the scorn that women writers must endure: "whore is scarce a more reproachful name / Than poetess," she says (lines 26–27). The irony with which Rochester's persona describes the world's disdain for women writers suggests more tolerance of women poets and sympathy with their plight than one might expect from this quintessential Restoration rake. Yet Artemisia's attitude toward her own talent and toward her presumption in undertaking the craft of poetry is apologetic, and she does feel subservient to male writers. Not so with Ardelia, who is confident and secure. When the snide Almeria makes scurrilous remarks about another woman poet, Ardelia is quick to defend the right of any woman to become a poet:

> Why shou'd we from that pleasing art be ty'd,
> Or like State Pris'ners, Pen and Ink deny'd?
>
> (208–09)

Here, as elsewhere in the poem, the identities of persona and poet are intertwined, so that Ardelia's remarks are also Finch's assertion of her own right to take up the pen.

Satire requires the reader to move back and forth from the fictive world of the poem to the real world; we test elements of a satiric work against the world we know, and we judge their validity accordingly. However, in Finch's poem a more significant issue is the extent to which the reader is led to identify the persona with the real poet.[8] To a woman writer for whom issues of authority and aesthetic liberation are crucial, the use of a persona may function as an enabling device with which to establish her poetic identity. Persona and poet may, in fact, form something of a symbiotic relationship.

The single most distinguishing aspect of Finch's poetic identity, here and elsewhere, is her consciousness of gender. She never forgets that she is writing as a woman and will also be read as a woman. And the reader of "Ardelia's Answer to Ephelia" never forgets that Ardelia the persona and Finch the poet often have intersecting identities.

In "Ardelia's Answer to Ephelia" Finch creates a revisionary version of Rochester's well-known satire. And because "A Letter from Artemisia in the Town to Chloe in the Country" is a major work by a contemporary male poet, she also creates a significant emancipatory revision of the pastoral satiric tradition.

Another poem that treats of the city/country theme through the pastoral convention and that involves the subverting of a patriarchal hegemony is "Adam Pos'd." Its finely polished, tightly executed verses consist of four heroic couplets and a triplet, concluding with an Alexandrine. This superb poem, as witty as it is skillful, deserves to be quoted in full:

> Cou'd our First Father, at his toilsome Plough,
> Thorns in his Path, and Labour on his Brow,
> Cloath'd only in a rude, unpolish'd Skin,
> Cou'd he a vain Fantastick Nymph have seen,
> In all her Airs, in all her antick Graces,
> Her various Fashions, and more various Faces;
> How had it pos'd that Skill, which late assign'd
> Just Appellations to Each several Kind!
> A right Idea of the Sight to frame;
> T'have guest from what New Element she came;
> T'have hit the wav'ring Form, or giv'n this Thing a Name.
> (149)

The basis of this satire is an anachronistic encounter between a "pos'd" or perplexed Adam and a Restoration coquette. The sophisticated nymph, transplanted with all her paint and courtly mannerisms to a natural country setting, would have been an instantly recognizable figure to Finch's contemporaries. The first half of the poem, furthermore, would have elicited immediate expectations from its readers, for the literary tradition of satiric attacks on feminine artificiality and the use of cosmetic arts, a tradition dating back to such ancient poets as Horace but revived during the Renaissance, was still a popular one during the seventeenth and early eighteenth centuries. Once again, however, Finch's use of tradition demonstrates her artistic finesse in handling feminine themes.

Finch is careful to place her Adam in a postlapsarian state: the thorns are in his path, he has the sweat of hard labor as he tills the ground (Gen. 3.18–19, 23), and he is clothed in skins (Gen. 3.21). By offering us an Adam already fallen, the poet intensifies his perplexity at confronting this nymph, for we know that he has already met Eve and named her (Gen. 3.20). What confuses him, then, is not that this nymph is of another sex; it is that her nature is so protean, her manner and appearance so changeable. Her fashions are "various," her faces are "various," and she performs with "all" her airs and "all" her antic graces. She is "fantastick" in the sense of being fanciful, capricious, and impulsive, but to Adam she is also, in an additional meaning of the word, something of a phantasm, an apparition, and outside the range of his rational knowledge. She is, in short, beyond definition, for to name is, at least in part, to define.

Adam's first act after being created is to name every living creature. Even before God has made Eve, he brings to Adam all the animals he has created, "to see what he would call them: and whatsoever Adam called every living creature, that was the name thereof" (King James Version, Gen. 2.19). Thus Adam's naming of things signifies that they are brought into some sort of schematic order, are made a part of the cosmic framework. And the reason he is perplexed with this court nymph is that she lies outside the scope of his understanding and, perhaps, his control. Adam may have unquestioning dominion over the creatures of the earth and the air and the sea, but this "wavering Form," this "Thing," has given him pause.

In her article "'Adam Pos'd': Metaphysical and Augustan Satire," Ann Messenger compares this poem to Donne's "Satyre 6," noting that the germinal idea for Finch's poem is the line in Donne that describes a courtier as "A thing, which would have pos'd Adam to name" (10). While one may differ with Messenger's reading of this poem as highly condemnatory of the nymph, her analysis of the poem's satire is astute. The persona of "Adam Pos'd," Messenger concludes, "is also quietly laughing at Adam, the mere male, vainly attempting to understand a modern woman" (11). This contemporary coquette is a vain, dissembling nymph, but she is also lovely, graceful, and perhaps somewhat enticing because of her very unpredictability. If Finch is gently satirizing feminine frivolity, her mood here is more amused than condemnatory. And it is the scene itself that causes her amusement. What is comical is not so much the nymph as the contrast between her and Adam. Clad in "rude, unpolish'd Skin," diligently plowing and weary from the drudgery of his labor, Adam suddenly confronts a frolicsome, frivolous, elaborately adorned lady, and she thoroughly befuddles this paradigm of patriarchy, this "first Father." Ultimately Finch allows the poem to turn upon itself, so that the nymph's very beauty and coquettish antics satirize Adam more than they satirize the nymph herself. The poem becomes a subtle assertion that women cannot be categorized nor molded into structures created and dominated by male rationality. When confronted by masculine control, female artfulness triumphs. Thus, at the poem's conclusion, this early feminist poet might almost be seen as lightheartedly thumbing her nose at Adam, that most formidable of patriarchal figures.

The country/city theme appears elsewhere in Finch's work, but it is not always handled satirically. "A Ballad to Mrs Catherine Fleming in London from Malshanger farm in Hampshire" (see app. A), which appears in the Wellesley manuscript, contains humorous verses addressed to a friend who has remained in town while the poet/persona has retreated to a country farm. In a series of pleasant images the poet contrasts the innocence and quiet of rural life with the noise and hectic pace of city dwelling. Only her friend's enticement, like the "sweet harmonious art" of Orpheus's song, could ever woo her away again (91). But if that happened, she cautions, then her beloved woods, "Charm'd like Birnam's . . . wou'd rise" and march with her into London, so startling the townspeople that she would be forced to return immediately. This is more gentle humor than satire, as she reminds us in her concluding stanza:

> Mean while accept what I have writ,
>   To shew this rural scene;
> Nor look for sharp satyrick wit,
>   From off the balmy plain:

The country breeds no thorny bays,
But mirth and love and honest praise.
With a fa-la-la-la-la-la.

This whimsical ballad, written in 1719, the year preceding Finch's death, demonstrates the versatility of the pastoral in her hands, as well as her persistent fondness for its themes. It also demonstrates an aspect of her pastorals that will be discussed more fully in the next chapter: the importance of pastoral friendships.

TEN

Elegiac and Edenic Visions

*T*he motif of friendship runs throughout much of Finch's pastoral verse. In "A Ballad to Mrs Catherine Fleming," for example, she turns the familiar country-versus-city theme into a poetic tribute to her friend: having retreated to the country after a recent visit to Fleming's London home, Finch welcomes in the poem the serenity of rural life and expresses a strong distaste for urban noise and confusion, yet she affirms that she will nonetheless return to the noxious city if it is the only way to enjoy the pleasure of her friend's company.

In addition to such occasional poems as "A Ballad to Mrs Catherine Fleming," Finch has numerous verse epistles in the pastoral mode that glorify friendship and honor individual friends. In the verse epistle "To My Sister Ogle, Dec³¹, 1688," for instance, she mourns the separation from her half-sister and speaks of the day when heaven shall restore them to each other's company.[1] Evoking an Edenic vision of a future when they will be reunited, she writes that

> Time, shall submitt to freindships pow'rs,
> And as we please, shall rest, or fly.
> (38, lines 11–12)

The poem concludes on a note of comfort: their present pains will be rewarded when they leave this life together,

> New arts to find, new joys to try,
> The height of freindship to improve.

The extraordinary significance Finch places upon friendship is not inimical to the pastoral tradition. Thomas Rosenmeyer traces in *The*

Green Cabinet the tradition of the epistle and its relation to the pastoral, noting that several of Theocritus's most successful poems are cast as letters to friends. He observes, moreover, that the epistolary medium has similarities to pastoral singing matches and to exchanges between lovers (106). Even more to the point is Rosenmeyer's assertion that in the pastoral, "proper freedom is possible only if it is enjoyed in a circle of friends" (105–07).

Inherent in the concept of the pastoral is the notion of freedom, whether from the responsibilities and restraints of sophisticated urban life or from the degradation and corruption of one's own age. Hence the yearning for a simple rural retreat, often created for us by the poet's evoking of a classical or a prelapsarian paradise. Whatever the philosophical issues treated in the pastoral, however, the notion of freedom is always central to the desire for retreat. As evidence for the corollary between friendship and retreat, we need only note that the personae in Finch's pastoral poems almost never seek solitude in their retreats. In "The Petition for an Absolute Retreat," for example, the poet would share her retreat with a sympathetic mate—"A *Partner* suited to my Mind"(68, line 72)—as well as with her friend Arminda, for whom she pleads:

> Give then, O indulgent Fate!
> Give a Friend in that Retreat."
> (Lines 196–97)

In one of the last poems she wrote, "On Lady Cartret drest like a shepherdess at Count Volira's ball" (see app. A), Finch's tribute to her friend becomes ultimately the means of resolving the pastoral dichotomy between nature and art.[2] Creating a whimsical visual image through the use of anachronism, as she does in "Adam Pos'd," the poet here reverses the use of this comic device; rather than bringing the present into the past (as when a modern coquette is placed before Adam), she inserts Arcadian shepherds into the midst of an elegant eighteenth-century masquerade ball.

The poem is in anapestic tetrameter, a measure difficult to sustain in English verse and seldom used before the nineteenth century. (Byron's "Destruction of Sennacherib" and Browning's "How They Brought the Good News from Ghent to Aix" are notable examples.) The rising meter of the anapests suggests unrest, a kind of unsettledness that borders on the awkward—all of which suits perfectly the disorientation conveyed through satirically humorous anachronisms.

A group of curious shepherds wander into a ballroom where they mingle unnoticed with the disguised revelers. And, like Adam, they, too, are "pos'd" by what they witness:

> Quoth the Swains who got in at the late Masquerade
> And never before left their flocks or their shade
> What people are here who with splendor amaze
> Or but with their antick variety please
> Who talk to each other in voices unknown
> And their faces are worse than their vizors when shown. . . .
>
> (W ms. 49)

The familiar art-versus-nature theme is explored as the shepherds quickly decide that these court ladies compare most unfavorably with their Arcadian nymphs. For all their cosmetics and costumes, these modern women, the young swains decide, are far less lovely than the nymphs they have left behind, and they also appear to be less virtuous (more "easily won").

Suddenly, however, Lady Carteret appears, dressed like a shepherdess and with such "innocent sweetness" and natural beauty that the shepherds immediately decide she surpasses all nymphs they have ever known. Moreover, she is supreme in virtue, for they have overheard the young gallants discussing her unshakable faithfulness to her husband. Returning to their valleys, the shepherds resolve never again to be enticed "by loud rumour or show" to leave, and they acknowledge that their Muses will henceforth be not Phillis or Silvia or Cloe but that fairest of all nymphs, Carteret.

The conflict between nature and art that is common to many pastoral poems is here resolved in the person of Lady Carteret herself, whose beauty of face is matched by her beauty of character. The poet's primary purpose, however, is not to present the philosophical questions inherent in the pastoral conventions but to pay tribute to a friend.

Finch's use of the pastoral tradition for friendship themes is not limited exclusively to poems about women, however, as her poem "Upon the Death of Sir William Twisden" demonstrates. Sir William, the great-grandson of the first countess of Winchilsea, Elizabeth Heneage, was not only someone whom Finch knew well and obviously respected greatly; he was also a relative of her husband. This splendid elegy of intense emotion is at once both pastoral and antipastoral. And what differentiates it from some of the most prominent poems in the pastoral elegiac tradition is a matter not just of gender but also of differences in theological and philosophical orientation.

There are reasons why the reader might expect to encounter pastoral conventions in this poem. For one thing, the poem opens by evoking precisely those images we associate with a pastoral elegy:

> Cou'd Rivers weep (as sometimes Poets dream)
> Cou'd neigh'bring Hills our sorrows know,
> And thoughtlesse Flocks, and faiding Flowers,
> Droop o're the pastures, and beneath the showers,
> To sympathize with Man, and answer to his Woe. . . .
>
> (61, lines 1–5)

Yet our anticipations are all deflated as the pastoral images collapse upon themselves. If these phenomena of nature could occur (as we have been led to believe by a long tradition of pastoral elegies), then, we are told, we should expect their fulfillment at this time of grief. But the poet's poignant cry of "Now," echoes in futile repetition: now should the streams become rivers of tears; now should the flocks forget to flourish and the flowers fail to bloom; and now should all of nature spread the doleful news "That Twisden is no more, their Matchlesse Patriot's dead" (line 19). The extended set of modal auxiliaries that the poet has built up culminates in a lengthy catalog of those occurrences of nature that we *should* experience but never will, for they are impossibilities.

Unlike Milton, whose announcement that Lycidas is dead is followed by tributes and emotional responses from personified flora and assorted watery gods, Finch follows the announcement of the death by a clear denial of any pathetic fallacy. Nature, we are told, cannot offer any comfort to man. Thus, by evoking the pastoral mode, she creates in the reader a set of expectations that she then subverts to heighten the poignancy of the death.

But oh! in vain, things void of sence, we call,
In vain, implore the murmuring sound
Of hollow groans, from underneath the ground;
Or court the loud laments, of some steep water's fall;
Of things innaninate, [*sic*] wou'd force,
Some share of our undivided greif,
Whilst Nature (unconcern'd for our relief)
Persues her settl'd path, her fixt, and steaddy course,
Leaving those ills, which Providence allows
To check our Pleasures, and contract our Brows,
Freely to act their uncontrouled part,
Within the center of the human breast.

(St. 2, lines 21–32)

This passage reveals much about Finch's attitude toward nature. In addition to recalling many traditional pastoral images, "Upon the Death of Sir William Twisden" also follows in structure many of the conventional divisions found in such pastoral elegies as "Lycidas." We have, for example, expressions of anguish at the loss of a dead friend, a procession of mourners (for Finch an expression of the grief of others that unites with her own grief), a digression (in stanza 7 she includes one that, like Milton's, centers around a church that will sorely miss the loss of so great a Christian), and a consolation based upon an affirmation of immortality. Yet she does clearly and unequivocally reject those aspects of pastoral elegiac convention that include mournful shepherds and shepherdesses with their flocks and that require all of nature to be drawn into grief for the deceased person. And the reason she defiantly rejects these conventions is that her sensibilities are in direct conflict with the concept of nature they embody. That concept of a moralized nature which Finch rejects was to grow throughout the eighteenth century and to culminate in the spiritualism of William Blake and the Romanticism of William Wordsworth. It was a concept that, as Albert J. Kuhn defines it in his article "Nature Spiritualized: Aspects of Anti-Newtonianism," viewed nature as "moral, redeemed, prophetic, indeed spiritual and spiritualizing."[3] And it was a concept antithetical to Finch's own philosophical and theological view of the universe.

After asserting that nature does not reverse her ordinary processes to mourn human loss, Finch continues, in the second stanza of her elegy, to widen the distance between mankind and nature. It is not simply that nature is aloof and indifferent to the suffering of men and women and can offer no comfort. Nature herself, in the face of human suffering, loses all attributes of beauty, calm, and endurance, to the extent that these attributes are dependent upon human perceptions of them. The state of mind so influences one's perceptions, she avers, that sorrow can reduce all of nature to desolation: the ancient flood of Noah is renewed, as

> All seems to dye, with a departed Friend,
> The Earth unpeopl'd seems, and all again is drown'd.
> (Lines 43–44)

The absence of classical names and the rejection of the pastoral concept of a nature in sympathy with humanity serve in this poem to heighten the sense of personal anguish. But there is an important gender difference between the two poems as well. The writing of a pastoral elegy, as Celeste M. Schenck observes, is "a literary gesture signifying admittance of the male novice to the sacred company of poets."[4] For the female elegist, however, the psychic models of the traditional elegy are inappropriate, and therefore the female elegist often writes from the displaced perspective of the woman mourner. Often, too, Schenck concludes, "[e]arly female elegists deplore their own inadequacies rather than the patriarchal constraints of the form" (14). In "Upon the Death of Sir William Twisden" Finch does precisely this. After affirming the apotheosis of Sir William, she rejects a conventional elegy closure. Rather than having her poet/persona, like Milton's young swain at the close of "Lycidas," move on to "fresh woods, and pastures new," she offers an apology for her lack of poetic skill:

> But far too weak, are these imperfect Lines,
> (Th' unskill'd attempts of an inferiour Muse)
> To paint a Mind, so exquisitely bright;
> To sett such Vertues, in their noblest light,
> Or in our anxious greif, pathetick thoughts infuse.
> (Lines 182–86)

These lines reflect the "anxiety of authorship" that Sandra M. Gilbert and Susan Gubar have traced in much women's literature prior to the twentieth century.[5] But as we have seen elsewhere in Finch's poetry, this self-demeaning posture, this seeming reluctance to empower herself with the identity of "poet" and assume an authoritative stance, in fact becomes an enabling device—a means of protecting herself from possible criticism. Her self-effacement becomes a feminine defense against silence, but there is, of course, a double irony, for her very act of writing is in itself subversive.

However, despite Finch's repudiation of a spiritualized nature and her revisionist handling of some of the elegiac conventions, "Upon the Death of Sir William Twisden" retains many ties with the pastoral elegiac tradition. In addition to the structural similarities to Milton's "Lycidas" that were noted above, the poem also has much in common with Edmund Spenser's "Astrophel."

First, both the Twisden elegy and "Astrophel" are essentially biographical, concerned with recalling the qualities of a deceased friend. Finch emphasizes Sir William's personal attributes: his patriotic service to his country, his exemplary courtly behavior, his Christian piety, and his great knowledge, particularly in antiquarian studies. He is praised as a lover of the arts, but she does not expound, as Milton does, on the nature of poetry and her own commitment to the craft. Similarly, Spenser eulogizes Sir Philip Sidney for his personal traits: he was a patriotic Englishman, a brave soldier, a skilled huntsman and athlete, and a faithful mate. And with the exception of a single brief reference to Sidney's being a poet (180, lines 67–68), no mention is made of art. As Richard Mallette observes in *Spenser, Milton, and Renaissance Pastoral*, rather than enunciating "truths on the nature of life, death, and immortality," Spenser avoids these issues in "Astrophel" and instead "concentrates on setting forth a pattern of manly perfection in the figure of his subject" (137)—a description that applies just as fittingly to Finch's approach in "Upon the Death of Sir William Twisden."

Second, these elegies express profound personal grief, rather than a general invective against death or a stylized lamentation for the loss of another creative human spirit. At the center of both poems is the poet's emotional response to the death. Spenser declares directly his deep personal affection for Astrophel:

The dolefulst beare that euer man did see,
Was *Astrophel,* but dearest vnto mee.

(149–50)

And Finch similarly describes with poignant analogies her "anxious greif, pathetick thoughts" (186). Both poets, moreover, use parenthetical asides to convey personal distress.

Other than structural differences and the apologetic disclaimer in the conclusion of Finch's poem, the primary difference between her elegy and "Astrophel" is that she rejects the rural setting, the classical names, and the traditional pastoral portrayal of a sympathetic nature.[6] And the philosophical reasons for these rejections lie at the very heart of her concept of nature.

We have seen how in poem after poem Finch uses the pastoral tradition as an enabling device for artistic freedom. We have also seen that though her vision of female friendship enriches her handling of the pastoral genre, her pastoral poems are not limited to the themes of female companionship and retirement. In addition to being able to create a grandly elegiac pastoral such as the poem for Sir William Twisden, Finch could also manipulate the pastoral tradition to explore gender issues, as in "An Invitation to Dafnis." And she could also use the pastoral lyric to develop a powerful political statement, as she does in "The Change."

In "The Change," written very shortly after the revolution of 1688, pastoral conventions become a vehicle for the politicization of the poet's public voice. That is, through use of the pastoral mode, she is able to express her opposition to contemporary political events in a way that might not otherwise have been possible for her—at least not without great personal risk during that time of upheaval. "The Change" is a bitter poem in which Arcadia is transformed by the recent events in English politics. At the opening of the poem we are presented with the vision of a desolate Arcadia, its fruitfulness and lush beauty spoiled by thinly veiled allusions to Restoration politics and the overthrow of the Stuart monarchy. Images of devastation are presented in a stanzaic progression that builds to a grim climax.

The poem opens with an apostrophe to a pastoral river now almost completely dried up. "What Nymph, or Swain, will near thee lie?" the persona/speaker asks (84, line 2). The water imagery developed in this stanza is of two kinds: the life-sustaining, refreshing water of the river, which can no longer either supply fish or quench the thirst of shepherds' flocks, and the mournful tears of the stream, which hide amid the rocks.

In the second stanza it is the sun that is addressed, and just as the Arcadian river has dried up, so, too, the Arcadian sun has disappeared. Only clouds remain as a permanent darkness covers the land, and all the imagery emphasizes that now the sun can supply neither light nor heat.

The third stanza focuses on some unidentified lofty structure that lies in the midst of a deserted meadow. Perhaps emblematic of man's architectural achievements and the hopes that even simple, primitive civilizations have for permanence, this mysterious building is now decaying with the ravages of time and frost—further symptoms of the collapse of the Golden Age. There are intimations of its previous glorious days, when it supplied shelter, "soft Nights," and "chearful Days" (line 35), but now it is left to rot with the earth for its tomb.

All the imagery of the preceding stanzas is united in the final stanza in a culminating apostrophe to man. As the stanza opens, the poet, who has earlier addressed the river, the sun, and the lofty structure, now turns to man, warning him that his fate is to be the same as theirs:

> No Love, sown in thy prosp'rous Days,
> Can Fruit in this cold Season raise:
> No Benefit, by thee conferr'd,
> Can in this time of Storms be heard.
> All from thy troubl'd Waters run;
> Thy stooping Fabrick all Men shun.
> All do thy clouded Looks decline,
> As if thou ne'er did'st on them shine.
>
> (85, lines 47–54)

The images all come together here in deepening levels of symbolic meaning. The river that once ran through Arcadia is here the troubled waters that run through the heart of James II, who is himself the landscape, just as the king is the country. The lofty structure is the stooping fabric of the troubled man, his bodily frame. And the sunless plains of Arcadia are the clouded looks on his sunless face. Man himself, then (symbolically both the king and, on another level, every English citizen as well), has become a fallen Arcadia, as all images of the previous stanzas combine to define his spiritual desolation. And in the final couplet the speaker urges this wretched man to repair to other worlds (a reference to France and perhaps to heaven as well) where old values might still be found. Arcadian England is now no more, and man can only look forward to a spiritual exile from the government of his country, if not a literal one.

Closely related to the re-creation of Arcadia or Eden in pastoral verse is the pastoral concept of time. For Finch, the use of anachronisms fulfills a variety of functions, ranging from the satiric and humorous to the didactic. But her concern with time goes far beyond the occasional juxtaposition of incongruous events or things for a desired effect. We find repeatedly in her verse an awareness of the profound implications of the pastoral mode. Perhaps her most serious attempt at the pastoral, however, is "A Pastoral," subtitled "Between Menalcus and Damon, on the appearance of the Angels to the Shepheards on Our Saviour's Birth Day."

"A Pastoral Between Menalcus and Damon" is cast in the form of a dialogue between two shepherds, one of whom, Damon, was present when the angels recently appeared to the shepherds to announce the birth of Christ. The context of the poem is decidedly Christian, but the biblical setting is infused with classical elements (such as the reference to Pan, lines 88–89). The plot is simple. To make the long night on the fields pass more quickly, Menalcus asks Damon to sing him a song, and Damon responds with sublimely beautiful verses describing the appearance of the Heavenly Host. Damon also offers a vision of what the earth will be like once the infant Savior grows to manhood and fulfills the prophecies. Damon's song elicits such joy and gratitude from Menalcus that he gives the poet/swain a treasured heirloom and asks that he repeat his song the following night.

What is most striking about this poem is that Damon does for Menalcus precisely what the pastoral poet does for all of us—he offers a glimpse of paradise, of a restored Eden. Through the shepherd poet, Finch presents in this poem an epiphany of sorts, in which heaven touches earth briefly and nature and man seem in perfect harmony with the universe. The tale of Damon and Menalcus becomes, then, a kind of parable about the redemptive powers of the pastoral poet and the function of the pastoral mode.

Martin Battestin's remarks on the importance of the concept of time in the pastorals of Pope are germane to this discussion of Finch's sense of the pastoral:

> The essence of pastoral, as Pope understood, is the recognition of the Fall and of our desire to repudiate the wretched legacy of Adam. In this life, in the final stages of Nature's decay and of man's moral decadence, the Golden Age of innocence and of perfect harmony between man and Nature is recoverable only through Art in the formal world of the eclogue itself. At the end of history, the true Golden Age will in fact be restored to men through the redeeming efficacy of Christ, the Logos and Messiah. . . . (61)

To Pope, and to Finch, art is a redemptive force for restoring Eden and is therefore, in Battestin's words, "man's compensation for the Fall" (60). And this vision that the poet offers us, a vision based upon Christian teleology, is brought about in pastoral verse by the poet's defeat of time.

The use of contrast within this poem—a device deeply seated in pastoral tradition—serves to heighten the teleological significance of the event that Damon's song celebrates. The opening stanza sets the scene: it is a winter night, the winds are harsh, and it is cold on the plains. Menalcus asks Damon for one of his songs, "To charm the season, and deceive the night" (216, line 6), and suggests a biblical story or song such as David would have sung while watching his flocks. The reader is thus set up for the sense of continuity in Christian history when Damon begins his story of the birth of the Redeemer of mankind. The beautiful lyrical descriptions of the approach of the Angelic Host and of the future restoration of an earthly paradise are in direct contrast to the harsh physical setting of the opening of the poem and emphasize that nature herself will also be a part of the fulfillment of this prophecy:

> Angels and God, shall dwell with men below,
> And men releas'd, to God, and Angels go.
> Peace, to the troubl'd World he shall restore,
> And bloody discord, shall prevail no more,

The Lamb, his side by the tam'd Wolff shall lay,
And o're the Aspicks den, the child shall play.
Contending Elements, his Pow'r shall own,
The Winds, shall att his word their rage lay down,
And the chaf't billows, shall forbear to frown.
Th' untun'd Creation (by the fall of man)
Shall move harmoniously as itt began.

(219, lines 109–19)

At the conclusion of Damon's song it is sunrise, and as Milton reminds us at the close of "Lycidas," our poet must move his flocks to fresh pastures. It is not Damon, however, who speaks the final words, but Menalcus, and he closes with praise not of God nor of the Savior child but of Damon, the shepherd whose song can create for others such an exalted vision. The poem is about the promised redemption of mankind, but it is also about the artist who through his pastoral song can restore the Golden Age, the renewed Eden. No rural gifts, Menalcus claims, are sufficient to express gratitude to Damon, so he gives him another artistic creation—a bowl said to have belonged to Joseph and passed down to Menalcus through "long inheritance." It is adorned with gold clusters of grapes that, when the bowl is filled, seem "to have produc'd the wine" (line 158); this wine, symbolic of the mystical blood of Christ, also, of course, renews.

The artist, Finch seems to be telling us, is the only one who can recapture repeatedly the vision of paradise or a restored Eden. And such a vision offers humanity at least temporary relief from the tribulations of life. Thus the poem closes with Menalcus's request that the shepherd poet repeat his song the following night, and his affirmation that then "The Season sha'nt be cold, nor shall itt then, be long." The poet, through his art, through her art, is able at least briefly to triumph over both nature and time.

ELEVEN

"The Spleen": Melancholy, Gender, and Poetic Identity

*I*t is a testimony to the vagaries of literary fashion that "The Spleen," the superb Pindaric ode for which Finch was best known in her lifetime and throughout the eighteenth century, should have been almost totally ignored since that time.[1] She herself would undoubtedly have found it ironic that a remark of Wordsworth's and a few atypical nature poems would form the cornerstone of her literary reputation for nearly two hundred years, while many of her greatest poems would be buried in the rubble of neglected Augustan philosophical and didactic poetry. Today, though a number of critics are examining eighteenth-century women authors in the light of feminist criticism and revision of the canon, interest is still focused primarily on Finch's nature poems or on those poems that deal overtly with women's issues, while her didactic poems remain essentially ignored.[2] Even Roger Lonsdale, who has performed a valuable service for literary scholarship with his recent edition of the Oxford *Eighteenth-Century Women Poets* anthology, prints "The Spleen" in an abridged version that eliminates the contextualized framework Finch establishes for her reflections on the spleen's effects and seriously falsifies the poem's tone.[3]

Though Finch is an eclectic poet and cannot be categorized by a single poem or group of poems, nevertheless "The Spleen" is representative, both in style and content, of a large body of her work. It contains several of her most serious recurrent topics and thematic approaches, including a general analysis of melancholy and its social and personal implications, an expression of Anglican faith and Royalist politics, a satirical criticism of contemporary society, an examination of the function of poetry, a defense of the right of women to become authors, and, finally, a reflection on her own role as a woman poet. Furthermore, in light of recent feminist theories regarding hysteria, madness, and the sexual politics of female ailments, "The Spleen" is of particular interest.

For most of her life Finch was afflicted with melancholy, a term then interchangeable with spleen, and her poetry contains numerous references to this malady. Even in her early twenties she was traveling to Tunbridge Wells to take the waters for her health. Moreover, as late as 1718, when she was close to fifty-seven years of age, she was still plagued by this nervous disorder that left her with a "temper frail and subject to dismay."[4]

Melancholy is difficult to define, for the term was applied to a vast range of clinical symptoms. While psychiatry textbooks today define it as "a severe depressive state" (Kaplan, Freedman, and Sadock 3: 3339), medical doctors of the seventeenth and early eighteenth centuries considered melancholy a physical ailment with accompanying mental symptoms. Finch's description of her own illness, in fact, comes close to what might now be diagnosed as a manic-depressive disorder, though the term, as William B. Ober notes, did not become part of the vocabulary of psychiatry until the end of the nineteenth century (232).

From the Renaissance through much of the eighteenth century, melancholy did not have the simple connotation of sadness or mournfulness that it does today. It was recognized as an ailment traced to black bile, one of the four primary humors; hence the word "melancholy," meaning "black bile."[5] It had, furthermore, both physical and psychological manifestations, as Robert Burton observes in this explanation of its symptoms from *The Anatomy of Melancholy:* "For as the body works upon the mind, by his bad humours, troubling the spirits, sending gross fumes into the brain, and so *per consequens* disturbing the soul, and all the faculties of it, . . . with fear, sorrow, &c. which are ordinary symptoms of this disease; so, on the other side, the mind most effectually works upon the body, producing by his passions and perturbations miraculous alterations, as melancholy, despair, cruel diseases, and sometimes death itself" (1: 288). Burton's remarks are of interest not only because the medical authenticity of all the symptoms he describes was still considered valid by the early eighteenth century but also because Finch mentions each of these symptoms in "The Spleen."[6]

The scholarship on medical dimensions of Restoration and eighteenth-century melancholy is plentiful and comprehensive.[7] There is, however, more direct evidence that this poem is a sound reflection of eighteenth-century medical thought: Dr. William Stukeley, a fellow of the Royal College of Physicians, published the poem in 1723 as an introduction to his medical treatise, *Of the Spleen, Its Description and History, Uses and Diseases, Particularly the Vapors, with Their Remedy.*

Melancholy had become so common an affliction by Finch's time that at least one scholar has referred to the first half of the eighteenth century as the Age of Melancholy (Moore, "English Malady"). Pope was known to suffer from occasional episodes of melancholy, and Swift's letters have repeated references to his own bouts with its symptoms (*Correspondence* 2: 360–61, 392, 429–30; 3: 382).

But melancholy was much more likely to afflict women than men and therefore had definite gender-discriminatory implications. By the time of Finch's birth the terms "hysteria" and "vapors" had already become interchangeable with "melancholy" or "spleen"—but were applied exclusively to female patients (Babb, *Elizabethan Malady* 28). As John F. Sena has observed, the eighteenth-century understanding of melancholy "served to lend medical credence to the timeworn notion that women were erratic and fickle creatures barely capable of holding on to the small measure of reason they possessed" ("Belinda's Hysteria" 142). Indeed, one contemporary writer went so far as to attribute the cause of the plague to "a poyson . . . retained in Histerick women."[8] The general trivializing of women's ailments and the readiness to apply the diagnosis of melancholy as a catchall for a great variety of women's complaints was experienced by Queen Anne herself. Following her accession to the throne in 1702, she was urged to reinstate Dr. Radcliffe as her personal physician. "No!" replied the new queen, sounding like a very modern woman; "Radcliffe shall never send me word again when I am ill, that my ailments are only vapours" (Strickland 12: 48).

A number of excellent studies, including Michel Foucault's *Madness and Civilization: A History of Insanity in the Age of Reason*, have examined the relationship between illness and society. Especially provocative is Ruth Salvaggio's *Enlightened Absence: Neoclassical Configurations of the*

Feminine. In analyzing the eighteenth century's linking of disease, madness, and women, she argues that the Enlightenment was established and sustained by the suppression of feminine phenomena: "If we can regard hysteria as a feminine configuration of madness, then woman's body becomes an object not only to be confined in the real world, but an object representative of a diseased and contagious otherness that the age felt compelled to contain. In this sense, we might think of feminine configurations of disease as constituting a kind of 'dis-ease,' an unsettling of material—bodily and social—that reasonable men tried to keep in place" (16). Relevant to Salvaggio's work are recent reevaluations of women's ailments and the efforts of such scholars as Phyllis Chesler and Carroll Smith-Rosenberg to trace the history of female disease as symptomatic of women's "dis-ease," of their sense of oppression and marginality in society.[9]

Many feminists point out that illnesses such as melancholy, which have manifestations that are at least partially psychological and that are peculiar to women, have been male-defined. They argue, moreover, that there has been a subtle collusion between a masculine culture and a masculine medical profession to keep women passive, subservient, and domestically confined, and that any deviation from these norms has been termed "illness." Such a view is expressed by Barbara Ehrenreich and Deirdre English, whose thesis in *Complaints and Disorders: The Sexual Politics of Sickness* is that "[m]edical science has been one of the most powerful sources of sexist ideology in our culture" (5). The myth of female frailty, they further insist, has been perpetuated by the medical profession for its own financial gain (23–25).

Such theories about women's ailments have at least some relevance to a reading of "The Spleen," particularly since spleen was largely a female disease. Finch was certainly aware of the fashionable aspect of the malady, as we see in her satiric portrait of the coquette who feigns melancholy, a passage that will be discussed later in this chapter. And moreover, she was cynical about the profit motive for physicians, since much of their income, she observed, was earned from upper-class women who were especially prone to the disease:

> Tho' the Physicians greatest Gains,
> Altho' his growing Wealth he sees

Daily increas'd by Ladies Fees,
Yet dost thou baffle all his studious Pains.
(252, lines 138–41)

But her poem is concerned with much more than only the social aspects of melancholy.

It might be well, at this point, to consider briefly the English tradition of melancholic literature, for Finch was in part reacting to it. That tradition has roots in the Renaissance and is endemic throughout the seventeenth century as well, though one might be likely, because of such poems as Robert Blair's "Grave" or Thomas Gray's "Elegy Written in a Country Churchyard," to associate melancholic lyricism solely with the eighteenth century. As Amy Reed notes in *The Background of Gray's Elegy: A Study in the Taste for Melancholy Poetry, 1700–1751*, "The eighteenth century . . . inherited from the seventeenth, a decided taste for poems of melancholy, and a considerable body of poetry which satisfied that taste" (78). The publication in 1621 of Robert Burton's three-volume study, *The Anatomy of Melancholy*, created further interest in the malady and helped stimulate its increased popularity as a literary idea. From John Donne's "Corona" sonnets to the Deity and Milton's "Il Penseroso" to numerous poems by Henry Vaughan and Abraham Cowley, melancholy lyrics were common throughout the seventeenth century. In the latter part of that century and the early eighteenth century, however, such melancholy themes as solitude, retirement, meditation, grief, the vanity of human life, sleep, and death became particularly abundant in English poetry.[10]

Finch has a number of poems typical of melancholic poetry of the period. The images that one finds in "A Nocturnal Reverie," for example, are common to melancholic verse: moonlight, an owl's screech, darkened groves and distant caverns, falling waters, winds, ancient ruins, and shadows that cast an eerie gloom over the entire isolated scene. The following lines from Thomas Warton the Younger's "Pleasures of Melancholy" contain, in fact, all of these images:

> Oh lead me, black-browed Eve, to solemn glooms
> Congenial with my soul, to cheerless shades,
> To ruined seats, to twilight cells and bowers,

Where thoughtful Melancholy loves to muse,
Her favourite midnight haunts. . . .

. . . .

Where through some western window the pale moon
Pours her long-levelled rule of streaming light;
Where sullen sacred silence reigns around,
Save the lone screech-owl's note, whose bower is built
Amid the mouldering caverns dark and damp,
And the calm breeze, that rustles in the leaves
Of flaunting ivy. . . .
(Bredvold, McKillop, and Whitney 565, lines 17–21, 31–37)

One is also reminded that the youthful Pope wrote melancholic verse, including "Elegy to the Memory of an Unfortunate Lady" and "Eloisa to Abelard." Indeed, the description of Eloisa's surroundings, though more grim and somber than anything in "A Nocturnal Reverie," is nevertheless evocative of many melancholic images in Finch's poem:

In these deep solitudes and awful cells,
Where heav'nly-pensive, contemplation dwells,
And ever-musing melancholy reigns. . . .

. . . .

But o'er the twilight groves, and dusky caves,
Long-sounding isles, and intermingled graves,
Black Melancholy sits, and round her throws
A death-like silence, and a dread repose:
Her gloomy presence saddens all the scene,
Shades ev'ry flow'r, and darkens ev'ry green,
Deepens the murmur of the falling floods,
And breathes a browner horror on the woods.
(*Poems* 2: 319, 325, lines 1–3, 163–170)

Not only the imagery of some of Finch's melancholic poems is common to contemporary meditative verse, but also her themes and subject matter. "The Petition for an Absolute Retreat," for example, bears resemblance to Thomas Parnell's "Hymn to Contentment" and also to John Pomfret's "Choice" (1700), a retirement poem that Samuel Johnson declared was "the composition oftenest perused in the English language" and that went through four editions during the first year of its publication (*Lives of the English Poets* 1: 302). Similarly, the vanity-of-life theme and the orthodox treatment of Judgment Day in her "All is Vanity" ode occur in Matthew Prior's lengthy "Solomon on the Vanity of the World," as well as in Blair's "The Grave," and Edward Young's "Last Day" and "Night Thoughts."

While the Christian consolation for death in a poem like "Night Thoughts" or "The Grave" is compatible with Finch's theology, the pensiveness and moody contemplation that mark these poems are antithetical to much of her verse. She never cultivates in her poetry a melancholic mood, as Thomas Warton does when he asks to be led "to solemn glooms / Congenial with my soul." Moreover, those poems of hers that do evidence gloom do not invite sadness for its own sake but, rather, have external causes for their melancholic mood. A number of such poems, including "To Death," "An Invocation to Sleep," "A Song on Greife," "All is Vanity," and "On Affliction," were written within a year or two following the Bloodless Revolution and reflect the great anxiety and upheaval experienced by Finch and her husband. Often these poems, while expressing a generalized grief and sense of loss, have a subtext that is highly politicized, making them more valid and less sentimental than much melancholic verse.

One poem written during this period that does pertain specifically to her affliction with spleen is "Ardelia to Melancholy." The opening lines, relying heavily upon martial imagery, plunge Ardelia into an adversarial role with her malady, a position she maintains throughout the poem, despite her dramatic declaration that she will resist its force no longer:

> At last, my old inveterate foe,
> No opposition shalt thou know.
> Since I by struggling, can obtain
> Nothing, but encrease of pain. . . .
>
> (15)

All the remedies she has applied are useless, she maintains, including mirth, music, friendship, and, finally, her own poetic impulse; her "dusky, sullen foe" overcomes all. Accepting realistically that the malady will remain with her throughout her life and will make her passage "sad, and slow," Ardelia declares that only heaven can set her free. The poem then concludes with the metaphor of herself as a conquered fort, ravaged and decaying. Yet even in this very personal poem—which, incidentally, she chose not to publish during her lifetime, despite the popularity of her melancholic poem "The Spleen"—there is an objectivity that balances the poem's intense emotion.

One marked way in which "The Spleen," like "Ardelia to Melancholy," differs from much melancholic poetry of the period is that Finch neither wallows in self-pity nor relinquishes all responsibility for her own misfortunes and afflictions. Never reluctant to fix blame upon society for its ills, she is nevertheless cautious, even in her most satirical verse, to remind others and herself that life is a continuous struggle for self-control. A poem that does share much with Finch's "Spleen," however, is Matthew Green's poem of the same name, first published in 1737 following his death and undoubtedly greatly indebted to its predecessor.

Green's "Spleen," written in the form of an epistle to his friend Mr. Cuthbert Jackson, sets forth in octosyllabic couplets the methods he has devised "In stormy world to live serene" (Fausset 210, line 42). Like Finch, he confronts the spleen as a detested affliction rather than an attitude congenial with his soul. And some of the remedies he applies to "cure the mind's wrong bias" (line 89) are those that she also applies: mirth, music, and the company of good friends. Moreover, Green's reliance on reason as the ruler of his passions, along with his general sense of self-control, are qualities Finch advocates in "The Spleen," though her orientation seems more overtly grounded in Christian theology than his. Green also distrusts religious enthusiasm and the somber, melancholic attitude of sectarians (lines 280–85), a distrust that Finch vehemently expresses in her poem, as will be noted later.

Green's verses are pleasant and contain an urbane wit combined with a heavy dose of good sense. He does not plumb the depths of personal anguish, as Finch does in her poem, nor does he develop the intimacy with the reader that she does. Though himself a splenetic, he maintains a consistent distance when discussing the ailment, reflecting the same sense of moderation that he advises other splenetics to adopt. Green's manner in his poem is genteel and at times almost jaunty. And it is quite different from Finch's poetic stance. It is, finally, a matter of tone that most markedly separates Finch's poem from Green's.

One must acknowledge, then, that Finch's melancholic poems share much in common with the melancholic poetry written in England during her lifetime and shortly after her death. But one must also conclude that "The Spleen" is unique among other melancholy poems of the period. One reason for this uniqueness is the individuating quality of its tone. Its intense personal appeal is tempered by a stark realism and a rigorous analytical approach. Finch is here describing what is most difficult to describe, for the spleen is neither a person, a place, nor a thing; it is a nervous disorder with physiological as well as psychological effects, and for Finch, herself afflicted with melancholy, it involved considerations that were both intrinsically personal and broadly social. Furthermore, the full implications of melancholy for one of her persuasion and intellectual integrity were immense. As noted earlier, it was a fashionable disease, and one more likely to afflict women than men. It was also an ailment whose symptoms and treatment had complex medical dimensions. Moreover, it had religious and political aspects that for the seventeenth-century English citizen were almost inextricably linked. And lastly, for Finch, who felt the debilitating effects of the disease most keenly as a detriment to her writing, melancholy raised issues regarding the nature of the poetic commitment and a woman's right to become a poet.

"The Spleen" is a Pindaric ode of 150 lines whose irregular strophic pattern marks the changing movements of the poem and complements its alternating moods. Never was her handling of her craft more subtle nor her sense of the poetic line more elegant than it is here. As already suggested, the tone of the poem is distinctive. Finch assumes the poetic stance of a public moralist, a spokesperson for society, while at the same time being intimately personal as well. And this tone and poetic stance are derived in large part from the fact that she knew firsthand the anguish of melancholy.

"The Spleen" opens with some basic general information about melancholy: it is mercurial in nature, assuming, like the sea god Proteus, a variety of shapes. Its symptoms ape those of other illnesses, and its cause remains elusive. The physical signs of the malady are described in imagery from the natural world, but these images are heavily suggestive of emotional states as well:

> Now a Dead Sea thou'lt represent,
> A Calm of stupid Discontent,
> Then, dashing on the Rocks wilt rage into a Storm.
> (248, lines 6–8)

Then follows, for the next fifty-five lines, a detailed account of the many symptoms of the malady. Melancholy was known to affect the sensory perceptions: in *The Anatomy of Melancholy* Burton wrote of splenic victims that "[a]ll their senses are troubled, they think they see, hear, smell, and touch, that which they do not. . ." (1: 442). Finch does not present the symptoms of spleen in random order, however, but arranges them by their impact upon the individual senses, in order to portray the immense inclusiveness of melancholic disorders. The opening images, which describe the varying moods of the splenetic, also suggest a kinesthetic aspect to the disorder. The Dead Sea and the storm hint at the physical stupor and involuntary bodily movements that may accompany melancholy, while the sense of movement is intensified by the word "dashing." The description of the torpor of fear that may overcome the victim forms a transition to the next category of senses: the visual.

The psychological manifestations of melancholy were well known to contemporary physicians, and here again, Finch's descriptions are precise and medically accurate. Insomnia, nightmares, and hallucinations plague the splenic victim:

> Thy fond Delusions cheat the Eyes,
> Before them antick Spectres dance,
> Unusual Fires their pointed Heads advance,
> And airy Phantoms rise.
> (Lines 16–19)

At this point she introduces a famous Roman melancholic figure, Brutus, whose nocturnal visions at Philippi preceded his downfall at the hands of Octavius. Her reference to Brutus is effective, particularly since Shakespeare's dramatization of that nocturnal scene is so well known for its ominous terror. Her choice of Brutus subtly reminds the reader that great persons may be afflicted with spleen and that it is not only hysterical females who are subject to its disorders. Moreover, Brutus is, or had been, as Mark Antony ironically reminds us in the scene of Julius Caesar's funeral, an "honorable man." But he is also a villain, one who, we remember, was assigned by Dante to the lowest circle of hell for betraying a friend. There is, then, an aspect of malevolence to him, just as there may be to the malady of melancholy itself if one romanticizes it or fails to struggle against its injurious effects. In the context of the entire poem, particularly in Finch's repudiation of the fashionable association between melancholy and wit and her attack on the Puritan cultivation of melancholic behavior as inimical to religion, the Brutus allusion is particularly apt.

The second stanza, which presents a series of olfactory images to describe the effects of spleen, continues the suggestion that there is something malefic about melancholy. The poet here identifies the malady with Original Sin, claiming that it is not the body that should be blamed for the disease but the soul:

> Falsly, the Mortal Part we blame
> Of our deprest, and pond'rous Frame,
> Which, till the First degrading Sin
> Let Thee, its dull Attendant, in. . . .
>   (Lines 26–29)

The idea that Original Sin is responsible for illness and bodily decay is standard orthodox theology, but Finch's reminder here intensifies the seriousness of melancholy. Throughout the poem she assails those who falsely represent the malady as desirable or cultivate a melancholic pose for their own self-serving ends. Melancholy is an enemy to honest human relationships, to peaceful domesticity, to all creative impulses, and to true religious sensibilities. It is not, then, something to be glorified, nor should its disorders be feigned by those who think it implies cleverness or genius.

The kinesthetic and visual imagery introduced in the first stanza is followed in this second stanza by a series of olfactory images, and these reinforce the theological point the poet has already made. When man and woman possessed paradise, she writes, all was fragrant, but now melancholy has corrupted Eden. In lines that are among the most famous from the poem,[11] Finch contrasts the perfections of paradise, described earlier, with the fallen Eden of the melancholiac:

> Now the *Jonquille* o'ercomes the feeble Brain;
> We faint beneath the Aromatick Pain,
> Till some offensive Scent thy Pow'rs appease,
> And Pleasure we resign for short, and nauseous Ease.
>
> (Lines 40–43)

The auditory symptoms of melancholy presented in the third stanza are as unpredictable as those affecting the other senses. The manic depressive stages that plague a splenetic are manifested in whispered fears and sorrows or loud, uncontrollable laughter, and again there is something sinister about the affliction. Under its influence the depressed victim utters malicious gossip based upon neurotic fantasies and the splenic wife becomes churlish and combative with her husband.

In the fourth stanza, which follows Finch's description of the various symptoms of the malady, she begins her consideration of the social aspects of melancholy. After briefly introducing the first of her several satirical targets, those who pretend to melancholy as a claim to genius or wit, she suddenly becomes subjective and personal. This transition from the objective to the subjective serves a dual purpose within the poem. By letting the reader know of her own affliction, she establishes her credibility as a satirist and social critic for all aspects of the spleen. Moreover, she creates an intimacy with the reader, thereby lending an element of pathos that heightens the seriousness of the poem. The personal passage is worth quoting in full:

> O'er me alas! thou dost too much prevail:
> I feel thy Force, whilst I against thee rail;
> I feel my Verse decay, and my crampt Numbers fail.
> Thro' thy black Jaundice I all Objects see,
>   As Dark, and Terrible as Thee,
> My Lines decry'd, and my Employment thought
> An useless Folly, or presumptuous Fault:
>   Whilst in the *Muses* Paths I stray,
> Whilst in their Groves, and by their secret Springs
> My Hand delights to trace unusual Things,

And deviates from the known, and common way;
   Nor will in fading Silks compose
   Faintly th' inimitable *Rose,*
Fill up an ill-drawn *Bird,* or paint on Glass
The *Sov'reign's* blurr'd and undistinguish'd Face,
The threatning *Angel,* and the speaking *Ass.*
                    (Lines 74–89)

These are powerful lines, poignant and self-revealing, yet free of self-pity or self-deception. Indeed, they are all the more powerful because of their painful honesty. And aesthetically they are absolutely essential, for they form the nexus of this exquisitely structured poem. In these sixteen lines Finch links together all the various implications of melancholy that for her are at once both highly personal and broadly social. It is no accident that this passage of deeply personal sentiment occurs in a stanza that opens and closes with satire. Her Augustan sense of harmony and proportion extends here to the balance between the individual tormented psyche and the objective rationality of the satirist.

Many of the sensory manifestations of melancholy that were detailed earlier in the poem come together in the poet's description of her own suffering. The overwhelming totality of the melancholic experience is suggested by its impact upon the senses. The emotional implosion that the malady inflicts upon her is documented in a flood of concurrent sensory responses that comes close to synesthesia. She feels melancholy through her entire body as a kinetic force. "I feel" is then repeated, both for emphasis and for transference of response from body to mind. "I feel my Verse decay," she writes, indicating a mental response that lies outside the reasoning faculties. The grammatical construction of this clause implies a painful progression in her distorted and morose view of her own poetry. Her verse does not suddenly appear decayed but, rather, decays increasingly under the influence of her splenic mood. These neurotic thoughts and the sense of kinesthesia are joined with visual and auditory impressions: all objects are seen through black, jaundiced eyes, and she imagines her lines "decry'd" by others. The depression that accompanies melancholy causes her to experience a sense of futility about her own writing and to imagine that her employment is "thought / An useless Folly, or presumptuous Fault."

Sandra M. Gilbert and Susan Gubar, commenting in *The Madwoman in the Attic* on this passage, see in it Finch's expression of her fear that wanting to be a writer is "crazy, neurotic, splenic"; this fear, they reason, suggests "that Pope's portrayal of her as the foolish and neurotic Phoebe Clinket had—not surprisingly—driven her into a Cave of Spleen in her own mind" (60–61). Here Gilbert and Gubar miss the point. Apart from their spurious assumption that Pope was indeed spoofing Finch, they seriously misread "The Spleen."

In examining manifestations of anxiety about authorship in pre-twentieth-century women's literature, Gilbert and Gubar perceptively define its form as "in many ways the germ of a dis-ease or, at any rate, a disaffection, a disturbance, a distrust, that spreads like a stain throughout the style and structure. . . ." Thus, they conclude, early women writers "struggled in isolation that felt like illness, alienation that felt like madness, obscurity that felt like paralysis to overcome the anxiety of authorship that was endemic to their literary subculture" (51). All very true. But to view Finch's treatment of melancholy within the context of this poem solely as a psychosomatic reaction to attacks upon her writing undercuts her satirical import and makes the poem little more than a piece of confessional verse. Finch did experience prejudice as a woman writer, as her comments in numerous poems indicate. But her concern here is with melancholy's destruction of her self-confidence and its debilitating effects upon her own writing. Her horror at the effects of spleen is due to her awareness that such distorted judgment about her own verse and about what others think of it is a paranoia resulting from the illness and runs contrary to reality. She is fully aware of the crippling depression the spleen brings upon her, and her salvation lies in her uncompromising honesty and her refusal to submit to this malady without a battle. To misunderstand this point is to miss the social criticism and the satirical thrust of the last half of the poem.

Despite the occasional self-deprecating poses and the apologies for her writing (which, as noted, were in part a matter of convention as well as a subversive means of achieving artistic liberation), Finch's belief in her art and in herself as a writer remained strong throughout her life. As a poet she had the continuous support of family members and friends, as well as the encouragement of such authoritative male writers as Pope and Swift. Though she was undoubtedly hurt by misogynist attacks and the lampooning of female writers, she never gave in to them. As evident in numerous poems, she ardently defends the right of women to become authors, and she never ceased, not even in the final years of her life, to define herself in her verse and to create her own artistic space.

In the last part of the fourth stanza of "The Spleen," Finch distinguishes between her own poetic impulses ("My Hand delights to trace unusual Things / And deviates from the known, and common way") and the meaningless employments that society thinks appropriate for women. The sort of contemporary prejudicial attitudes toward women writers that she is here objecting to found expression in the following remark from an unsigned essay in the *Spectator* (no. 606, October 13, 1714), which appeared just one year following the publication of Finch's small volume of verse:

> What a delightful Entertainment must it be to the Fair Sex, whom their native Modesty, and the Tenderness of Men towards them, exempts from Publick Business, to pass their Hours in imitating Fruits and Flowers, and transplanting all the Beauties of Nature into their own Dress, or raising a new Creation in their Closets and Apartments. How pleasing is the Amusement of walking among the Shades and Groves planted by themselves, in surveying Heroes slain by their Needle, or little *Cupids* which they have brought into the World without Pain!
>
> This is, methinks, the most proper way wherein a Lady can shew a fine Genius, and I cannot forbear wishing, that several Writers of that Sex had chosen to apply themselves rather to Tapestry than Rhime.

In "The Spleen" Finch juxtaposes her own desires to just such expectations as these. And by moving from personal considerations back to general social ones, she creates a strong irony. She defiantly rejects the pseudoartistic pursuits traditionally reserved for women, such as painting, tapestry, and embroidery. The results of these pursuits, she observes, tend to be devoid of artistic merit, so that the conventional bird is expectedly "ill-drawn." There is also subtle political irony from this steadfast Jacobite in her description of the fashionable subjects for such art:

The *Sov'reign's* blurr'd and undistinguish'd Face,
The threatning *Angel,* and the speaking *Ass.*

The ambivalence about the cause of the "undistinguish'd Face" can be taken as intentional; England's reigning monarch at the time this poem was written was still William of Orange, successor to the Finches' beloved, deposed James II. Moreover, she reinforces the bitter irony by placing in juxtaposition to the image of William of Orange a reference to the biblical tale of Balaam's ass and the angel. In the familiar narrative the prophet Balaam, intent upon conquering the Israelites, disregards God's will until he is rebuked by his own ass. Seeing in her path a threatening angel, whose appearance has not been visible to the rider on her back, Balaam's ass turns him aside from his destination and speaks to him with God's words: "I went out to withstand thee, because thy way is perverse before me" (Num. 22.32). Ultimately Balaam realizes the error of his ways and turns from his original plan, thereby leaving the Israel nation free, as, by implication, the usurper William has not done with England.

The remainder of the poem is devoted to the more public, social aspects of melancholy. As Finch well knew, the malady was too serious an affliction to be taken lightly. She therefore has no sympathy for those such as the ill-natured husband, the shrewish wife, or the drunkard who claim melancholy as an excuse for their behavior:

Patron thou art to ev'ry gross Abuse,
The sullen *Husband's* feign'd Excuse,
When the ill Humour with his Wife he spends,
And bears recruited Wit, and Spirits to his Friends.
The Son of *Bacchus* pleads thy Pow'r,
As to the Glass he still repairs,
Pretends but to remove thy Cares,
Snatch from thy Shades one gay, and smiling Hour,
And drown thy Kingdom in a purple Show'r.
(Lines 90–98)

She also lashes out against those who pretend to be its victims for desired ends, such as the frivolous coquettes who delight in melancholic posturing to attract male attention:

When the *Coquette,* whom ev'ry Fool admires,
   Wou'd in Variety be Fair,
   And, changing hastily the Scene
   From Light, Impertinent, and Vain,
Assumes a soft, a melancholy Air,
And of her Eyes rebates the wand'ring Fires,
The careless Posture, and the Head reclin'd,
   The thoughtful, and composed Face,
Proclaiming the withdrawn, the absent Mind,
Allows the Fop more liberty to gaze,
Who gently for the tender Cause inquires;
The Cause, indeed, is a Defect in Sense,
Yet is the *Spleen* alledg'd, and still the dull Pretence.

(Lines 99–111)

    To understand Finch's attack against such melancholic imposters, it is necessary to remember that two fundamentally opposite concepts of melancholy appear throughout Elizabethan and Stuart literature. The concept derived from Galen and medical tradition is found essentially in the melancholic lover, the malcontent, and the grief-stricken dramatic figure. The view of melancholy embodied in this tradition is that it is a debilitating and degrading malady, and literary figures evidencing this type of melancholy are generally the object of scorn or laughter. The other tradition, which derives from Aristotle, is that melancholic disorders are an attribute of superior intellect and genuine piety (Babb, *Elizabethan Malady* 175–85). An introspective figure such as Hamlet would therefore be viewed as typifying the dignity of the illness. From this tradition is derived what Finch sees as the most despicable and destructive of all melancholic poses, that of the sanctimonious, morose Puritan:

      By Thee *Religion,* all we know,
      That shou'd enlighten here below,
      Is veil'd in Darkness, and perplext
    With anxious Doubts, with endless Scruples vext,
And some Restraint imply'd from each perverted Text.
    Whilst *Touch* not, *Taste* not, what is freely giv'n,
Is but thy niggard Voice, disgracing bounteous Heav'n.

From Speech restrain'd, by thy Deceits abus'd,
To Deserts banish'd, or in Cells reclus'd,
Mistaken Vot'ries to the Pow'rs Divine,
Whilst they a purer Sacrifice design,
Do but the *Spleen* obey, and worship at thy Shrine.
(Lines 116–27)

These are harsh lines, far different in tone from the humorous portrayal of fops and coquettes, or the gibe, occurring toward the conclusion of the poem, at physicians whose greatest financial gain is
from splenic patients. As we have seen repeatedly, Finch is incensed
at hypocrisy in any form, but what she sees as the false piety of the
Puritans is particularly odious to her. The religious fanaticism and ex-
cessive fear of damnation that Puritanism cultivated, and that had such
devastating political ramifications for England during the seventeenth
century, were still objects of distrust to Finch, a child of the Restoration.

So strong was the association between Puritanism and melancholy
in the Restoration and eighteenth century that many antisectarians
regarded Puritan zeal as a manifestation of a melancholic mental disorder.[12] Thus many writers of the period, distinguishing between true
and false enthusiasm, viewed Puritan behavior as the result of a disease
that required medical treatment. Robert Burton had declared in 1621
in *The Anatomy of Melancholy* that Puritan enthusiasts were "certainly
far gone with melancholy, if not quite mad, and have more need of
physic than many a man that keeps his bed, more need of helebore than
those that are in Bedlam" (3: 372). Echoing Burton, the Cambridge
Platonist George Rust averred in his 1683 *Discourse of the Use of Reason
in Matters of Religion* that the hallucinations and delusions of Puritans
are "no better then Frenzies and Symptoms of Melancholy" (33). And
the year prior to publication of Finch's "Spleen," John Locke noted in
a chapter added to the fourth edition of his *Essay Concerning Human
Understanding* that "in all ages, men, in whom melancholy has mixed
with devotion . . . often flattered themselves with a persuasion of immediate intercourse with the Deity" (2: 431). There was, then, ample
precedence for Finch's linking of Puritan religiosity with melancholy
and for such later satirical attacks on Puritans as Swift's in *A Tale of a
Tub*. Joseph Addison's allegation in number 494 of the *Spectator* that "a

sorrowful countenance . . . eaten up with spleen and melancholy" is the Puritan norm for piety seems to have been widely accepted.

The anger Finch displays in "The Spleen" is an outburst against that which violates her basic religious sensibilities. The Puritan obsession with sin and the emphasis on repression are inimical to her Anglican faith. For her, melancholic despair has little to do with a true sense of sin; indeed, once sin is acknowledged and forgiven, the best way to worship God, she believes, is with a joyful heart. This theme of the affinity between true piety and a happy spirit is a recurrent one in her verse. In one of the first poems she wrote, the song "Love, thou art best of Human Joys," God is said to recognize the love between a man and a woman as having great spiritual worth because its pleasures elevate the soul. The love of human beings for one another, even passionate love for one's spouse, is not, for Finch, very far removed from love for God. Even during the final period of her life, when she was plagued with chronic melancholy and ill health, her religious verse was never morbid. In "A Suplication for the joys of Heaven" (see app. A) she writes that when she is eventually united with God, she will be steadfastly "spiritualiz'd and gay" (W ms. 108). And in "An Hymn of Thanksgiving after a Dangerous fit of sickness in the year 1715" (also in app. A) she offers jubilant alleluias to God, who has restored her health, claiming that her praise of him will allay any fear of recurring attacks of spleen:

> In Allelujahs who'l proceed
> Shall find all objects praises breed
> Nor fear the spleen
> Shou'd come between
> By Allelujahs freed.
> (W ms. 77, st. 11)

Finch believes that one should always be cheerful in praising God, for to be otherwise implies a lack of true gratitude for what one has been given. Thus the austerity and dour manner of the Puritans are, as she notes in "The Spleen," "disgracing bounteous Heav'n."

In summary, then, Finch's religious persuasion, her perspective as a female writer, and her Augustan rationality all blend to make "The Spleen" an extraordinary poem. Its reflective sentiments are checked by its author's unflinching satirical eye, so that the poem is both sub-jectively emotional and objectively rational. Throughout "The Spleen" Finch maintains a balanced stance that is at once both public and pri-vate, both general and specific, both publicly moralistic and intimately confessional. Though the poem, in both a literary and a scientific sense, has roots in the Renaissance and seventeenth-century understanding of melancholy, it strongly reflects its author's originality. Furthermore, Finch does not cultivate a melancholic mood as appropriate and desir-able for the expression of intensely personal and emotional sentiments, as many eighteenth-century melancholic poets do.

Bouts with melancholy were to torment Finch throughout her life. "My old inveterate foe" she called it in her early "Ardelia to Melan-choly," as noted earlier, and the martial imagery in that poem is appro-priate to the war she was to wage against the ailment even in her final years.[13] Taken as a group, her melancholy poems reveal a wide range of moods, from somber to satiric to lighthearted. Above all, they dem-onstrate her individuating tone and her refusal to approach melancholy from a popular viewpoint.

TWELVE

The Final Years

*I*n many ways Finch's final years were as full of adversity as those early years following the revolution. And just as her personal anguish during the revolution is reflected in a number of poems from that period, so, too, her distress toward the end of her life is evident in her later poetry. Though she continued to write poems of personal friendship ("An Epistle to Mrs. Catherine Fleming"), gentle humor ("After drawing a twelf cake at the Honble Mrs. Thynne's"), public commemoration ("On the Death of the Queen"), and biting satire ("Sir Plausible"), much of her later verse is marked by a predominance of religious themes and probings into the meaning of human suffering. The titles of some of these poems suggest her preoccupation with spiritual matters: "A Prayer for Salvation," "An Act of Contrition," "Mary Magdalen at our Saviour's Tomb, a Fragment," "No Grace," "A Suplication for the joys of Heaven," "The happynesse of a departed soul," and a number of poems, such as "On these Words, Thou hast hedg'd in my way with thorns," that are reflections on biblical passages.

It is ironic that Heneage Finch's accession to the peerage, rather than easing the couple's difficulties, should have brought them additional displacement from much of the political life of London and from the court circle, increased their financial problems, and made them no less vulnerable to fear of further persecution and reprisals.

In addition to the stress brought about by serious financial problems, the tangled series of court trials and appeals must have been painfully reminiscent to Anne Finch of her earlier experiences with the legal system when her husband was tried for Jacobitism following the revolution and perhaps also during her childhood. And with the reinstatement of the Whig government in 1714, the political atmosphere in England was once again menacing for people like the Finches. Many Tories, who feared that a Hanoverian succession with George I would abolish legitimate authority and revive the situation that existed in England during the Interregnum, wanted a restoration of the Stuarts. Historian Paul Kleber Monod notes that "Jacobitism excited, between October 1714 and August 1715, the most widespread political disturbances of any comparable period in English history" (194). Several Tory leaders approached James III (the "Pretender") with offers to support an uprising in the western part of England, and reports spread of intrigues between the Pretender and both Russia and Sweden (Handasyde 139–50; Michael 130–32). Tory ministers were impeached and imprisoned, rebel Jacobites were brought to trial and had their estates seized by the government, and seditious riots occurred frequently in London.[1]

One highly publicized incident occurred in front of St. James's Palace, which was directly across the street from the residence of the new Lord and Lady Winchilsea on Cleveland Row. In May 1715, on the anniversary of King George's birthday, the Foot Guards demonstrated outside the palace, protesting their discontent with the king's economic policies and complaining that their uniforms were in need of replacement. "Look at our Hanover shirts," they shouted, as they threw their military uniforms into the gardens of St. James's (Sinclair-Stevenson 73). Finch and her husband, widely recognized as seasoned Jacobite sympathizers, had good cause to be uneasy.

Several months later, on October 18, she addressed a prose and verse epistle from London to her friend Arabella Marrow.[2] Entitled simply "A letter to Mrs Arrabella Marow," the poem reflects the tremendous tensions that Finch experienced during this Jacobite uprising, as does the brief note affixed to it: "The favour of such an agreeable & most obliging letter as I recieved from dear Mrs Marow ought much sooner to have been acknowledged by me & it has been my daily intention tho' still detain'd by reflecting on the great cautiousness with which we must write to our friends under the present posture of affairs & I was very unwilling when addressing my self to you to be under that necessity of being dull which that great reserve imposes" (W ms. 82–83).

The opening stanzas of the accompanying poem give several allusions to topical events that would warrant the "great cautiousness" the note refers to:

> For can our correspondence please
> Who must report no news
> Least Messengers our Person's ceaze
> Who have confin'd the Muse.
>
> Marr in the North a trumpet blows
> And Ormond's dreaded here
> Where none a softer passion knows
> Then dull suspence or fear.
>
> (83)

A note in the left margin of the Wellesley manuscript, in the same handwriting as that in which the poem is transcribed, identifies the Muse of line 4 as "Mr. Prior." Matthew Prior, with whom Finch was personally acquainted, had been charged with Jacobitism and turned over to the sergeant at arms for the House of Commons on June 9, 1715; though he subsequently took the oath of allegiance, he nevertheless remained under house arrest for a full year.[3] The persecution of this poet with whom she shared political allegiances would have been most distressing to her.

The second stanza of this poem attests to the prevailing mood of "dull suspence or fear" and alludes to two men who figured prominently in the 1715 Jacobite rebellion. John Erskine, sixth earl of Mar, had held the position of secretary of state for Scotland under the ministry of the earl of Oxford and on September 6, 1715, had published a declaration in support of James III (Ehrenpreis 3: 19). James Butler, second duke of Ormonde, was deprived of his offices and commands following the accession of George I, but he remained highly regarded by the general populace for his integrity and came to symbolize the Tory peace policy (Monod 173, 180; Swift *Correspondence* 2: 103–04; Boyer 9: 333). He eventually fled to France, and on October 10, one week before the date of Finch's verse epistle, James III appointed him captain general and commander in chief of his forces in England and Ireland. That same month three Irish soldiers, attempting to fill up the ranks of their Foot Guards company with Jacobite loyalists in preparation for the duke of Ormonde's planned landing, were executed (Boyer 10: 354, 385–88; 11: 504; Monod 109).

The third stanza brings the current crisis within a personal domestic realm.

> Cornwallis breaks up every seal
>   To guard the state from harms
> How can we then our hearts reveal
>   Or Arrabella's charms?

Charles, the fourth Baron Cornwallis, had recently been appointed joint postmaster general, and it was therefore his job, she declared with some cynicism, to break open "every seal / To guard the state from harms." The recent order to break seals and read letters from persons suspected of seditious acts or intents is one that she implies is effectively silencing her; under the present injunction, she can neither praise Arabella's charms nor reveal her own thoughts and sentiments. As the opening lines have warned her friend, one must report "no news" of any substance, no word of one's true political concerns, or else risk retribution from the state.

In this poem Finch successfully intertwines discourses of politics with discourses of gender. While the references in the first ten lines are all to male figures who are part of the power structure and who are shaping the course of England's history, the remaining forty lines shift focus to a feminine world, a substratum of the body politic. And though this female substratum, this marginal society, is displaced doubly, both by its political sensibilities and its gender, it becomes empowered through female friendship and love. If the influence of Arabella's charms could be freely revealed and those silenced hearts (which include the poet's own) could speak openly, then Cornwallis would know the true strength of his Jacobite foes:

> For shou'd their influence be declared
>   In numbers or in prose
> He'd know 'gainst whom they were prepared
>   Must fear an host of foes.[4]

The poem continues with a catalog of women, including Marrow herself, who have departed from London during these dangerous times, leaving their friends "dejected and opprest." The poet concludes that her own relief and that of her suffering friends could be restored only by Marrow's loving presence,

> Whilst but the noise of war and steel
> Can other minds molest.

This society of women friends is therefore oppositional to the state and its dominant values, and it becomes, in the course of the poem, a powerful counteractant to "the noise of war and steel."

There was additional cause for Finch to be distressed during the political unrest following the accession of George I and to feel the personal threat of danger, for the new countess of Winchilsea and her husband were actively involved with the Nonjuring segment of the Church of England.

When Heneage Finch was elevated to the peerage, an account of the event (quite different from Swift's) was furnished by the scholarly Thomas Hearne: "This Day Sennight died the R Honble. Charles Finch Earl of Winchilsea in the 40th Year of his Age, and having no Son, he is succeeded in Honour and Estate by his Uncle Col. Heneage Finch, a very honest Worthy Non Juror, & an excellent Antiquary, to ye great Joy and Content of the Writer of these Matters" (3: 427). Hearne, once a librarian at Oxford University, was himself a Nonjuror, and for his refusal to take the oaths of allegiance to William and Mary and subsequent monarchs, he had been deprived of his position and debarred from the Bodleian Library (Rupp 16). He therefore had cause to welcome a fellow Nonjuror's rise to a position of prestige.

The term "Nonjuror" is difficult to define. In a general way the Nonjuring movement refers to a schism within the Church of England that occurred during the 1688 revolution and lasted at least through the first half of the eighteenth century. Many of the people who categorized themselves as Nonjurors saw the issue as one of obedience to conscience, but the term had political implications as well as theological ones. Though in one sense the terms "Nonjuror" and "Jacobite" are not necessarily synonymous, as Monod observes, "In an age that took oaths very seriously, Nonjuring was a very strong political statement" (139). Nonjurors were people who, along with the archbishop of Canterbury and a number of his episcopal colleagues, refused to swear allegiance to William and Mary because they believed that their prior oaths to James II were inviolable and that hereditary monarchies ruled by divine right. For their act of conscience, three to four hundred clergy and an unknown number of laity were suspended, deprived of office, and excluded from public life (Hart 104–15).

The issue of conscience was a recurrent one, for, as Gordon Rupp notes in *Religion in England, 1688–1791*: "The Non-Jurors were a proscribed community, on whom the authorities might swoop as they did in dangerous times, as 1715 . . . when oaths would be proffered them, on pain of arrest and fine, if not imprisonment (23). Anne and Heneage Finch were certainly aware of their vulnerability as widely recognized Nonjurors. Yet despite the personal risks involved, they remained deeply committed to the Nonjuring cause, and there is ample evidence of their repeated efforts to aid others who shared their commitment. One authority on Church of England history acknowledges the couple as closely identified with Nonjurors (Overton 274–75), and another scholar goes so far as to call Heneage Finch "a kind of god-parent to the movement" (Rupp 24).

Within months of receiving his title, Heneage Finch was one of two witnesses at the consecration of three Nonjuring bishops in a private ceremony, and later, in 1721, he was a witness at the consecration of two more bishops. Samuel Hawes, one of the bishops whose consecration the new Lord Winchilsea witnessed in 1713, was later deprived of his income and removed from his house, after which it was reported that he went "down with Lᵈ Winchilsea to live Wᵗʰ him in Kent" (qtd. in Overton 133).[5] Bishop Hawes's will, drawn up in 1722 shortly before his death, still identified him as "Samuel Hawes of Eastwell in Kent," an indication that he must have resided at Eastwell for the remainder of his life (Overton 134).

Anne Finch was in her own right an active Nonjuror. Among the English Theology manuscripts in the Bodleian is an exchange of letters between Finch and the prominent theologian Thomas Brett. Widely recognized as a scholar of liturgiology, Brett refused in 1715 to take the oaths that a new act of Parliament required following the accession of George I to the throne. He subsequently retracted his earlier condemnation of Nonjurors and on St. Paul's Day, 1716, was consecrated a Nonjuring bishop (Overton 138–41).

Shortly thereafter a controversy developed within the Nonjuring movement between two groups known as Usagers and Non-Usagers. At issue were certain practices relevant to administering the Eucharist, and Brett, as an authority on ancient liturgy, quickly became embroiled in the controversy (Overton 290–308). On October 9, 1717, Finch wrote to Brett regarding her concern about the "growing dissensions" within their religious community and pleaded with him to appease the "dangerous and unreasonable" branch that was threatening schism (English Theology ms., c. 26, 99–100). Brett replied in an erudite four-page letter that set forth his position and appealed to liturgical practices dating back to the primitive church (English Theology ms., c. 38, 263–66). In November he wrote again (possibly in answer to further correspondence from Finch that is no longer extant), supplementing his minor treatise on the doctrine of transubstantiation with an outline of the steps he was taking to unify the two religious factions (English Theology ms., c. 38, 273–75).

The Finch/Brett correspondence is significant for several reasons. Her letter to Brett indicates her keen awareness of theological matters and her desire to protect the Nonjuring segment from further fragmentation. But even more revealing of the strength and independence of Finch's intellect are Brett's letters of response. His care to acknowledge and attempt accommodation of her requests might well be due in part to her aristocratic title and the role that her husband played in supporting the Nonjuring cause. The extent and level of his scholarly explanations, however, and the lack of any condescension in his tone to her, suggest his high regard for her intellectual attributes and his awareness of the influential position that she herself held within the Nonjuring community.

Another instance of the generosity and courage of Anne and Heneage Finch is their aid to the Reverend Hilkiah Bedford. Bedford had earlier been deprived of his rectory in Northamptonshire after refusing to take the oaths. He was subsequently wrongly accused of having written *The Hereditary Right of the Crown of England Asserted*, and after being tried in the Court of King's Bench in February 15, 1714, he was fined a thousand marks and sentenced to prison.[6] Even after he received his pardon in April 23, 1718, his difficulties continued, for the following year he was "suspected to be a dangerous and disaffected person to his . . . Majesty" and had to appear before two magistrates to be questioned about the oaths (Bodl. Rawlinson ms., Letters 42, folio 3).

There is much evidence of the Finches' support for Bedford. "To the Rev^d. Mr. Bedford," a poem in the Wellesley manuscript that was probably written during his period of imprisonment or soon after his release, was prompted by Anne Finch's unsuccessful efforts to solicit a favor from some lord on his behalf (see app. A). The poem describes humorously in tetrameter couplets her response upon receiving Bedford's note:

> Your note recieved down stairs I fly
> My gown unpin'd my hood awry
> With Mrs Mary at my heels
> Who as she this disorder feels
> Here gives a twitch there aims a pin
> But cannot reach to fix it in
> Yet does with lengthen'd strides aproach
> And throws my ruffles in the coach
> I finishing the best I can
> Now drop my gloves and then my fan
> As Jehu scours along the street
> And swears at every thing he meets
> Till to his Lordship's door he comes.
>
> (78)

With levity obviously meant to lift the spirits of the friend she is trying to help, she describes the officious lord who, suspecting the nature of her errand, feigns a previous appointment in order to be rid of her, and then rushes off,

> Whilst in the parlour I remain
> O'ercome with sorrow and disdain
> Yet with a Roman virtue scorn
> The Land depraved where I was born
> Where men now wealthy grown and great
> En bagatell our sufferings treat.

Thus she abandons her humorous tone in the narrative to relate her genuine sympathy for Bedford's plight and her outrage at the distorted values of her countrymen in positions of power. However, she reassures him, "Yet still I will your cause persue."

Correspondence among the Rawlinson manuscripts in the Bodleian Library at Oxford indicates some of the extent of the Finches' help for the Bedford family. A letter from Heneage Finch on August 5, 1719, concludes with messages for Bedford and his wife from their daughter, who at the time was with the Finches at Malshanger Farm, the Hampshire estate that Heneage managed for his wife's nephew, William Kingsmill.[7]

The Finches must have kept the Bedfords' daughter under their care for some time, for she is mentioned again in a letter to the Reverend Bedford the following year. This lengthy letter, sent from Eastwell on April 12, 1720, is one of the few extant letters by Anne Finch, and it is of special interest for what it reveals about her life just a few months before her death.

Much of the letter pertains to some financial matters that are referred to in what is most likely an intentionally oblique manner: "When ye have ye mony I desire you will employ it with what else is in your hands of ours in ye use mentioned to you when I saw you last" (Rawlinson ms., Letters 45, folios 158–59). Above the letter is a note, signed and dated in Finch's hand, which requests that half a year of the annuity left to her be turned over to Bedford. (This is possibly part of her inheritance from her father.) It appears that the financial arrangements pertain to the Nonjuring cause, whether or not they are meant to help Bedford directly.

The letter expresses personal concern for the welfare of the Bedfords' daughter, who is ill in bed, and Finch confesses to being "at a loss what to do for her[,] being ignorant of ye habits of her indisposition. . . ." Another person mentioned in the letter is Samuel Hawes. She mentions nursing him for a bad stomach and also attempting to cheer him, for she worries that he continues to be "low in spirits." And her own husband, she mentions, is still sick with a bad cough.

At the time Finch wrote this letter she was fifty-nine years old, in poor health, and still experiencing the adversities imposed upon her and her husband by their religious and political principles. Her chronic depression, or melancholy, left her in her later years with what she described as a "temper frail and subject to dismay" (W ms. 108). Moreover, in 1715 she suffered a serious illness, alluded to in several poems, that left her on "the verge of the devouring grave" (W ms. 140). The exact nature of this illness is undisclosed, but the political turmoil during that year and the renewed persecution of Nonjurors must have seriously exacerbated her nervous disorder.

Finch was as productive a poet in her fifties as she had been in her twenties, and with the publication in 1713 of her *Miscellany Poems*, her reputation spread throughout London's literary circles (see chapter 7). Despite tension from the political climate and from financial difficulties, she continued to delight in the company of friends and to participate in social and literary events. The poems written in the final years of her life reveal a fun-loving, good-natured woman who enjoyed people. Young Alexander Pope, the brightest new star on London's literary scene, was a frequent visitor at her townhouse, and she attended lively literary gatherings at the home of her husband's grandniece Lady Hertford.[8] She often exchanged visits with family members and friends, played with the children and grandchildren of relatives, took part in lively card games, and spent pleasant afternoons riding with female companions through St. James's Park. Once a week she regularly visited another of her husband's grandnieces, Lady Carteret, who resided with her husband at their nearby home on Arlington Street.[9] There were also trips outside the capital to Malshanger Farm and frequent returns to her beloved Eastwell.

In "A Contemplation," the final poem included in the Wellesley manuscript, Finch writes what might almost be taken as a summation of her theological and philosophical views (see app. A). It deals with issues of political and social concern, as well as personal ones, and it provides a great deal of insight into the way in which her religious beliefs were deeply intertwined with all aspects of her life.

The central theme of "A Contemplation" is the vanity of human wishes. The poem's mood of solemnity is created, in part, by the use of the hymnal stanza, a form consisting of quatrains in strict iambic accentual-syllabic meter with alternating tetrameter and trimeter lines. The poem opens with a reflection on heaven as the only proper focus for one's ambitions, but this heaven is not an amorphous, incorporeal state of vapid spirituality. In "The Spleen," one may recall, Finch expresses her dislike for the *"Touch* not, *Taste* not" dictum that leads Puritans to denigrate the physical senses and repress all pleasures of the body. Her heaven, as one might expect, is vibrant and gloriously sensuous, a fulfillment of bodily and spiritual delights. It is, in short, the realization of what it means to be human in the richest physical, mental, and spiritual sense, and her hymn of praise offers a description of heaven that becomes, in part, an exaltation of the human senses. In heaven, she writes, our sight will know only the beauty of "th'incorruptable Face," our bodies will know exhilarating "Agility in pace or flight," our ears will hear "Praises in Seraphick Sounds," and our noses will inhale

> Such balmy Odours. . .
>   As from the Bridegroom's pores
> The holy Canticles rehearse.
>   (143)

In contradistinction to this vision of perfection, which the poet believes men and women yearn for, is the picture of a tainted world in which mortal suffering is inevitable. The heaven she portrays in "A Contemplation" is notable not only for what it possesses but also for what it lacks: illness and decay, usurpation, thievery, and the common miseries of the human condition.

The political overtones in this poem are strong. Amid heaven's "large Possessions," she writes, "none usurps anothers Lands"—a reference to the recent Hanoverian usurpation of Stuart claims to England's throne. And as her vision of heaven unfolds, it affirms her Stuart allegiances:

> With Christ there Charles's Crown shall meet
>   Which Martirdom adorns
> And prostrate lye beneath his feet
>   My Coronet of Thorns.

The crown of the martyred Charles I will be welcomed by Christ himself, while the poet's own "Coronet of Thorns" (a symbol that relates her coronet as countess to the crown of thorns that both Christ and Charles have borne) is offered up in humility before the feet of Christ. She then explains more fully the suffering which she and her husband have endured:

> The Lord to whom my life is joyn'd
>   For Conscience here opprest

> Shall there full retribution find
> And none his Claimes molest.

In her customary manner Finch then proffers laudatory verses for a female friend. Lady Coventry, she writes, will also be crowned in heaven, in recognition of her numerous acts of charity:[10]

> There Coventry of Tufton's Line
> For piety renown'd
> Shall in transcending virtues Shine
> And Equally be Crown'd
>
> Around her shall the Chains be spread
> of Captives she has freed
> And ev'ry Mouth that she has fed
> Shall testify the deed
>
> Whilst Scools supplied to mend our youth
> Shall on the List be shown
> A Daughter and a Mother both
> In Her the Church shall own
>
> The Gospell crosse the seas rehearst
> By her diffusive aid
> And fifty-thousand pounds dispers'd
> Shall there be largely paid.

As she does in other poems as well, Finch moves from private concerns back to broader social ones, here depicting the vanity of human wishes and decrying economic inequities by use of the examples of Cardinal Wolsey and John Churchill, duke of Marlborough:

> And Mammon wert thou well employ'd
> What Mansions might be wonne
> Whilst Woolsey's Pallace lyes destroy'd
> And Marlbrough's is not done.

The poet imagines what worthy "monuments" might have been built if Mammon had been "well employ'd," rather than pandering to greed and corruption. Juxtaposed to the crowns of Charles I and Lady Coventry are two testimonials to a perverted Mammon: Hampton Court Palace and Blenheim Palace. Hampton Court, built by Cardinal Wolsey, was offered by him to Henry VIII in a futile attempt to retain kingly favor. When Sir Christopher Wren remodeled Hampton Court for William and Mary, he tore down portions of the original palace, and hence the reference to its lying destroyed (Hedley 23). The duke of Marlborough, who epitomized for many Tories the war and the profiteering that the Whig government represented, had begun Blenheim in 1705; it was still unfinished a decade and a half later.

The poem concludes with a gentle admonition that we must look to heaven for the fulfillment of our hopes and ambitions. If we learn to be contented with little, desiring no more for ourselves on earth than "A Sweet Repose at Night" and placing our trust in an afterlife, then, the poet affirms, our earthly sufferings are much easier to bear.

In the last years of her life Finch must have felt in many ways as if she had come full circle, returning, after retirement to the country, to a more public life, residing near the Court of St. James, and even, for a brief period, finding her Tory party welcomed to power. In the end, however, both she and her husband remained victims of the vagaries of English government. But her life, despite adversity, still focused upon what had always been of primary importance to her: her family and friends, her religious faith, and her poetry.

Anne Finch, countess of Winchilsea, died at 9 P.M. on August 5, 1720, at her home on Cleveland Row. In those last months her health had deteriorated, though the exact cause of her death is undisclosed.[11] According to her own wishes, her body was taken to Kent, where she was buried at Eastwell in the little church that now lies in ruins. The following obituary sketch, which her husband transcribed and preserved in his personal diary, is an eloquent tribute to her:

> On Friday, the 5th instant, died, at her own in Cleveland Row, the R[t] Hon[ble] Anne, Countess of Winchelsea, and was on Thursday following (privately, according to her own Desire) carried down to East-Well in Kent, the ancient Seat of that noble Family, and interred there. She was a Daughter of Sir William Kingsmill of Sidmonton, a very ancient Family in Hampshire, and had been Maid of Honour to her late Majesty Queen Mary, when Dutchess of York, 'till married to the Honourable Colonel Heneage Finch,

who, on the Death of his Nephew, the late Earl of Winchelsea, succeeded to that Honour. To draw her Ladyship's just Character, requires a masterly Pen like her own (She being a fine Writer, and an excellent Poet); we shall only presume to say, she was the most faithful Servant to her Royal Mistress, the best Wife to her Noble Lord, and in every other Relation, publick and private, so illustrious an Example of all moral and Divine Virtues: in one Word, a Person of such extraordinary Endowments, both of Body and Mind, that the Court of England never bred a more accomplished Lady, nor the Church of England a better Christian.[12]

As commendatory as this sketch is, Finch's poems themselves offer the fullest tribute to her as a writer and as a human being. Her sense of herself as a friend, relative, and spouse, as a devout Christian, as an English citizen, as a chronic melancholic, and as a committed female poet is unified. As a Nonjurist and a Jacobite she had to cope with religious and political upheavals that shook the foundations of English life and threatened the personal welfare and safety of herself and her husband. As a victim of melancholy she had to wage a lifelong battle to overcome the emotional ravages of her affliction and to resist yielding to despair. And as a woman writer she had to struggle to achieve identity in a literary world and a literary tradition dominated by men. She fought hard to develop her own identity and to maintain integrity—in her domestic and social relationships, in her political allegiances, in her religious faith, and, above all, in her art. She fought hard, in frequent skirmishes and in occasional decisive conflicts. And she triumphed.

Some Poems from
the Wellesley Manuscript

On Lady Cartret drest like a shepherdess
at Count Volira's ball.

Quoth the Swains who got in at the late Masquerade
And never before left their flocks or their shade
What people are here who with splendor amaze
Or but with their antick variety please
Who talk to each other in voices unknown
And their faces are worse than their vizors when shown
Where the Nymphs we have left if amongst y^{m} wou'd seem
More fair than the dazies which grow by the stream
Yet cold to the men who no title cou'd show
As our fields when the flocks are not seen for the snow
Whilst these appear kind & as easily won
As our apples are mellowed by age or the sun.

But just as the Coridons this had expres't
Lady Cartret came by like a shepherdess dress't
The innocent sweetness observed in her eyes
Agreeing so well with her rural disguise
Her lips & her skin which in pastoral disputes
They used to extoll by their flowers & their fruits
Exceeding comparisons drawn from the plains
At once discontented & ravish't the Swains

For Strephon who curious had stray'd thro' the rooms
And felt on the sheep that was wrought in the looms
Soon told them the courtship they made on the downs
Wou'd on Cartret be lost or occasion her frowns
For he heard the gallants who in feathers & lace
Did busily crowd & encumber the place
Declare that no favour of her's wou'd be shown
To any on earth but a Lord of her own.

Then back they resolved to their valleys they'd go
And no more thence be brought by loud rumour or show
Nor shou'd Phillis they said in her holiday cloaths
With a pink in her hat in her bosom a rose
Nor Silvia who with the best cream in her bowl
Set a gloss on her forehead & breeded her role
Or light hearted Cloe who laugh't ere she spoke
For ever hereafter their muses provoke
But all the green springs which their youth shou'd behold
Or chimnies where tales must revive them when old
Shou'd hear them repeat how they Cartret admired
Which said as they came they unheeded retired.

(W ms. 49–50)

The puggs   a dialogue between an old & young dutch Mastiff.

What dogs can do & what they'd say
The Fable writers do convey
Is not all known yet sure their talents
Are not outdone by modern gallants
For 'tho' they neither read nor write
If they make love can play & fight
Are comb'd & powder'd & appear
At either park & call'd my dear
If they know how to push their fortune
And the best giver can importune
To supple they've their masters lick't
The very moment they've been kick't
Have all fidelity maintain'd
Untill by larger proffers gain'd
Who can pretend to go beyond 'em

Or blame such patrons as defend 'em
But I've too long my tale omitted
To which this prologue has been fitted
And now must tell you that I know
A young Dutch dog in Cleaveland Row
Who wou'd had he been taught & letter'd
His own complaints perhaps have better'd
But being left to me I must
To all his jealous cares be just.

This dog who so much matter yeilds
Wou'd visit pug in Leicester feilds
A dog in all sage prudence learn'd
And for the Provinces concern'd
Tho' naturealiz'd he was of late
And grown a member of our State
Extreamly civil was their meeting
And thus the elder pug did greet him
My namesake whelp't amongst the ditches
And offspring sure of noblest bitches
Permit me tho' our race but traded
Till we our neighbours rights invaded
With saple paws thus to embrace you
And on the upper hand to place you
For truly this kind favour done me
Has to your service throughly won me
But something in your face appears
Too melancholy for your years
Unfold then all your griefs & dangers
We're now esteemed as mungril strangers
Time was—but here a sigh was vented
And the harangue by that prevented.

Then quoth the dog from Cleaveland Row
I meant this visit long ago
But kept so close whilst chief in favour
I cou'd not show my good behaviour
Till now of that incumberance quitted
I'm farther liberty permitted
And may imploy my time & feet

May court or quarrel in the street
Might hang my self had I but garters
Nor shou'd be mist in my old quarters
And certainly that dog's a puppy
That stays when any one wou'd drop ye.

'Tis right young pug the elder cry'd
My age these changes oft has try'd
Now hugg'd & priz'd shut up & hamper'd
Then lash'd & spurn'd & gladly scamper'd
Or cring'd till it did so endear me
That not a servant durst come near me
And all who did not love must fear me.

A favorite till he domineers
Is a poor dog below the spheres
But then the dog that fires the sky
Is not so curish or so high.

But we have all enough to do
To keep our masters just & true
Since often they but little care
For what we eat or what we wear
See how they've hagl'd my bavaire
And as that were not scorn enough
Have snipt my cravat to a ruff
Made me asham'd to walk my rounds
From Doll's to Colemeer's were my bounds
And grave respect was allways paid
By those who my strict watch survey'd
But grief talks all & I'm to blame
Now tell how your misfortunes came
And if you master served or dame

Quoth t'other when his speech was ended
'Twas on a Lady I attended
And frisk'd & fawn'd till I was tired
As long as she my airs admired
Prefer'd each word & smile of hers
To all that cou'd be done for curs
Securely wou'd her house have kept

And never but dog sleep have slept
Tho' being of a sturdy head
I've to a cup of ale been bred
In Southwark taught by Mrs Cary
And still 'twas fill'd by Mrs Mary
Yet I for that was never blamed
Tho' sometimes ridiculed & sham'd
But 'twas comparison disgraced me
And in my Lady's sight debas'd me
A lovelier thing she met with one day
O! fatal sight O! fatal monday
But may it ever be forgotten
And Yanica lye dead & rotten.

Tho' Yanica is small & jetty
Sleek as a mole & wondrous pretty
Her beauty in its youthfull splendor
Such enbonpoint so soft so tender
Minyion even when she's most untoward
Genteely coy & chastly froward
A bitch that any heart cou'd soften
And no wise dog wou'd see her often
Yet had you heard my dame commend her
You wou'd have wish't a rope might end her
Such never ceasing praise she gave her
And wou'd have lost us all to have her
Then tell me can it be supported
When one has been carest & courted
Call'd handsome fellow stroak'd & patted
And regularly lodged & fatted
To be thrown off & hear a pother
Kept day & night about another
When Ladies never yet cou'd pardon
The men who others fix regard on
And she whose prayse not highest rises
Or whom the Swain not chiefly prizes
All other court or praise dispises.

Friend quoth old pug you're in the wrong
You came I find to town but young
And by rehearsing of this matter

Have lived on t'other side the water
But you must alter now depend on't
Since you're removed to the court end on't
Must swallow wrongs for which by nature
Your mouth seems a convenient feature
Must sooth the dog your betters fondle
And all things take by the right handle
Favour tho' you perhaps may share it
Will come & go & all must bear it
D'ye think my Knight tho' much refin'd
Is always courteous always kind
No sometimes he'll not let me stir
Then presently take out the cur
Who now am strip't of every rag
And for my diet force't to beg
Then be content where chance has set ye
Nor let your Lady's coldness fret ye
If not till now her love has wander'd
Think her one woman of an hundred.

Fondness dear pug is all a jest
And never yet was long possest
But if you'd only live at ease
Who changes least strive most to please.
                                        (W ms. 50–54)

[handwritten note beside title: Mary of Modena d. 1718]

On the Death of the Queen.

Dark was the shade where only cou'd be seen
Disasterous Yew that ever balefull green
Distructive in the field of old when strung
Gloomy o'er graves of sleeping warriors hung
Deep was the wild recess that not an ear
Which grudged her praises might the accents hear
Where sad ARDELIA mourn'd URANIA's Death
In sighs which seem'd her own expireing breath
In moving Sylables so often broke

That more then Eloquence the anguish spoke
Urging the tears which cou'd not give relief
But seem'd to propagate renewing grief
Lamira near her sat and caught the sound
Too weak for ecchoing rocks which fixt the bound
For Clifts that overlook't the dangerous wave
Th'unhappy Vessels or the Sailors grave
The pittying Nymph whom sympathy constrain'd
Ask't why her friend thus heavily complain'd
Why she retired to that ill omen'd spot
By men forsaken and the World forgot
Why thus from light and company she fled
And living sought the mansions of the Dead
Her head reclined on the obdurate stone
Still uttering low but interrupted moan
In which URANIA she to all prefer'd
And with her seem'd unactive or interr'd
As if all virtues of the polish't mind
All excellencies of the female kind
All wining graces in Urania join'd
As if perfection but in her was seen
And Her least dignity was England's Queen.

Thou hast discrib'd her pleas'd ARDELIA cry'd
As thou hadst known her awfull without pride
As thou in Her Domestick train hadst stood
And seen her great and found her warmly good
Duely maintaining her exalted place
Yet condescending with attractive grace
Recall'd be days when ebon locks o'erspread
My youthfull neck my cheeks a bashfull red
When early joys my glowing bosom warm'd
When trifles pleas'd & every pleasure charm'd
Then eager from the rural seat I came
Of long traced Ancestors of worthy name
To seek the Court of many woes the source
Compleated by this last this sad divorce
From her to whom my self I had resign'd
The Sovereign Mistress of my vanquish't mind
Who now survive but to attend her hearse

With dutious tribute of recording verse
In which may truth with energy be found
And soft as her compassion be the sound
Bless't were the hours when thro' attendance due
Her numerous charms were present to my view
When lowly to her radiant eyes I bowed
Suns to my sight but Suns without a cloud
Towards me their beneficial aspect turn'd
Imprest my duty and my conduct warn'd
For who that saw the modest airs they cast
But from that pattern must be nicely chast
Peculiar Souls have their peculiar sighs
And thro' the eye the inward beauty shines
Then who can wonder if in hers appear'd
Superior sense to be reveer'd & fear'd
Endearing sweetness to her happy friends
And Holy fire which towards the alter tends
Bles't my attention was when drawing near
(My places claim) her crouded audience chair
I heard her by admiring States addrest
With embasies in different tongues exprest
To all that Europe sent she gave replies
In their own speech most eloquent & wise
Soft was her talk and soothing to the heart
By nature solid perfected by art
The Roman Accent which such grace affords
To Tuscan language harmonized her words
All eyes all listning sense upon her hung
When from her lovely mouth th'inchantment sprung
What Livia was when Rome Augustus sway'de
And thro' a woman's wit the world obey'd
What Portia was when fortitude and love
Inflected wounds which did her firmness prove
And forcing Brutus to applaud her worth
Drew with the steel th'important secret forth
Such was URANIA where they most excell'd
And where they fail'd by nobler zeal upheld
What Italy produc't of glorious names
Her native Country & her kindred Dames
All virtues which Antiquity cou'd boast

She equal'd but on Stormy Britain tost
They lost their value on a northern Coast
Yet who can wonder if to her we grant
What Poets feign when they Diana paint
What Legends write when they enthrone a Saint
What now ARDELIA speaks with conscious sense
Of Real Worth & matchless excellence
Never such lustre strove against the light
Never such beauty satisfied the sight
Never such Majesty on earth was found
As when URANIA worthyly was crown'd
As when superior airs declared her birth
From Conquerours o'er the Monarchs of the Earth
And large excuse did for their Maxim bring
That Roman Ladies stoop'd to wed a King
If Royalty had then arose from choice
And merit had compell'd the publick voice
All had allow'd URANIA claimed the most
In view of whom all other charms were lost
Her's in Meridian strong in their decay
But sweetly sinking like declining day
In grief but veil'd as when a rainy cloud
The glorious Sun does yet transparent Shroud
And whilst it softens each resplendent beam
Weeps o'er the land from whence the vapour came
O'er Brittain so her Pious sorrows fell
Less for her Woes then that it cou'd rebell
Yet thence arose the shades her life o'ercast
And worldly greatness seldom made to last
Thence in a foreign clime her Consort died
Whom death cou'd never from her thoughts divide
Thence Sable weeds & cyprus walks she chose
And from within produc't her own repose
Yet only pray'd for those she cou'd not calm
As fragrant trees tho' wounded shed but balm
Nor ceas't to live till vindicated Heaven
Shew'd that in vain were such examples given
Who held her light to three great Kingdoms forth
And gave her Sufferings to dilate her worth
That Gallia too might see she cou'd support

Monastick rules and Britains worst effort
Now peacefull is the spirit which possest
That never blemish't that afflicted breast
Closed are such eyes as paradise might boast
Seen but in Eve e'er innocence she lost
The solemn grave with reverence takes her down
And lasting wreaths succeed th'unstable crown
For rude Huzza's in mercenary streets
All Hail in her triumphant way she meets
Who shall in silent Majesty repose
Till every tomb shall every guest disclose
Till Heaven which does all human loss repair
Distinguishing the attoms of the fair
Shall give URANIA's form transcendant beauty there
And from the beams Iradiating her face
(Which here but wanted that suspended grace)
Shall shew the Britains how they strove in vain
To strip that brow which was consign'd to reign
Tho' Polititians strove to guide the round
Of miscall'd fortune & prescribe its bound
Till the contested Earth shou'd be no longer found.

Here she concludes Lamira thinks it just
Such pious tears shou'd wait such Royal Dust.

(W ms. 68–71)

An Hymn of Thanksgiving after a Dangerous fit of sickness in the year 1715.

To thee encreaser of my days
My ransom'd Soul my voice I raise
O may thy love
My warmth improve
And guide my future days.

2.

With Allelujah's now I come
From terrours rescued and the tomb

To pay my thanks
Amidst the ranks
Devoted from the womb.

3.

With Allelujahs let me try
To penetrate the vaulted sky
　Till all thy train
　Endulge the vein
And Allelujah cry.

4.

For health restored and will to please
For softened passions and for ease
　O let me give
　Whilst I shall live
In Allelujahs praise.

5.

By Angels who their tents display'd
Around my curtains gloomy shade
　Now I their charge
　Am set att large,
Be Allelujahs paid.

6.

With Allelujahs I aspire
To mix with that Celestial choire
　Accept my heart
　Without the art
Which does their songs inspire.

7.

Till to thy Courts thou dost me bring
Where I like them shall touch the string
　With zeal and will
　And equal skill
Their Allelujahs sing.

8.

For Providence my ample feild

My food my raiment and my shield
 Thro' life my trust
 Rejoice I must
And Allelujahs yeild.

9.

For scaping dangers in my way
The deadly shaft which fly's by day
 The hasty fright
 That comes by night
I Allelujahs pay.

10.

For this the gift by Heaven assign'd
With verse to sooth my active mind
 To every thought
 Which there is wrought
Be Allelujah join'd.

11.

In Allelujahs who'l proceed
Shall find all objects praises breed
 Nor fear the spleen
 Shou'd come between
By Allelujahs freed.

12.

To Allelujahs till I dye
May I my chearfull hours apply
 Then to the blest
 In ceasless rest
With Allelujahs fly.
     (W ms. 76–78)

To the Rev^d. Mr. Bedford

On me then Sir as on a friend
You say your interests now depend
And may you be no longer mine

When your least service I decline
But tho' my will is all on fire
To compass that which you desire
Success from others must proceed
Towards which observe my restless speed
Your note recieved down stairs I fly
My gown unpin'd my hood awry
With Mrs Mary at my heels
Who as she this disorder feels
Here gives a twitch there aims a pin
But cannot reach to fix it in
Yet does with lengthen'd strides aproach
And throws my ruffles in the coach
I finishing the best I can
Now drop my gloves and then my fan
As Jehu scours along the streets
And swears at every thing he meets
Till to his Lordship's door he comes
Who spyes me thro' a suite of rooms
And forward moves with courtly pace
Till noting my requesting face
He puts on a refuseing air
And bids his footman call a chair
Then draws his watch—'tis two and past
You find me in prodigious haste
He crys as he on tiptoe stands
Yet Madam what are your commands
I'll serve you to my utmost power
The Houses have been met this hour
Shall I conduct you to my wife
I have no interest on my life
I'm ruin'd if I come too late
W'ere like to have a warm debate
I promis't Solon to attend
Tis he my Lord must help my friend
I barely hint as he goes on
Who Madam crys it can't be done
Your humble servant you forgive
You see in what a round we live
From morning hurried thus till night

Madam I hope you take me right
When I've a moment to dispose
I'll come and hear what you propose
Make haste ye blockheads—up they weigh
My Lord and to the house convey
Whilst in the parlour I remain
O'ercome with sorrow and disdain
Yet with a Roman virtue scorn
The Land depraved where I was born
Where men now wealthy grown and great
En bagatell our sufferings treat
Yet still I will your cause persue
Th'unrighteous Judge the harden'd Jew
As soon might be at rest as I
Will leave them till they all comply
Or if no good from thence I draw
They still are Jews without the Law.

(W ms. 78–79)

Sir Plausible

[untitled in manuscript]

Sir plausible as 'tis well known
Has no opinions of his own
But closes with each stander by
Now in a truth now in a lie
Fast as Camelions change their dye
Has still some applicable story
To gratify or Whig or Tory
And with a Jacobite in tatters
If met alone he smoothly flatters
Is full of service and accosts
Knows each mans interests and his toasts
Uncivilly wou'd no one treat
To save his Honour or estate
Greets friend and foe with wishes fervent
And lives and dies your humble servant.

(W ms. 87)

A Ballad to Mrs Catherine Fleming in London
from Malshanger farm in Hampshire

From me who whileom sung the Town,
    This second Ballad comes;
To let you know we are got down,
    From hurry, smoke, & drums:
And every visitor that rowls,
In restless Coach from Mall to Paul's.
    With a fa-la-la-la-la-la.

2.

And now were I to paint the seat,
    (As well-bred poets use;)
I shou'd embellish our retreat,
    By favour of the muse:
Tho' to no villa we pretend,
But a plain farm at the best end.
    With a fa-la &c.

3.

Where innocence & quiet reigns,
    And no distrust is known;
His nightly safety none maintains,
    By ways they do in Town:
Who rising loosen bolt and bar,
We draw the latch and out we are.
    With a fa-la &c.

4.

For jarring sounds in London streets,
    Which still are passing by;
Where cowcumbers with Sand ho meets,
    And for loud mastry vie:
The driver whisling to his team,
Here wakes us from some rural dream.
    With a fa-la &c.

5.

From rising hills thro' distant views,
    We see the Sun decline;

Whilst every where the eye persues,
    The grazeing flocks and kine:
Which home at night the Farmer brings,
And not the Post's but sheeps bell rings
    With a fa-la &c.

6.

We silver trouts and Cray-fish eat,
    Just taken from the stream;
And never think our meal compleat,
    Without fresh curds and cream:
And as we pass by the barn floor,
We choose our supper from the door.
    With a fa-la &c.

7.

Beneath our feet the partridge springs,
    As to the woods we go;
Where birds scarce stretch their painted wings,
    So little fear they shew:
But when our outspread hoops they spy,
They look when we like them shou'd fly.
    With a fa-la &c.

8.

Thro' verdant circles as we stray,
    To which no end we know;
As we o'er hanging boughs survey,
    And tufted grass below:
Delight into the fancy falls,
And happy days and verse recalls.
    With a fa-la &c.

9.

Oh! why did I these shades forsake,
    And shelter of the grove;
The flowring shrub the rusling brake,
    The solitude I love:
Where Emperours have fixt their lot,
And greatly chose to be forgot.
    With a fa-la &c.

10.

Then how can I from hence depart,
    Unless my pleasing friend;
Shou'd now her sweet harmonious art,
    Unto these shades extend:
And like old Orpheus powerfull song,
Draw me and all my woods along.
        With a fa-la &c.

11.

So charm'd like Birnam's they wou'd rise,
    And march in goodly row;
But since it might the town surprize,
    To see me travel so:
I must from soothing joys like these,
Too soon return in open chaise.
        With a fa-la &c.

12.

Mean while accept what I have writ,
    To shew this rural scene;
Nor look for sharp satyrick wit,
    From off the balmy plain:
The country breeds no thorny bays,
But mirth and love and honest praise.
        With a fa-la-la-la-la-la.
                (W ms. 89–91)

The white mouses petition
to Lamira the Right Hon:^{ble}
the Lady Ann Tufton now Countess of Salisbury.

With all respect and humble duty
And passing every mouse in Beauty
With far more white than garden lillies
And eyes as bright as any Phillis
I sue to wear Lamira's fetters
And live the envy of my betters
When I receive her soft caresses

And creeping near her lovely tresses
Their glossy brown from my reflection
Shall gain more lustre and perfection
And to her bosom if admitted
My colour there will be so fitted
That no distinction cou'd discover
My station to a jealous Lover
Her hands whilst they're my food bestowing
A thousand graces will be shewing
And smiles enliven every feature
Whilst I engage her youthfull nature
To mind my little tricks and fancies
My active play and circling dances
And if by a genteel behaviour
'Tis but my lot to gain her favour
To her my life shall be devoted
And I as her first captive noted
Shall fill a mighty place in story
And share in that ambitious glory
To which so many hearts are growing
Where loss of freedom shall be owing
To her whose chain my value raises
And makes me merit all your praises.

(W ms. 92–93)

An Apology for my fearfull temper
in a letter in Burlesque upon the firing
of my chimney At Wye College March 25th 1702.

'Tis true of courage I'm no mistress
No Boadicia nor Thalestriss
Nor shall I e'er be famed hereafter
For such a Soul as Cato's Daughter
Nor active valour nor enduring
Nor leading troops nor forts securing
Like Teckley's wife or Pucell valiant
Will e'er be reckonded for my talent
Who all things fear whilst day is shining

And my own shadow light declining
And from the Spleen's prolifick fountain
Can of a mole hill make a mountain
And if a Coach that was invented
Since Bess on Palfrey rode contented
Threatens to tumble topsy turvy
With screeches loud and faces scurvey
I break discourse whilst some are laughing
Some fall to chear me some to chaffing
As secretly the driver curses
And whips my fault upon the horses
These and ten thousand are the errours
Arising from tumultuous terrours
Yet can't I understand the merit
In Female's of a daring spirit
Since to them never was imparted
In manly strengh tho' manly hearted
Nor need that sex be self defending
Who charm the most when most depending
And by sweet plaints and soft distresses
First gain asistance then adresses
As our fourth Edward (beauty suing)
From but releiving fell to wooing
Who by Heroick speech or ranting
Had ne'er been melted to galanting
Nor had th'Egyptian Queen defying
Drawn off that fleet she led by flying
Whilst Cesar and his ships crew hollow'd
To see how Tony row'd and follow'd
Oh Action triumph of the Ladies
And plea for her who most afraid is
Then let my conduct work no wonder
When fame who cleaves the air asunder
And every thing in time discovers
Nor council keeps for Kings or Lovers
Yet stoops when tired with States and battles
To Gossips chats and idler tattles
When she I say has given no knowledge
Of what has happen'd at Wye College
Think it not strange to save my Person

I gave the family diversion
'Twas at an hour when most were sleeping
Some chimnies clean some wanted sweeping
Mine thro' good fires maintain'd this winter
(Of which no FINCH was e'er a stinter)
Pour'd down such flakes not Etna bigger
Throws up as did my fancy figure
Nor does a Cannon ram'd with Powder
To others seem to Bellow louder
All that I thought or spoke or acted
Can't in a letter be compacted
Nor how I threatn'd those with burning
Who thoughtless on their beds were turning
As Shakespear says they serv'd old Prium
When that the Greeks were got too nigh'em
And such th'effect in spite of weather
Our Hecuba's all rose together
I at their head half cloath'd and shaking
Was instantly the house forsaking
And told them 'twas no time for talking
But who'd be safe had best be walking
This hasty councel and conclusion
Seem'd harsh to those who had no shoes on
And saw no flames and heard no clatter
But as I had rehears'd the matter
And wildly talk't of fire and water
For sooner then 'thas took to tell it
Right applications did repell it
And now my fear our mirth creating
Affords still subject for repeating
Whilst some deplore th'unusual folly
Some (kinder) call it melancholy
Tho' certainly the spirits sinking
Comes not from want of wit or thinking
Since Rochester all dangers hated
And left to those were harder pated.

(W ms. 98–100)

A Suplication for the joys of Heaven.

To the Superior World to Solemn Peace
To Regions where Delights shall never cease
To Living Springs and to Celestial shade
For change of pleasure not Protection made
To Blissfull Harmonys o'erflowing source
Which Strings or stops can neither bind or Force
But wafting Air for ever bears along
Perpetual Motion with perpetual Song
On which the Blest in Symphonies ascend
And towards the Throne with Vocal ardours bend
To Radial light o'erspreading Boundless space
To the safe Goal of our well ended race
To shelter where the weary shall have rest
And where the wicked never shall molest
To that Jerusalem which ours below
Did but in type and faint resemblance shew
To the first born and ransom'd Church above
To Seraphims whose whole composures love
To active Cherubins whom wings surround
Not made to rest tho' on imortal ground
But still suspended wait with flaming joy
In swift commands their vigour to employ
Ambrosial dews distilling from their plumes
Scattering where e'er they pass innate perfumes
To Angells of innumerable sorts
Subordinate in the etherial Courts
To Men refin'd from every gross allay
Who taught the Flesh the Spirit to obey
And keeping late futurity in view
Do now possess what long they did persue
To Jesus founder of the Christian race
And kind dispenser of the Gospell grace
Bring me my God in my accomplish't time
From weakness freed and from degrading crime
Fast by the Tree of life be my retreat
Whose leaves are Med'cin and whose fruit is meat
Heal'd by the first and by the last renew'd

With all perfections be my Soul endued
My form that has the earthly figure borne
Take the Celestial in its Glorious turn
My temper frail and subject to dismay
Be stedfast there spiritualiz'd and gay
My low Poetick tendency be rais'd
Till the bestower worthily is prais'd
Till Dryden's numbers for Cecilia's feast
Which sooth depress inflame and shake the breast
Vary the passions with each varying line
Allow'd below all others to outshine
Shall yeild to those above shall yeild to mine
In sound in sense in emphasis Divine
Stupendious are the heights to which they rise
Whose anthems match the musick of the skies
Whilst that which art we call when studied here
Is nature there in its sublimest sphere
And the pathetick now so hard to find
Flows from the gratefull transports of the mind
With Poets who supernal voices raise
And here begin their never ending layes
With those who to the brethren of their Lord
In all distress a warm relief afford
With the Heroick Spirits of the brave
Who durst be true when threatn'd with the Grave
And when from evil in triumphant sway
Who e'er departed made himself a prey
To sanguine perils to penurious care
To scanty cloathing and precarious fare
To lingring solitude exhausting thoughts
Unsuccour'd losses and imputed faults
With these let me be join'd when Heaven reveals
The judgment which admits of no appeals
And having heard from the deciding throne
Well have ye suffer'd wisely have ye Done
Henceforth the Kingdom of the blest is yours
For you unfolds its everlasting doors
With joyfull Allelujahs let me hail
The strength that o'er my weakness cou'd prevail
Upheld me here and raised my feeble clay

To this felicity for which I pray
Thro' him whose intercession I implore
And Heaven once enter'd prayer shall be no more
Loud acclamations shall its place supply
And praise the breath of Angells in the sky.

Finisht February 6th 1717/18

(W ms. 108–09)

Written after a violent and dagerous fit of sicknesse in the Year 1715.

Snatch'd from the verge of the devouring grave
What with his Creature wou'd her Maker have
Speak for thy Servant hears and ready stands
To yield her lengthen'd life to thy Commands
If not enough this Chastisement appears
For Idlenesse or long offending years
Oh yett again lett me thy Rod endure
Nor rashly ask the hast'ning of my Cure
Till bow'd with Grief and sinking on the Flore
I hear it utterr'd Go and Sin no more
And now methinks I hear that healing Voyce
Seem to reply and bid my Soul rejoyce
Depart in peace it sais and rest secur'd
Thy groanes are finish'd and thy ease procur'd
A Ransom is receiv'd God's only Son
Has pay'd the Price of all that thou hast done
Thy Prayers thy sighs through him accesse have found
And no one Tear unpittied dew'd the ground
His watchfull Providence unloos'd thy Bands
And he again upheld thy lifted hands
Strength to thy feeble knees from him there came
Again to bear thy Supplicating Frame
This Intercessor for that Mercy made
Which thy unslak'd and threatning heats allay'd
Rebuk'd the Feaver as in Peter's house
He drove it from the Mother of his Spouse

Temper'd thy blood in ev'ry beating vaine
And gave its just Dominion to the Brain
Baffling the spite of those who envy bore
And said she's fallen now to rise no more
But o're the waves of Misery and Care
He bid thee walk nor sink into Dispair
'Tis true indeed O my Redeeming Lord
By thee again to ease and breath restor'd
In Thee I think my Father reconcil'd
And I again acknowledg'd as a Child
I now again my clouded hopes renew
And future glory keep in present view
Entitled to the Church my mothers breast
In Christs clean Robe the Wedding garment dresst
I now again her Sacraments draw near
In Love in Trust in Penitence in Fear
Whilst in my Thoughts still this suggestion falls
Be of good Comfort rise thy Saviour calls
I come Lord Jesus at thy Call I come
O my good Shepheard bring thy wanderer home
Then shall the Hands the Knees the Heart the Brain
Which to their use thou hast restor'd again
Be all employ'd to Glorify thy Name
And thy sweet Service be my future aim
Make me O Lord whom thou hast deign'd to raise
An humble Instrument to spread thy Praise
Lett my weak pen thy tender Servants lead
To pious meltings when my Verse they read
Lett my Recovery which I here Record
Teach ev'ry fainting Soul to trust the Lord
And if sometimes when Flesh that quickly tyres
Some relaxation some new Theam requires
I sink to trifle for a little space
Let no revengefull Spleen my page disgrace
Whilest general Vice I strive to ridicule
And prove the Sinner is the witty Fool
In grave or chearfull numbers lett me try
Lesse to divert then warmly Edefy
And if I'm blest to compass that dessign
As thine the Gift the Glory too be thine

All that I am all that I had or have
Since my first dawn of life thy Mercy gave
And now renews delivering from the grave
To thee be Glory from my Heart and Pen
And with me joyn all Angels Saints and Men
Lett every thing extoll him that has breath
Who here adjourns hereafter Conquers Death

All Glory be to God

(W ms. 139–40)

A Contemplation

Indulg'd by ev'ry active thought
    When upwards they wou'd fly
Nor can Ambition be a fault
    If plac'd above the sky

When humbld first we meekly crave
    Remission for the past
We from the fore-tasts which we have
    May guesse our Joys at last

Then let my Contemplations soar
    And Heav'n my Subject be
Though low on Earth in nature poor
    Some prospect we may see

And now that scene before me stands
    And large Possessions there
Where none usurps anothers Lands
    And Theives we do not fear

All Care all Sorrow all Surprise
    Fly from that World of peace
Where tears are wip'd from clouded Eyes
    And Sighs for ever cease

Decay or Sicknesse find no place
   In that untainted Air
But still th'incorruptable Face
   Shall as at first be fair

Agility in pace or flight
   The Blessed shall convey
Where e're the Lamb more fair then light
   Shall lead the radiant way

Whilst Praises in Seraphick Sounds
   The blisfull road shall trace
And musick seem to passe the bounds
   Even of unbounded Space

Such balmy Odours shall disperse
   As from the Bridegroom's pores
The holy Canticles rehearse
   Fell on the Bolts and Doors

When to his Spouse the well belov'd
   More white then Jordans Flocks
Spake whilest her hand the Barrs remov'd
   And dew-drops fill'd his locks

The Crosse shall there triumphant rise
   And ev'ry Eye shall scan
That promis'd Ensign in the skies
   Close by the Son of Man

With Christ there Charles's Crown shall meet
   Which Martirdom adorns
And prostrate lye beneath his feet
   My Coronet of Thorns

The Lord to whom my life is joyn'd
   For Conscience here opprest
Shall there full retribution find
   And none his Claimes molest

Hypocrisy and feign'd pretence
  To cover foul Dissigns
Shall blusshing fly as far from thence
  As to the deepest Mines

We there shall know the use of Foes
  Whom here we have forgiven
When we shall thank them for those woes
  Which pav'd our way to Heaven

There all good things that we have mist
  With Int'rest shall return
Whilst those who have each wish possest
  Shall for that fullnesse mourn

There Coventry of Tufton's Line
  For piety renown'd
Shall in transcending virtues Shine
  And Equally be Crown'd

Around her shall the Chains be spread
  Of Captives she has freed
And ev'ry Mouth that she has fed
  Shall testify the deed

Whilst Scools supplied to mend our youth
  Shall on the List be shown
A Daughter and a Mother both
  In Her the Church shall own

The Gospell crosse the seas rehearst
  By her diffusive aid
And fifty-thousand pounds dispers'd
  Shall there be largely paid

My Heart by her supporting Love
  In all its Cares upheld
For that, to see her Crown improve
  With transports shall be fill'd

From Gratitude what graces flow
    What endlesse pleasures spring
From Prayers whilst we remain below
    Above whilst Praise we Sing

And Mammon wert thou well employ'd
    What Mansions might be wonne
Whilst Woolsey's Pallace lyes destroy'd
    And Marlbrough's is not done.

Whilst to this Heav'n my Soul Aspires
    All Suff'rings here are light
He travells pleas'd who but desires
    A Sweet Repose at Night

                (W ms. 143–46)

Poems in Tribute to
Anne Finch

Apollo Outwitted
To the Hon. Mrs. Finch,
(since Countess of Winchilsea,)
under the Name of Ardelia

Phoebus now short'ning every Shade,
   Up to the *Northern Tropick* came,
And thence beheld a lovely Maid
   Attending on a Royal Dame.

The God laid down his feeble Rays;
   Then lighted from his glitt'ring Coach;
But fenc'd his Head with his own Bays,
   Before he durst the Nymph approach.

Under those sacred Leaves, secure
   From common Lightning of the Skies,
He fondly thought he might endure
   The Flashes of *Ardelia's* Eyes.

The Nymph, who oft had read in Books
   Of that bright God, whom Bards invoke,
Soon knew *Apollo* by his Looks,
   And guess'd his Business, e'er he spoke.

He in the old Celestial Cant,
 Confess'd his Flame, and swore by *Styx*,
Whate'er she would desire, to grant;
 But wise *Ardelia* knew his Tricks.

Ovid had warn'd her to beware
 Of stroling Gods, whose usual Trade is,
Under Pretence of taking Air,
 To pick up Sublunary Ladies.

Howe'er, she gave no flat Denial,
 As having Malice in her Heart;
And was resolv'd upon a Tryal,
 To cheat the God in his own Art.

Hear my Request, the Virgin said;
 Let which I please of all the Nine
Attend whene'er I want their Aid,
 Obey my Call, and only mine.

By Vow oblig'd, by Passion led,
 The God could not refuse her Prayer:
He wav'd his Wreath thrice o'er her Head,
 Thrice mutter'd something to the Air.

And now he thought to seize his Due,
 But she the Charm already try'd,
Thalia heard the Call, and flew
 To wait at bright *Ardelia's* Side.

On Sight of this celestial Prude,
 Apollo thought it vain to stay,
Nor in her Presence durst be rude;
 But made his Leg, and went away.

He hop'd to find some lucky Hour,
 When on their Queen the Muses wait;
But *Pallas* owns *Ardelia's* Power;
 For Vows divine are kept by Fate.

Then full of Rage *Apollo* spoke,
    Deceitful Nymph! I see thy Art;
And though I can't my Gift revoke,
    I'll disappoint its nobler Part.

Let stubborn Pride possess thee long,
    And be thou negligent of Fame;
With ev'ry Muse to grace thy Song,
    May'st thou despise a Poet's Name.

Of modest Poets thou be first,
    To silent Shades repeat thy Verse,
Till *Fame* and *Eccho* almost burst,
    Yet hardly dare one Line rehearse.

And last, my Vengeance to compleat;
    May you descend to take Renown,
Prevail'd on by the Thing you hate,
    A Whig, and one that wears a Gown.

JONATHAN SWIFT

IMPROMPTU, *To Lady* WINCHELSEA.
Occasion'd by four Satyrical Verses on Women-Wits, in the Rape of the Lock.

In vain you boast Poetick Dames of yore,
And cite those Sapphoes wee admire no more;
Fate doom'd the fall of ev'ry female Wit,
But doom'd it then when first Ardelia writ.
Of all examples by the world confest,
I knew Ardelia could not quote the best,
Who, like her Mistresse on Britannia's Throne,
Fights and subdues in quarrells not her own.
    To write their Praise you but in vain essay,
Ev'n while you write, you take that praise away,
Light to the Stars the Sun does thus restore,
But shines himselfe till they are seen no more.

ALEXANDER POPE

APPENDIX C

Genealogical Charts

A Winchilsea Genealogy

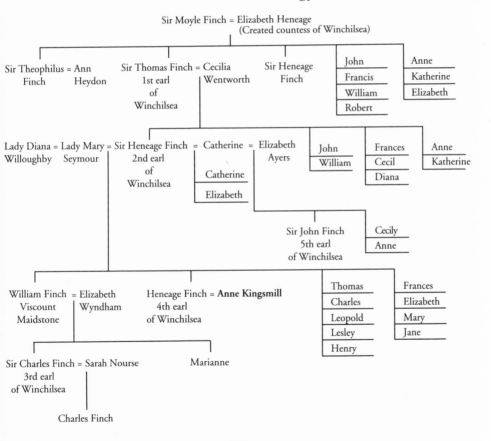

Sir Moyle Finch = Elizabeth Heneage
(Created countess of Winchilsea)

Sir Theophilus = Ann Finch Heydon

Sir Thomas Finch = Cecilia Wentworth
1st earl of Winchilsea

Sir Heneage Finch

John
Francis
William
Robert

Anne
Katherine
Elizabeth

Lady Diana = Lady Mary = Sir Heneage Finch = Catherine = Elizabeth Ayers
Willoughby Seymour 2nd earl of Winchilsea

Catherine
Elizabeth

John
William

Frances
Cecil
Diana

Anne
Katherine

Sir John Finch
5th earl of Winchilsea

Cecily
Anne

William Finch = Elizabeth Wyndham
Viscount Maidstone

Heneage Finch = **Anne Kingsmill**
4th earl of Winchilsea

Thomas
Charles
Leopold
Lesley
Henry

Frances
Elizabeth
Mary
Jane

Sir Charles Finch = Sarah Nourse
3rd earl of Winchilsea

Marianne

Charles Finch

225

A Kingsmill Genealogy

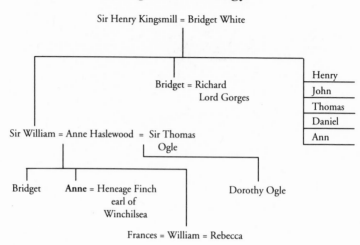

Sir Henry Kingsmill = Bridget White

Bridget = Richard
Lord Gorges

Henry
John
Thomas
Daniel
Ann

Sir William = Anne Haslewood = Sir Thomas
Ogle

Bridget   Anne = Heneage Finch   Dorothy Ogle
             earl of
             Winchilsea

Frances = William = Rebecca

Notes

Introduction: "Alas! a woman that attempts the pen"

1. The standard source for biographical information about Anne Finch has been the introduction by Myra Reynolds to her 1903 edition. Though an ambitious work, it is marred by some factual inaccuracies and very incomplete, as is the collection of poems itself. More recently Katharine Rogers has edited a small volume of the poems, which contains none of the previously unpublished poetry from the last two decades of Finch's life, and Denys Thompson has also brought out a slim volume of *Selected Poems*.

2. Unless otherwise noted, all poetry quotations and passages quoted from Finch's prose preface to the folio manuscript will be from the Reynolds edition. Numbers following each passage refer to page numbers in that edition; line references are given as well for longer poems.

3. "Politics of Difference" 377. This is the introductory essay in *Eighteenth-Century Studies* 23 (1990); the entire issue (no. 4), which Felicity Nussbaum has edited, is noteworthy for anyone interested in theoretical issues in contemporary eighteenth-century studies. See also the title essay in Meese for a discussion of difference.

4. For a cogent analysis of the controversies in contemporary feminist criticism see Nussbaum and Brown 1–22.

5. Newton warns against creating what she calls "an inevitable and tragic essentiality" (126). Other feminist theorists, like Nancy Chodorow, Jane Flax, and Carol Gilligan, have also emphasized that ideologies of gender are constructions of history.

6. Williamson defines this position, which she herself uses in her splendid book *Raising Their Voices*, as viewing the construction of subjectivity as "a continuous process, produced not only by external social patterns and discourses

but through the individual's interaction with such discourses and cultural practices." She adds, "Such thinking does not compel a choice between the extremes of the essentialist feminine subject and the genderless subject produced by discourse" (10). A similar position is held by de Lauretis, especially in *Alice Doesn't*, and by Alcoff.

7. Perry explores this seeming paradox in Mary Astell's views in *The Celebrated Mary Astell*; see particularly the chapter "A Monarch for Life" (150–80). Her article "Mary Astell" is also relevant.

8. Williamson's arguments for a continuous feminist history (15) dispute Smith's conclusion that because many seventeenth-century women writers did not become political activists their private ideas were "truncated" and only later revived (192). My own view coincides with Williamson's. Her book is compelling reading for anyone interested in early British women writers.

9. A noncritical edition of the Wellesley poems, not available for purchase, was privately printed in Italy in 1989 by Jean M. Ellis D'Alessandro. It is, unfortunately, not an acceptable edition; it has no critical or content notes, there is no description of the manuscript and no attempt to identify the handwriting, the editor's introduction does not mention any recent Finch scholarship, no acknowledgment is given for those poems that have been published elsewhere, and the transcriptions contain numerous textual errors. My fully annotated critical edition of these Wellesley manuscript poems, under advance contract with the University of Georgia Press, is forthcoming.

1. Childhood Years

1. The often-quoted phrase is from Finch's poem "To my Sister Ogle." Gosse, who is responsible for discovering in the late nineteenth century the folio manuscript of her poems (now in the Folger Shakespeare Library), wrote of her in his 1891 *Gossip in a Library* and also in his introduction to Thomas Ward's 1880 edition of *The English Poets*. He, like Murry ("Countess of Winchilsea" in *Countries of the Mind*), offers a portrait of her that occasionally wanders into fantasy. Reynolds's introduction to her edition of Finch's poems is more accurate but still somewhat romanticized.

2. Burke, *Landed Gentry*. Little has been published about Finch's life. As noted earlier, Reynolds's introduction to the *Poems* contains some valuable biographical information. A more reliable source is Cameron's thesis, which adds new material to the Reynolds biographical sketch and corrects some of her errors.

3. Eames's 1986 article contains much genealogical information about the Kingsmill family. See also Kingsmill and Doubleday and Page 4: 252–53.

4. The entry for 1654 in Northamptonshire Record Office, Parish Register Extracts, ROP 925, is as follows: "The publicon of Matrimonie was publisht betwixt Sr. William Kingsmill of Didmount [sic] in the County of Southampt. Knight, and Mrs. Anne Haslewood daughter of Sr. Anthony Haslewood, Knight, and Elizabeth his Lady Three several Lords Dayes in ye Parish Church of Maidwell at the time of morning exerstise. The above named Sr. Willia Kingsmill and Mrs. Anne Haslewood was married the one and twentith day of ffebruarie 1654."

5. Eames 128–36 provides a full account of Kingsmill's treatment during the Civil War.

6. Northamptonshire Record Office, Parish Register Extracts 10, lists Bridget's birth. Eames suggests that William may have been conceived, if not born, prior to the marriage (137). But the most reliable source is F-H ms. 2754, a writ for the execution of a decree of Chancery. This document gives William's age during Michaelmas term in 1664 as four years and thereby places his birth sometime in early 1660 or late 1659.

7. The Kingsclere Parish Register 2 in the Hampshire Record Office records Sir William Kingsmill's burial at Kingsclere on Sept. 3, 1661.

8. In this assessment I agree with John Eames, who has recently brought to light an unpublished manuscript of Sir William's poems housed in the Lichfield Cathedral Library.

9. Some idea of how much 1,500 pounds was worth can be gained from Gregory King's 1696 estimate of average family incomes within different classes in England, reprinted in Clark 25. Among the higher classes, a knight averaged 650 pounds a year, an esquire 450 pounds, and a gentleman 280 pounds, each supporting a household averaging from 8 to 13 people. For a more accurate indication of how a single woman might survive if she chose to live independently and with few needs, one can measure against the average shopkeeper or tradesman who supported an estimated 4½ persons in his household and took in a yearly average of 45 pounds, or the clergyman who supported a family of 5 on 50 pounds. How much annual income could have been earned from 1,500 pounds invested would vary greatly.

10. The license, issued by the archbishop of Canterbury's Faculty Office on Oct. 7, 1662, was for "Sir Thomas Ogle Kt., of Wickin, in Bardwell, Co. Suffolk, Bach^r [bachelor], 24, and Dame Anne Kingsmill of Sydmonton, Co. South^{ton}, widow, above 30" (Cokayne and Fry).

11. PRO PCC, Prob. 11/314. A portion of the will reads as follows: "And out of the assurance I have of the prudent love and care of my deare husband Sir Thomas Ogle I doe wholly give assign and remitt and bequeath the education and government of all my Children unto my said deare husband Sir

Thomas Ogle to be brought up in the feare of God and good nurture according to their Quality as he in his Dyscretion shall think fitt."

12. Though nothing is known about Sir Richard, the name Campion does occur frequently in the Northamptonshire Parish Register, suggesting that Dorothy may have been raised in the vicinity of Maidwell, seat of her mother's family, the Haslewoods. Furthermore, Dorothy's will was drawn up at Maidwell, an indication that she probably lived there for at least part of her youth and remained there until she died unmarried at the age of twenty-nine. In her will, dated Aug. 8, 1692, she identifies herself as "Dorothy Ogle of Maidwell in ye County of Northton." The will, probated also in 1692, is in the PRO.

13. For more information on Langham see *Burke's Peerage*. For Lucy see the *DNB*.

14. PRO Chancery records, Index: 1604 Book, Kingsmill v. Ogle. In addition, the incomplete F-H ms. 2754 (only the first page remains) is a writ of execution for a decree of Chancery.

15. H. Pearson 115; Edwards 229–34; *London Encyclopedia* "Charing Cross." I am very grateful to Paula Backscheider for sharing with me her extensive research on the historical importance of the Charing Cross area.

16. See Hampshire Record Office, Kingsmill Family Papers, items 1158, 1160, 1591, and 1607–11.

17. Numerous items in the Hampshire Record Office's holdings of the Kingsmill Family Papers document Lady Kingsmill's management of the family's affairs; see, for example, items 155, 156, 1163, 1166, 1168, and 1363. Eames has a relevant discussion of her financial dealings (127–28).

18. Lady Kingsmill's will, dated July 13, 1670, with a codicil dated Mar. 9, 1672, was proved on Aug. 30, 1672.

19. First discovered and privately printed in 1875 in an edition of only one hundred copies by Walter Rye, the diary has now been translated and published in a scholarly edition.

20. Pepys wrote on Oct. 24, 1667, of hearing "one Monsieur Prin, play on the Trump. Marine, which he doth beyond belief . . ." (8: 500).

21. The Latin inscription on her tombstone in Lamport Church reads, "Mathematices et Algebrae imprimis supra sexum et annos ad miraculum" (Isham, introd. 112). Thus her family singled out her genius as a mathematician and algebraist as being "miraculous" for one of her sex and young age.

22. Among the papers at the Northamptonshire Record Office in Delapre Abbey is a manuscript (F-H ms. 1140) containing an inventory of the contents of the house at Maidwell. That inventory, taken after Sir William's death in 1682, reveals a well furnished home containing, among other things, ten paintings, "forest tapestry hangings," and a library of books.

23. In rare nostalgic reflection on her youth, Finch wrote in "On the Death of the Queen," composed in 1718 for Mary of Modena, that she came to court directly from the rural seat of the family (W ms. 69). Following her grandmother's death, then, she remained in her uncle's household at the family seat of Maidwell until she reached maturity.

2. Court and Courtship

1. Clark 81–110 contains a good analysis of the Catholic issue in Restoration politics. See also Ashley, *James II* 112–26, 131–41; and C. Hill, *Century* 242–54.

2. Gilbert Burnet, bishop of Salisbury, was the most famous and influential of the Latitudinarian bishops who gained power following the accession of William of Orange. His comments on Mary are quoted in Oman 47.

3. Her four-line poem entitled "Under the picture of Mr. John Dryden" is in the W ms. (103).

4. Ashley, *James II* 94–95. Ashley inaccurately describes Lady Bellasyse as a maid of honor.

5. Cameron's chronological listing of all her poems and plays is reliable in most instances.

6. *DNB*; I'Anson 52–55. For an explanation of the fourteenth-century connection between the Finch family and the town of Winchilsea see Cokayne 12: 773–74 note h. Orthographic differences between the name of the town and the family title Winchilsea are explained on 775 note f.

7. A letter from John Thorys to William Trumbull, dated 1613 and included in the Downshire manuscripts published by the HMC (4: 68), contains the following remark: "Of creations there is now spoken of but one and that at the Count Palatine's suit, to benefit some of his for a gratuity. I think that it will be Sir M. Finche."

8. HMC, *Finch* 1: 365 contains a letter, dated Mar. 23, 1665, to the duchess of Somerset from Heneage Finch's father, in which the earl thanks the duchess and duke of Somerset for looking after the five children he left with them, and particularly for seeing that Heneage was sent to Chelsea and his brother William to Cambridge.

9. Anne Finch's six-line elegy "Upon the Death of the Right Honorable William Lord Maidstone" commemorates the death of the young war hero (32).

10. *Calendar of State Papers, Domestic, March 1, 1678, to December 31st, 1678,* 337, 354. A document from the earl of Winchilsea to Sir J. Williamson, dated Aug. 1, 1678, from Eastwell, reads as follows: "By the bearer, my son Heneage, who is one of my colonels of foot in this county, I desire you to speak to his

Majesty that he will be pleased to make him also one of my deputy lieutenants. I hope his Majesty will not quite forget me, but give me some occasion abroad or at home to serve him, and I hope I shall not want your kindness in putting him in mind of me as occasion may require." On Aug. 10 Williamson sent notice to the earl of Winchilsea of the "Approbation by the King of the Hon. Heneage Finch to be one of the deputy lieutenants for Kent."

11. Henning 2: 324. For a discussion of the political climate see 1: 29–44.

12. BL Add. ms. 4224 contains a biographical note on the conferring of the degree. Wood also mentions it (5: ii, 389).

13. Reference to Sir William's letter, dated Dec. 3, 1683, to the attorney general, along with the Haslewood sisters' petition, is found in *Calendar of State Papers, Domestic, October 1, 1683–April 30, 1684*, 244. Anne Finch remained particularly close to Elizabeth Haslewood and, after her cousin's marriage to Viscount Hatton, was a guest at Kirby Hall, their estate in Northamptonshire.

14. The pardon was granted from Windsor Castle. See *Calendar of State Papers, Domestic, May 1, 1684–February 5, 1685*, 53.

15. Reynolds, in quoting the license in her introduction, comments on the "delicious bit of coquetry" she sees the twenty-two-year-old Kingsmill evidencing in the "spinster ab. 18 years" phrase (xxv). However, such vagueness about the age of women is fairly common in marriage licenses for that time. Possibly a sense of propriety caused some men who issued marriage licenses to make a polite estimate of a woman's age, without exacting much in the way of response. The license of Anne Finch's own mother when she married Sir Thomas Ogle, for example, gives her age simply as "above 30."

16. A report on the coronation, made by J. Collinson in 1727, is quoted in *Sussex Archaeological Collections* 15: 192.

17. Henning 2: 324. Hythe, as one of the Cinque Ports, had its own representative institution and regularly sent "barons" to the House of Commons. These members of Parliament were traditionally nominated by the lord warden, but James II retained for himself the office of lord warden and made all the Cinque Port nominations himself, choosing a slate made up almost entirely of men who held appointments in his court (Henning 2: 271). During his term, which began on Apr. 3, 1685, Heneage Finch served on seven committees, though they were all of minor importance politically. The charter for the corporation of Hythe was surrendered in 1686, and no replacement was issued until the charter was remodeled in September 1688 (Henning 2: 497–98).

3. "*Hymen's* Endearments and Its Ties": Poems on Love and Marriage

1. In *The Troublesome Helpmate* Rogers offers a comprehensive study of the tradition of misogynist themes and archetypes, while Nussbaum's *Brink of All We Hate* focuses on attacks against women in Restoration and eighteenth-century English satires. Also valuable is Roger Thompson's *Unfit for Modest Ears*, which examines sexual attitudes of the period, particularly as evidenced in the pornographic and obscene literature whose effect was most assuredly demeaning to women.

2. Woolf's essay "Professions for Women" makes an impassioned plea for the destruction of this image as an essential prerequisite to freedom for women.

3. As Perry demonstrates in *The Celebrated Mary Astell* (120–48), Astell believed that the single, chaste life was essential if women were to maintain their freedom and individuality.

4. Several of the essays in the valuable collection that Nussbaum edited for the recent issue of *Eighteenth-Century Studies* devoted to "The Politics of Difference," for example, demonstrate the error in such bipolar categorization.

5. Williamson offers a good brief analysis of Restoration sexual ideologies and the critique of marriage in Restoration drama (134–39).

6. 28–34. Gardiner discusses this issue in relation to Aphra Behn.

7. Weber decides that the status of women may, in fact, have declined during the last part of the seventeenth century (144). Masek, though acknowledging that more research is needed in this area, finds evidence that at least the economic role of women was stronger in the Elizabethan and Stuart periods than it was during the Restoration (144). Other relevant material may be found in Trumbach, particularly in the chapter "Settlement and Marriage" (69–117). Bridget Hill's anthology gives an indication of contemporary attitudes toward marriage and the position of women, especially 69–122.

8. See, for example, "Ardelia's Answer to Ephelia" or her prose preface.

9. Among the standard history books on the second half of the century is Ogg's *Charles II*, which contains ample information on the Great Fire of 1666 and the Anglo-Dutch Wars. The conflict between England and Scotland is covered in Ogg's later work, *James II and William III* 263–80. A briefer and thoroughly readable history is Ashley's *England*.

10. See his discussion of the companionate marriage in ch. 8 of *Family, Sex and Marriage*.

11. The frequent vagaries in Finch's spelling are here evident in the discrepancy between her spelling of "Dafnis" in the title and "Daphnis" in the poem itself.

12. Todd comments on the need for eighteenth-century women to assume a "sentimental passive stance" in their prefaces (*Dictionary* 8). Also relevant is Smith's discussion of Katherine Philips and her frequent protestations and apologies for writing (154–56). See Mallinson 35–43 for her discussion of Finch's apologies.

13. The play opened at the Theatre Royal in Drury Lane on Feb. 22, 1714. It was successful both as a performance and as a publication, having gone through two editions that same year. See Pedicord's introduction to the play (Rowe xiii).

4. The Revolution and Its Aftermath

1. Longknife briefly compares *Triumphs* to Beaumont and Fletcher's *Philaster* and to Shakespeare's *Othello* (73–75, 80–81).

2. Prall's chapter "James II and the Descent into Tyranny" relates the unfolding of events that led to Parliament's actions (89–165). See also Nenner.

3. Ashley offers a succinct analysis of these options in his chapter "Defeat and Departure" in *James II* 249–64. Carswell's analysis is also valuable (183–214).

4. Reresby records the incident in his diary for 1688 (536). Innes gives the full text of James's letter to Winchilsea, dated Feversham, Dec. 12, 1688: "I am just now come in here, having been last night seased by some of this towne, who telling me you were to be here this day, I would not make myself known to them, thinking to have found you here; but that not being, I desire you would come hither to me, and that as privately as you could do, that I might advise with you concerning my safty, hoping you have that true Loyalty in you, as you will do what you can to secure me from my Enemys, of which you shall find me as sensible as you can desire" (app. 6). A note following the letter, by Rev. John Creyke, chaplain to Heneage Finch, fourth earl of Winchilsea, verifies that he has copied the letter exactly from the original, which had been in the earl's possession until his death.

5. Clark 143. The date is in the Old Style English reckoning and hence ten days behind the New Style used on the Continent.

6. The Hatton family letters, BL Add. mss. 29548–96, a selection from which was published by Hatton, are a valuable source of information about the Hatton and Finch families.

7. The Nonjuring movement is discussed more fully in the final chapter. Monod has a good analysis of the movement (138–45).

8. Lord Winchilsea's will, made out on Aug. 18, was proved by his widow on Sept. 10 (PRO PCC 131). See also Luttrell 1: 578 and *DNB*.

9. This information about the circumstances of the arrest is found among the Le Fleming manuscript papers at Rydal Hall in Westmoreland, which have been published by the HMC. Sir Daniel Fleming, active in Westmoreland county business, arranged to have news from London supplied to him regularly by clerks in the office of Sir Joseph Williamson (iv). The brief news item regarding the arrest of Heneage Finch is dated May 6, 1690.

10. I am extremely grateful to Norman Evans, Head of Research at the PRO, for helping me explore all the possibilities as I tried to locate the relevant records for Heneage Finch's trial. It is Mr. Evans who first suggested the implications of nonexistent records for the warrant.

11. For information on the complex war and England's relations with France, see Clark 160–75; Lunt 470–72; and Haley.

12. The vicar of Godmersham at the time was Rev. James Christmas, but I can find no record of who actually rented the priory house or lived there with Finch during that year. Most likely the temporary residence was arranged for her through either a sympathetic clergyman or a member of her husband's family from nearby Eastwell. The information about Godmersham has been passed on to me through the kindness of George V. Allen of Ashford, Kent, and is based upon Canterbury records and papers left by S. G. Brade-Birks, a former Godmersham vicar. These papers, which I refer to as the Godmersham mss., are located in the Ashford PRO and the Ashford Library.

13. The second-century historian Pausanius tells the tale of the unfortunate Aristomenes. Reynolds discusses *Aristomenes* briefly (introd. to *Poems* ci–ciii).

14. The poem is titled "A Letter to the Same Person" in the Reynolds edition, which relies more heavily upon the folio manuscript. The poem is dated only in the table of contents of the earlier octavo manuscript.

5. Settling Down

1. The quarrel had to do with ownership of the contents of the Eastwell house, the countess claiming that some things belonged to her as part of her jointure, and Lady Maidstone claiming that the former earl had left them to his heir in a deed of gift. In a letter dated Dec. 22, 1689, Leopold William Finch, writing on behalf of the family to Lord Weymouth, summarized the dispute and asked his brother-in-law for advice. The case was ultimately settled in a hearing before the Court of King's Bench, but Leopold William's letter suggests some of the tension the family experienced at that time (Longleat Thynne Papers 208–09). See also the letter from Charles, third earl of Winchilsea, to the earl of Nottingham dated Nov. 18, 1689 (HMC, *Finch* 2: 261). The verdict, decided in Lady Winchilsea's favor, may be found in *English Reports* 87: 257.

2. The drawing, done quite likely as an illustration for Hasted, is now in the British Museum.

3. Philip G. Dormer, a resident on the grounds of the original Eastwell estate, has kindly given me some of the documents he has collected on the history of Eastwell. He has also written a pamphlet about Eastwell.

4. See, for example, Dr. Thomas Brett's letter to Dr. William Warren, president of Trinity Hall, Cambridge, which recounts a visit to Eastwell during which Heneage Finch repeated the tale. That portion of the letter is printed in Peck.

5. The parish register was made available by the kind permission of Rev. John Gleadall, vicar of Boughton Aluph Church in nearby Ashford, Kent.

6. These monuments and the history of their preservation and removal to the Victoria and Albert Museum are Physick's subject.

7. During World War II, soldiers were stationed at Eastwell Park, and a great deal of damage occurred to the church at that time. Dormer reports that blasting during training operations weakened the church's structure. One local resident told me, however, that the damage was due in part to a German plane that unloaded its remaining bombs on its way back to Germany (a common practice), and inadvertently hit the little church with one. In any case, in 1951 the roof finally collapsed, along with the central pillars and the arch (Dormer 14). A description of the church before its destruction may be found in Igglesden (9–33).

8. Two letters are in the library of the marquess of Bath at Longleat House, Thynne Papers 282–83, 313. The other two are at the Bodleian Library, English Theology ms., c. 26, 99–100, and Rawlinson ms., Letters 45, ff. 158–59.

9. The date appears in the octavo (F-H ms. 283) only in the table of contents after the title of the poem and not on the ms. of the poem itself.

10. The table of contents to the octavo ms. concludes with the previous poem, "A Song. Quickly Delia," and does not list this poem at all.

11. For instance, the title "To the R^t Honble the Lady C. Tufton Upon Addressing to me the first letter that ever she writt at the age of ———" on p. 298 of the folio ms. is in her handwriting. See Cameron 75–77, 120, for commentary on the dating of the folio.

12. Reynolds cites the 1701 Gildon's miscellany poems as her first appearance in print and thus is off by a full decade.

13. Wood 4: 664. Leopold William Finch was the son of the second earl of Winchilsea and his second wife, and hence a half-brother of Charles's father. He had been warden of All Souls College since 1686.

14. Finch's own note draws recognition to Charles's noble descent (and, by extension, also her husband's) from a daughter of Henry VII.

15. His painful affliction with gout, first diagnosed four years earlier, probably prevented him from joining his wife on her frequent walking excursions.

16. Alnwick ms. 22 (BL microfilm 289, reel 10) contains a six-page letter by Heneage Finch, included with Mrs. Thynne's directive to the executor's account of Lord Weymouth, describing a historical seal and a medal that belonged to Lord Weymouth. See also Heneage Finch's letter to John Battely (BL Add. ms. 17301) of October 1700, also printed in Nichols's *Illustrations* 4: 95–96. Reynolds discusses some of Heneage Finch's scholarly interests in the introduction to the *Poems* (xlv–xlviii).

17. For the contemporary view on the link of gout with diet, see the *OED* 1704 entry from Francis Fuller's *Medicina Gymnastica*. A fuller contemporary description of the disease and its treatment may be found in Palmer (78, 119–20).

18. In 1688, for example, W. Finch (presumably Leopold William Finch) wrote to Viscount Weymouth from Wye College (Longleat Thynne Papers 17: 208; BL microfilm 904, reel 9). The pamphlet *Wye College* contains information on the history of the college, its division into a college and a grammar school, and the arrangement by which the Finch family became involved with it. Early history of Wye College may also be found in Hasted 3: 172–76.

6. "Nature Unconcern'd": Nature Poems and Humanistic Sensibilities

1. The poems that belong in this category are "The Bird," "The Nightingale," "A Nocturnal Reverie," "The Petition for an Absolute Retreat," "To the Countess of Hertford who Engaged Mr. Eusdon to Write upon a Wood," "To the Eccho," and "The Tree."

2. In addition to the monumental 1985 *Norton Anthology of Literature by Women*, some excellent women's literature anthologies containing some of Finch's poetry have appeared in the past two decades. Among these are the collections by Goulianos, Bernikow, and Ferguson. The Rogers and McCarthy anthology is the first to include several of Finch's later poems. Most welcome is Lonsdale's recent publication. That most popular of English literary anthologies, *The Norton Anthology of English Literature*, gave Finch the distinction of being the only woman included in vol. 1 of its third edition (1974), but it included just "A Nocturnal Reverie" and "On Myself." It is surely a sign of the growing concern with canon revision that the 1986 edition of that volume has ten women authors represented, though, alas, Finch still has only two poems included—"A Nocturnal Reverie" and "The Introduction."

3. "The Spleen," which is discussed in the penultimate chapter of this book,

remained her most anthologized poem throughout the eighteenth century.

4. Messenger's "Selected Nightingales" explores the complexity of dualisms underlying the dialectic movement of "To the Nightingale." Her thesis is provocative and convincingly argued.

5. Finch's poems constitute a third of the collection, which also includes poems by Anne Killigrew, Laetitia Pilkington, and Jane Warton. For a discussion of Wordsworth's editing of Finch, see Greer (4–8).

6. Some of the recent scholarship on English gardening includes Martin's *Pursuing Innocent Pleasures* and Maccubbin and Martin's *British and American Gardens*, which contains Morris R. Brownell's comprehensive survey of current thought regarding the history of British landscaping. See also Battestin's controversial discussion of the theological basis for supporting the gardening movement. Of additional interest is Mack's eloquent *Garden*.

7. For a good evaluation of the fallacies and distortions that may result from using the term "Augustan" to define a single humanistic tradition or world view see Fabricant 2–5. For other challenges to critics such as Martin Battestin and Paul Fussell, who have advanced theories generalizing an "Augustan outlook" shared by a number of eighteenth-century writers, see Rawson's *Fielding* and also his *Gulliver* and his article "Order and Misrule."

8. P. 114. See also the entire chapter "Anne Finch Placed and Displaced" (105–26).

9. P. 273. The "Arachnologies," Miller believes, involve both interpretation and reappropriation of a tale with "interwoven structures of power, gender, and identity inherent in the production of mimetic art" (272).

7. London and Its Literary Life

1. Finch's poem "A Letter to the Hon:ble Lady Worsley at Long-leate" (W ms. 100) documents the Leweston and Longleat visits. Heneage Finch's letter of Aug. 14, 1704, to Lord Weymouth makes reference to the anticipated Kirby visit (Longleat Thynne Papers 302–03).

2. For a good discussion of the involvement of the press see Backscheider's *Defoe*, 76–83.

3. For a discussion of the circumstances surrounding the death of James II see Sinclair-Stevenson 17–22.

4. BL Dartmouth ms. 3: 147. The relationship with Lady Marrow is discussed in Chapter 8.

5. There is, unfortunately, a gap in the rate books for the Westminster district for the years 1708–18, but Heneage Finch, earl of Winchilsea, is listed as a ratepayer to the Overseers of the Poor of the Parish of St. James's Westmin-

ster in 1718. (See vols. D23 and D24 of the rate books, which are housed in the Westminster City Library.) Other evidence of their Cleveland Row residence can be found in BL Harleian ms. 7316, 44–46, and F-H ms. 4477, but these do not help fix the date when they first moved there. However, Finch's poem "The Puggs" refers to her Cleveland Row house and also to Sir Andrew Fountaine's living at Leicester Fields. Swift, a friend of Fountaine's, records in his *Journal to Stella* that Fountaine moved from Leicester Fields in May of 1711, so the poem must have been written prior to that date.

The street was named for Barbara Villiers, mistress of Charles II, who created her duchess of Cleveland (Bebbington 90–91).

6. It is likely that Charles Finch, author of the first poem in the volume, was responsible for the inclusion of "The Spleen" in Gildon's miscellany.

7. According to Arber 3: 645, Tonson's sixth *Poetical Miscellanies* was published in May or June of that year, but the date must have been closer to April or the first of May, given Steele's reference to it in the May 3 *Tatler*. In any case, Swift and Finch had already become friends at least four or five months earlier (see below), though the exact date of their first meeting is not known.

8. 2: 446. Barber's reputation as a publisher is discussed in Backscheider, *Defoe* 148, and in *The Life and Character of John Barber* 10–11. For additional information on Barber's friendship with Swift see Downie 175; and Ehrenpreis 2: 610, 633–35.

9. Heneage Finch also received the title Baron FitzHerbert of Eastwell, Kent, which had been created for his father in 1660 and became extinct in 1729 (Cokayne 12, ii: 780). For reasons explained in chapter 2, some reference books list Heneage Finch as fifth earl of Winchilsea, rather than fourth.

10. Pp. lii–liii. After Prior's death in 1721, his executor, Adrian Drift, found the poem among Prior's papers and attributed it to Finch. The poem is not included in the Wellesley ms., and no other copy of it is known.

11. William Douglas, born in 1696, succeeded his father as earl of March in the autumn of 1705 (Cokayne "March"). Prior was in England during the years 1706–11.

12. Jervas lived at Bridgewater House on Cleveland Court, by St. James's (Sherburn 69).

13. Though the publication date on the book is 1714, the miscellany, according to Iolo A. Williams, actually appeared in December 1713 ("Poetical Miscellanies").

14. Only one of the eight, a poem addressed to Pope, appears in the Reynolds edition. The other seven are "An Invocation to the Southern Winds, inscrib'd to the Right Honourable Charles Earl of Winchelsea at his Arrival in London, after having been long detained on the Coast of Holland," "An Epistle

to the Honourable Mrs. Thynne, persuading her to have a Statue made of her youngest Daughter, now Lady Brooke," "On a double Stock July-flower, full blown in January; presented to me by the Countess of Ferrers," "The Toad undrest," "The Mastiff and Curs, a Fable inscrib'd to Mr. Pope," "A Fable," and "The Fall of Caesar."

15. Bruckmann offers an account of Catholics in England during the reign of William and Mary (82–88). For other accounts that include subsequent years see Monod 132–38 and Humphreys 142–43.

16. *Poems* 1: 210, st. 6. Lady Frances Scudamore lived at Coleshill with her cousin, Robert Digby, who was a good friend of Pope's. She and Finch shared a close mutual friend in Mrs. Catherine Fleming.

8. Female Friendships and Women Writers

1. "A Tale of the Miser and the Poet" (191, lines 32–33). "On the Death of the Queen" in the Wellesley ms. also contains a nostalgic remembrance of her days as a court attendant.

2. Lady Worsley was the Thynnes' only daughter (also named Frances), who in 1690 married Sir Robert Worsley.

3. I am grateful to the current duke of Northumberland for allowing me permission to see these letters, now on microfilm at the British Library. Hughes, who did a thorough study of the manuscripts in the library at Alnwick Castle, quotes extensively from these letters in *Hertford*. See especially p. 6 for mention of Finch's visits.

4. Traditional Twelfth Night festivities included the serving of a large decorated cake with a bean baked inside it. Whoever received the slice with the bean was then designated "king" or "queen" of the feast. An 1863 reference to Chambers's *Book of Days* cited in the *OED* indicates that in the eighteenth century "Twelfth-Night cards represented ministers, maids of honour, and other attendants of a court." A citation from Thackeray's 1866 *The Rose and the Ring* refers to "funny painted pictures of the King, the Queen, the Lover, the Dandy, the Captain, and so on—with which our young ones are wont to recreate themselves at this festive time."

5. The name of Mrs. Higgons occurs frequently in the Alnwick manuscript letters quoted in Hughes's *Hertford*. Lady Weymouth refers to her as "my cozin Higgons."

6. Heneage Finch records the wedding date in his diary (F-H ms. 282, 42).

7. The poem appeared in Steele's *Poetical Miscellanies* of 1714 and also in Pope's 1717 *Miscellany*. The existence of such uncollected poems in isolated manuscripts, and, of course, the omission of all the Wellesley manuscript

poems from the Reynolds edition, underscores the serious need for a good scholarly edition of Finch's complete writings.

8. Lawrence Eusden, a now obscure poet, was appointed England's Poet Laureate in 1718, just months after this incident most likely occurred.

9. Percy Family Letters and Papers 22: 56 (2nd pagination), from the Alnwick manuscripts quoted by Hughes in *Hertford*.

10. BL Dartmouth ms. 3: 147, qtd. in Reynolds's edition of the *Poems* xliv.

11. Not much is known about Catherine Fleming, to whom Finch directed a number of poems written between 1718 and 1720. As noted earlier, she was a friend of Lady Frances Scudamore, cousin of Pope's friend Robert Digby.

12. Morgan pieces together thinly veiled autobiographical material from Manley's narratives and verifiable facts from other sources to create a coherent biography.

13. The first to identify these poems in Manley's texts was Anderson. Anderson corrects a mistaken assumption made by Reynolds, that Anna Seward's quoting in 1763 a slightly different version of "Progress of Life" than is found in the 1713 *Miscellany* is evidence of its having been changed through oral transmission.

14. As noted earlier, Heneage Finch transcribed the ode in a sloppy, hurried hand at the end of the octavo manuscript, apparently some time after the octavo had been abandoned for preserving future poems of his wife's. There are idiosyncratic annotations and other marginalia, whole passages are obliterated, words are crossed out with corrections above them or written boldly over them, and in several places the revised passages have been pasted over the original lines. It appears that the blank pages at the end of the octavo were used for a rough draft of the ode, and that as Finch made revisions, her husband added them to his original transcription. The differences in his handwriting between the original transcription and the emendations, and the variations in ink, suggest that these revisions were made at a later time and quite likely in several stages. Unlike the ode itself, however, the seventy-line hymn affixed to it is transcribed in the neat hand Heneage Finch employed in the rest of the octavo and in the folio and Wellesley manuscripts. Only one minor correction appears, and that is quite possibly due to a mistake in copying. Moreover, neat explanatory notes at the conclusion of the poem refer back to the ode, and the place and date of composition are given in a final note.

15. Reynolds could locate only one other poem attributed to Randolph, "On the much lamented death of the Incomparable Lady, the Honorable Lady Oxenden. A Pindarique Ode," which is preserved in a commonplace manuscript in the British Library (Introd. to *Poems* lii). My own efforts to find out more about Randolph have been similarly unsuccessful.

16. A commendatory poem by William Shippen appears with Randolph's panegyric at the beginning. Randolph's poem makes no mention of Finch's great odes, especially "The Spleen" (1691), for which she had already received critical acclaim.

17. Most likely this friend was Anne Owens, known by Philips as her "dearest Lucasia."

18. Two very recent excellent works that offer discussions of the relationships between Finch, Philips, and Behn are Williamson and Mermin. Mermin looks at common conditions that aided these three women in becoming writers. Williamson's book is an extremely valuable study of early British women authors and the relationships of text and context in the various current discourses that these writers were involved with. Especially relevant are her chapters "Orinda and Her Daughters" (64–133) and "Behn and Her Daughters" (134–207).

19. Perry's *Celebrated Mary Astell*, a scrupulously researched and well-written book, offers a discussion of the friendship theme in Astell's works. See 136–42 and 265–68.

9. Arcadian Anachronisms: Place and Time in the Pastorals

1. P. 342. Mermin offers a valuable analysis of the literary contexts that enabled Philips, Behn, and Finch to become England's earliest "important" poets. She focuses particularly on the methods that each of these poets devised in order to accommodate a woman's point of view.

2. Greg, whose *Pastoral Poetry and Pastoral Drama* was long regarded as the standard history of English pastoral poetry, declines to give a concise definition of pastoral, claiming that "[a]ny definition sufficiently elastic to include the protean forms assumed by what we call the 'pastoral ideal' could hardly have sufficient intension to be of any real value" (2). More recently, Rosenmeyer, commenting on the "extraordinarily rich and flexible" tradition of the pastoral, similarly warns that "[i]n all probability a tidy definition . . . is beyond our reach" (3).

3. There are numerous valuable studies of the pastoral, including Kermode's introduction to his anthology, though it stops short of the period in which Finch began to write. Particularly outstanding is Congleton's *Theories of Pastoral Poetry*, which focuses upon the two distinct types of pastoral poetry prevalent toward the end of the seventeenth century, the neoclassic and the rationalistic. Congleton demonstrates repeatedly that serious philosophical issues, both moral and aesthetic, continued to be present in Augustan pastorals. His book thus counters Evans's assumption that by the eighteenth

century the pastoral had declined into "decorative idyll or rustic realism" (95), or Toliver's assertion that "the bulk of the pastorals written during the hundred years after the publication of *Paradise Lost* are uninspired reapplications of new makeup to an aging countenance" (17). Mack's *Garden* provides an elegant analysis of the English pastoral tradition and of the way in which classical texts had by the eighteenth century been "so often culled, so often translated, paraphrased, and imitated that they had become part of the mind of England . . ." (21).

4. This is an instance in which Reynolds's dating appears to be more accurate than Cameron's. Cameron places the composition of the poem at some time between 1691 and 1697, but Reynolds observes that *Description de tout l'Univers* by Nichols and Guillaume Sanson, the geography book referred to in line 26 of the poem, was published in 1700 (418).

5. Piper's introduction to his anthology (3–153) contains a lengthy discussion of this form. Though his concern is essentially with the heroic couplet as a political vehicle, particularly for Dryden and Pope, his historical survey and his analysis of some of the subtle variations in handling the poetics of the couplet are perceptive.

6. For an account of the early publication of this poem see Vieth's introduction to his edition of the *Poems* xxxiii. Vieth calls it Rochester's "masterpiece" (xl), a view with which Pinto concurs (*Enthusiast in Wit* 121).

7. The significance of the nymph in Augustan satire is examined by Rees. Cosmetic paint, she notes, "is the emblem of art, flesh the emblem of natural beauty; and this kind of distinction crosses over from satire to pastoral" (3).

8. Gill makes the same point with regard to Pope.

10. Elegiac and Edenic Visions

1. The date of this poem is significant and makes the sentiments all the more poignant, for just days earlier, on Dec. 18, William of Orange first entered the capital. (See ch. 4.) At the time the poem was written, James II had gone into exile with his family and Anne and Heneage Finch had fled the court, taking temporary refuge at Kirby Hall, Lord Hatton's estate in Northamptonshire.

2. Frances Carteret, daughter of Robert and Frances Worsley, was, like the countess of Hertford, another of the third generation of Thynnes who was on very affectionate terms with her great-aunt. Frances Worsley's husband, John Carteret, baron of Hawnes, left England on June 1, 1719, to assume his duties as ambassador of Sweden (*DNB* "Carteret"). It was during his absence that Lady Carteret attended the ball described in Finch's poem. While in Sweden Lord Carteret sent Finch a miniature of Charles XII of Sweden, which

prompted her prose and verse epistle of Jan. 13, 1720, "To His Excellency the Lord Cartret at Stockholm Upon recieving from him a picture in miniature of Charles the Twelth [,] King of Sweden" (W ms. 66).

3. P. 412. Kuhn's article traces in eighteenth-century theological thought the view of external nature as a manifestation of God's grace and a confirmation of Christian revelation and mystery. Wasserman's "Nature Moralized" is also valuable in distinguishing the Augustan concept of nature from what would come to be identified as the Romantic one.

4. P. 15. Some of the other gender differences that Schenck finds in her study of women's pastoral elegies, such as the refusal to move from mourning to an acclamation of transcendence, do not pertain to Finch.

5. See particularly the chapter "Infection in the Sentence: The Woman Writer and the Anxiety of Authorship" in *Madwoman* (45–104).

6. "Astrophel" is here considered without its appended "Dolefull Lay of Clorinda." See 500–07 in vol. 7 of the *Variorum Edition* of Spenser for the controversy regarding the "Lay" and its questionable authenticity.

11. "The Spleen": Melancholy, Gender, and Poetic Identity

1. After its first publication in Gildon's 1701 miscellany, it was reprinted numerous times thereafter, being apparently the most popular of all the poems in her 1713 collection.

2. A notable exception is Salvaggio's chapter on Finch, which offers a highly suggestive poststructuralist reading of "The Spleen" (123–26) in the context of Finch's other poetry and the general exclusion of the feminine from Enlightenment discourses.

3. Lonsdale deletes the first seventy-three lines and begins at the most personal section of the poem: "O'er me alas! thou dost too much prevail."

4. "A Suplication for the joys of Heaven," dated Feb. 6, 1717/18, W ms. 108.

5. See chs. 2 and 3 of Babb's *Elizabethan Malady* (21–71) for an explanation of the scientific theory of melancholy.

6. Katharine M. Rogers's recent article, "Finch's 'Candid Account,'" places the poem in its medical context, as does Sena's earlier "Melancholy."

7. In addition to the works already cited, see Babb, "Cave of Spleen"; Doughty; Randolph; and Riddell. This literature easily refutes Lyons's claim that by the early seventeenth century, particularly because of Harvey's discovery in 1628 of the circulation of blood, melancholy became obsolete as a medical category and existed solely as a literary idea (xiv–xv).

8. The author, a Tomlinson whose identity has thus far eluded me, is cited

in the *OED* under the entry for "hysteric." The quotation is from his 1657 *Renou's Disp.* 25.

9. Smith-Rosenberg, writing of the sexist ideological implications of hysteria, concludes that large numbers of nineteenth-century women chose hysteria "as their particular mode of expressing malaise, discontent, anger, or pain" (198). Chesler is also a valuable study of female mental health and the norms that have defined it. Bernheimer's introduction to *In Dora's Case* offers a useful history of hysteria (2–7).

10. Sena's *Bibliography* supplies ample evidence of the interest in melancholy during this period and the later eighteenth century as well. This bibliography is conveniently divided into poetry, prose, and medical works and contains a valuable list of scholarly works on the subject. For a discussion concentrating on the time at which "The Spleen" was published, see the chapter entitled "The Taste for Melancholy in 1700" in Reed (27–79), which demonstrates that a good many writers around 1700 wrote about melancholic themes.

11. See Reynolds's notes to the *Poems* 430–31 and Brower 70–71 for brief discussions of how both Pope and Shelley apparently borrowed from these lines.

12. Sena's "Melancholic Madness" examines anti-Puritan literature of the period and the changes that occurred in the nature of the attacks. Noting that earlier charges of ignorance and hypocrisy leveled against Puritans were replaced by the middle of the seventeenth century with claims of melancholic madness, Sena documents that these claims were founded upon contemporary medical theory.

13. Reynolds assumes that Finch's health problems improved in later years (introd. to *Poems* xliv), but the Wellesley manuscript contradicts this assumption. Her later verse contains references to the spleen in at least half a dozen poems, including "A Suplication for the joys of Heaven," dated just two years before her death.

12. The Final Years

1. For background on the arrests and trials see Monod 179–94. Nicholas Rogers offers a description of the London riots.

2. Though this letter is undated in the Wellesley manuscript, it is dated in its slightly altered version in BL Add. ms. (Birch) 4457, 56 v. The poem makes reference in line 2 to the death of Arabella Marrow's mother, Lady Marrow, who died Oct. 19, 1714, so perhaps the epistle was meant to reach the bereaved daughter on the first anniversary of her mother's death.

3. See ch. 7 for an account of the relationship between Finch and Prior.

Details of his ill use by the Whigs may be found in Eves 327–56.

4. In the variant stanza in BL Add. ms. 4457 a similar meaning is expressed:

> Which if describ'd in moving Lines
> In this suspicious Age
> He'd think did she affect Designs
> They'd half mankind ingage.

5. In addition to Hawes, those consecrated at the 1713 ceremony on Ascension Day were Jeremy Collier and Nathaniel Spinckes. On Jan. 25, 1721, Hilkiah Bedford and Ralph Taylor were also consecrated. See Overton 133–34; *DNB* "Hickes"; and F-H ms. 282, 17.

6. Hearne 4: 311, 316; 5: 40–41, 75, 77, 323; 6: 81, 170, 196, 292. Heneage Finch frequently mentions Bedford in his personal journal (F-H ms. 282).

7. Bodl. Rawlinson ms., Letters 45, folio 157. Heneage Finch made note of some of the accounts for Kingsmill's estates in his journal (F-H ms. 282, 8, 129–30, 140.

8. Pope's letter to John Caryll of Aug. 6, 1717, refers to his regular visits to Lord Winchilsea's home (1: 417–18). "To the Right Honourable Frances Countess of Hartford who engaged Mr Eusden to write upon a wood enjoining him to mention no tree but the Aspin & no flower but the King-cup" recounts events at one of these literary gatherings (W ms. 72). See ch. 8 for a mention of activities with female friends.

9. "To Mrs. Catherine Flemming at ye Lord Digby's at Coleshill in Warwickshire" (BL Add. ms. 84338) contains a reference to her Arlington Street visits:

> In Street of Arlington I spend
> Each Week one pleasing day
> And in the evening with my friend
> At Serious Ombre play,
> But w^n I should be mindfull still,
> I think of you & loose Codill
> With a fa la la la la.

The Westminster City Library ms. F 5437, p. 5, contains verification that Lord and Lady Carteret lived on Arlington Street, just a few blocks from the Finch townhouse on Cleveland Row.

10. Margaret Tufton, wife of George, third baron of Coventry, apparently performed numerous good works on behalf of the Society for the Propagation of the Gospel, which her brother helped found. She died in 1710 (*DNB*).

11. Several years later, in the letter to Lady Hertford quoted in full in ch. 8, Heneage Finch repeated his gratitude to her and her husband for their kindness to his wife during her "decline and sickness."

12. F-H ms. 282, 47. Hearne also preserved the sketch in his memoirs (7: 155–56).

Bibliography

MANUSCRIPT SOURCES

Alnwick Castle Library, Alnwick, Northumberland
  Percy Family Letters and Papers, vols. 21 and 22
Ashford Library, Kent
  Godmersham mss. (Brade-Birks Papers)
Bodleian Library, Oxford
  English Theology ms., c. 26, c. 38
  Rawlinson Letters mss. 42, 45
British Library, London
  Additional mss. 4224, 4457 (Birch), 4807 (Pope's Original Mss. of the Trans-
    lation of *The Iliad*), 5507, 17301, 27989, 28101, 29548–96 (Hatton Family
    Letters), 80287, 84338
  Dartmouth ms.
  Harleian ms. 7316 (Second Quarto Book, Satyrs and Lampoons)
  Percy Family Letters and Papers, microfilm 320 (mss. at Alnwick Castle)
  Sloane ms. 3962
  Swift Correspondence mss. 4804–06
  Thynne Papers, microfilm 904/9 (mss. at Longleat House)
Folger Shakespeare Library
  Anne Finch folio ms., "Miscellany Poems with Two Plays by Ardelia"
Hampshire Record Office
  Kingsclere Parish Register
  Kingsmill Family Papers
Litchfield Cathedral Library
  Sir William Kingsmill ms., "Vana non Ludibria. Carmina Ventosa."
Longleat House Library, Warminster, Wiltshire

Portland Papers, vol. 19
Thynne Papers, vol. 17
Northamptonshire Record Office, Delapre Abbey, Northampton
    Finch-Hatton mss. 258, 282 (Heneage Finch's Journal), 283 (octavo ms. of
        Anne Finch's "Poems on Several Subjects, Written by Ardelia"), 759, 948,
        1140, 1898, 2754, 2755, 3211, 3224, 3871, 4477, 4430, 4434, 4435
    Parish Register Abstracts, ROP 925
    Parish Register Extracts 10
Public Record Office, Ashford, Kent
    Canterbury Records and Godmersham mss.
Public Record Office, Chancery Lane, London
    Court of Chancery records, Index to Entry Books: 1604 Book C33 223; 1614
        Books 233–53
    Patent Henry VIII, 1542, C66/720, membrane 32
    Prerogative Court of Canterbury records, Prob. 11
Society of Genealogists
    Kingsmill Records ms., ed. W. K. Cook-Kingsmill
Wellesley College, Margaret Clapp Library
    Anne Finch ms., Poems
Westminster City Library, London
    Ms. F 5437
    Rate Books
Dr. Williams Library, London
    Roger Morrice. "Entering Book" ms. 3 vols.

OTHER SOURCES

Adburgham, Alison. *Women in Print: Writing Women and Women's Magazines
    from the Restoration to the Accession of Victoria.* London: Allen, 1972.
Alcoff, Linda. "Cultural Feminism Versus Post-Structuralism: The Identity
    Crisis in Feminist Theory." *Signs* 13 (1988): 405–23.
Allibone, S. Austin. *A Critical Dictionary of English Literature, and British and
    American Authors Living and Deceased: from the earliest accounts to the Middle of the
    Nineteenth Century. Containing Thirty-Thousand Biographies and Literary Notices:
    with Forty Indexes of Subjects.* 8 vols. Philadelphia: Childs and Peterson, 1859.
Anderson, Paul B. "Mrs. Manley's Texts of Three of Lady Winchilsea's
    Poems." *Modern Language Notes* 45 (1930): 95–99.
Arber, Edward. *The Term Catalogues, 1668–1709 A.D.; with a Number for Easter
    Term, 1711 A.D.: A Contemporary Bibliography of English Literature in the Reigns*

of Charles II, James II, William and Mary, and Anne. 3 vols. London: privately printed, 1903–06.

Archaeologia: or Miscellaneous Tracts Relating to Antiquity. 2 vols. London: Society of Antiquaries of London, 1770.

Ashley, Maurice. *England in the Seventeenth Century (1603–1714)*. Pelican History of England, vol. 6. Baltimore: Penguin, 1960.

————. *The Glorious Revolution of 1688*. New York: Scribner's, 1966.

————. *King James II*. Minneapolis: U of Minnesota P, 1977.

Aubrey, John. *The Natural History and Antiquities of the County of Surrey*. 2 vols. London, 1718.

Ault, Norman, ed. *Seventeenth Century Lyrics from the Original Texts*. 2nd ed. New York: Sloane, 1950.

Babb, Lawrence. "The Cave of Spleen." *Review of English Studies* 12 (1936): 165–76.

————. *The Elizabethan Malady: A Study of Melancholia in English Literature from 1580 to 1642*. East Lansing: Michigan State College P, 1951.

Backscheider, Paula R. *Daniel Defoe: His Life*. Baltimore: Johns Hopkins UP, 1989.

Ballard, George. *Memoirs of several Ladies who have been celebrated for their writings or skill in the learned languages, arts and sciences*. Oxford: W. Jackson, 1752.

Barlough, J. Ernest., ed. *Minor British Poetry, 1680–1800: An Anthology*. Metuchen: Scarecrow, 1973.

Bateson, Frederick, ed. *The Cambridge Bibliography of English Literature*. 4 vols. New York: Macmillan; Cambridge: Cambridge UP, 1941.

Battestin, Martin C. *The Providence of Wit: Aspects of Form in Augustan Literature and the Arts*. Oxford: Clarendon, 1974.

Bebbington, Gillian. *London Street Names*. London: Batsford, 1972.

Behn, Aphra. *The Works of Aphra Behn*. Ed. Montague Summers. 6 vols. New York: Bloom, 1967.

Berger, Joseph. *New York Times*, Jan. 6, 1988: B6.

Bernheimer, Charles, and Claire Kahane, eds. *In Dora's Case: Freud—Hysteria—Feminism*. New York: Columbia UP, 1985.

Bernikow, Louise, ed. *The World Split Open: Four Centuries of Women Poets in England and America, 1552–1950*. New York: Vintage, 1974.

Biographia Brittanica. London, 1763.

Birch, Thomas, et al. *The General Dictionary*. 10 vols. London: G. Strahan, 1734–41.

Blackmore, Richard. *A Treatise of the Spleen and Vapours: or, Hypochondriacal and Hysterical Affections*. London: Pemberton, 1725.

Boswell, James. *The Life of Samuel Johnson.* 2 vols. London: Oxford UP, 1946.

Boucé, Paul-Gabriel, ed. *Sexuality in Eighteenth-Century Britain.* Manchester: Manchester UP; New York: Barnes, 1982.

Boyer, Abel. *The Political State of Great Britain.* 40 vols. London: J. Baker, 1711–40.

Brashear, Lucy. "Finch's 'The Bird and the Arras.'" *Explicator* 3 (1981): 21–22.

Bredvold, Louis I., Alan D. McKillop, and Lois Whitney, eds. *Eighteenth Century Poetry and Prose.* 2nd ed. New York: Ronald, 1956.

Brower, Reuben A. "Lady Winchilsea and the Poetic Tradition of the Seventeenth Century." *Studies in Philology* 42 (1945): 61–80.

Bruckmann, Patricia. "Catholicism in England." *The Age of William III and Mary II: Power, Politics and Patronage, 1688–1702.* Ed. Robert P. Maccubbin and Martha Hamilton-Phillips. Williamsburg: College of William and Mary, 1988. 82–88.

Bullen, A. H., ed. *Musa Proterva: Love-Poems of the Restoration.* London: privately printed, 1880.

Burke, John. *A Genealogical and Heraldic History of the Landed Gentry.* 5th ed. 2 vols. London: Burke's Peerage, 1871.

Burke, John Andrew. *Burke's Genealogical and Heraldic History of the Peerage, Baronetege, and Knightage, Privy Council and Order of Precedence.* London: Burke's Peerage, 1907–37.

Burnet, Gilbert, bishop of Salisbury. *History of My Own Times.* 2 vols. London: Thomas Ward, 1724–34.

Burton, Robert. *The Anatomy of Melancholy.* 3 vols. London: Bell, 1926.

Bush, Douglas. *English Literature in the Earlier 17th Century, 1600–1660.* Oxford: Oxford UP, 1945.

Buxton, John. "The Poems of the Countess of Winchilsea." *Life and Letters* 65 (1950): 195–204.

———. *A Tradition of English Poetry.* New York: St. Martin's, 1967.

Calendar of State Papers, Domestic Series, March 1, 1678, to December 31, 1678, Preserved in the Public Record Office. Ed. F. H. Blackburne Daniell and Francis Bickley. London: HMSO, 1913.

Calendar of State Papers, Domestic Series, January 1 to June 30, 1683, Preserved in the Public Record Office. Ed. F. H. Blackburne Daniell. London: HMSO, 1933.

Calendar of State Papers, Domestic Series, October 1, 1683–April 30, 1684. Ed. F. H. Blackburne Daniell and Francis Bickley. London: HMSO, 1938.

Calendar of State Papers, Domestic Series, May 1, 1684–February 5, 1685. Ed. F. H. Blackburne Daniell and Francis Bickley. London: HMSO, 1938.

Calendar of State Papers, Domestic Series, of the Reign of William and Mary: May 1690–October 1691. Ed. William John Hardy. London: HMSO, 1898.

Cameron, William J. "Anne, Countess of Winchilsea: A Guide for the Future Biographer." Thesis. Victoria College, Wellington, N.Z., 1951.

Carswell, *The Descent on England: A Study of the English Revolution of 1688 and Its European Background.* New York: Day, 1969.

Case, Arthur Ellicott. *A Bibliography of English Poetical Miscellanies, 1521–1750.* Oxford: Bibliographical Society, 1935.

Chalmers, Alexander. *The Works of the English Poets.* 21 vols. London: J. Johnson, 1810.

Chamberlayne, Edward. *Anglia Notitia.* 16th ed. N.p.: for R. Chiswel, T. Sawbridge, G. Wells, and R. Bentley; and sold by Matthew Gilliflower, and James Partridge, 1687.

Chesler, Phyllis. *Women and Madness.* New York: Avon, 1972.

Cheyne, George. *The English Malady: or A Treatise of Nervous Diseases of All Kinds, as Spleen, Vapours, Lowness of Spirits, Hypochondrical and Hysterical Distempers.* London: Strahan, 1733.

Chodorow, Nancy. "Feminism and Difference: Gender, Relation and Difference in Psychoanalytic Perspective." *Socialist Review* 46 (1979): 51–69.

——— . *The Reproduction of Mothering: Psychoanalysis and the Sociology of Gender.* Berkeley: U of California P, 1978.

Cibber, Theophilus. *The Lives of the Poets of Great Britain and Ireland, to the time of Dean Swift.* London: R. Griffiths, 1753.

Clark, Sir George. *The Later Stuarts: 1660–1714.* 2nd ed. Oxford: Clarendon, 1965.

Cokayne, G. E., and E. A. Fey, eds. *Calendar of Marriage Licenses Issued by the Faculty Office, 1632–1714.* London: Index Library, 1905.

Cokayne, George Edward. *The Complete Peerage; or, A History of the House of Lords and All Its Members from the Earliest Times.* Ed. Geoffrey H. White and R. S. Lea. 12 vols. London: St. Catherine, 1959.

Colman, George, and Bonnell Thornton, eds. *Poems by Eminent Ladies.* 2 vols. London: R. Baldwin, 1755.

Congleton, J. E. *Theories of Pastoral Poetry in England, 1684–1798.* New York: Haskell, 1968.

Connell, Neville. *Anne the Last Stuart Monarch.* London: Butterworth, 1937.

Cooper, Helen. *Pastoral: Mediaeval into Renaissance.* Totowa: Rowman, 1977.

Councer, C. R. "The Medieval and Renaissance Painted Glass of Eastwell." *Archaeologia Cantiana* 59 (1940): 109–13.

Cowper, Joseph, ed. *Roll of the Freemen of the City of Canterbury, from A.D. 1392 to 1800.* Canterbury, Eng.: Cross and Jackman, 1903.

Cullen, Patrick. *Spenser, Marvell, and Renaissance Pastoral.* Cambridge: Harvard UP, 1970.

Curtis, Gila. *The Life and Times of Queen Anne*. London: Weidenfeld, 1972.

Dalton, Charles. *English Army Lists and Commission Registers*. London, 1892.

Day, Martin S. *History of English Literature, 1660–1837*. New York: Doubleday, 1963.

de Lauretis, Teresa. *Alice Doesn't*. Bloomington: Indiana UP, 1984.

Dictionary of National Biography. Ed. Leslie Stephen. 63 vols. London, 1885–1901. Supplements 1901–60.

Dormer, P. G. *Eastwell: The "Royal" Village*. Ashford, Eng.: privately printed, 1986.

Doubleday, H. Arthur, and William Page, eds. *The Victoria History of Hampshire and the Isle of Wight*. 5 vols. Westminster: Constable, 1900–12.

Doughty, Oswald. "The English Malady of the Eighteenth Century." *Review of English Studies* 2 (1926): 257–69.

Dowden, Edward. *Essays Modern and Elizabethan*. London: Dent, 1910.

Downie, J. Alan. *Jonathan Swift: Political Writer*. London: Routledge, 1984.

Drabble, Margaret, ed. *The Oxford Companion to English Literature*. 5th ed. Oxford: Oxford UP, 1985.

Dryden, John. *Essays of John Dryden*. Ed. W. P. Ker. 2 vols. New York: Russell, 1961.

———. *Works of John Dryden*. Gen. eds. Edward Niles Hooker and H. T. Swedenberg, Jr. 20 vols. to date. Berkeley: U of California P, 1956–.

Duncombe, John. *The Feminiad or Female Genius*. London, 1751.

D'Urfey, Thomas, ed. *Wit and Mirth; or, Pills to Purge Melancholy*. New York: Folklore Library, 1959.

Eames, John. "Sir William Kingsmill (1613–1661) and His Poetry." *English Studies: A Journal of English Language and Literature*. 67.2 (1986): 126–56.

Edwards, George W. *London*. Philadelphia: Penn Pub. House, 1922.

Ehrenpreis, Irvin. *Swift: The Man, His Works, and the Age*. 3 vols. Cambridge: Harvard UP, 1967.

Ehrenreich, Barbara, and Deirdre English. *Complaints and Disorders: The Sexual Politics of Sickness*. Glass Mountain Pamphlet No. 2. Old Westbury: Feminist, 1973.

Empson, William. *Some Versions of Pastoral*. 1935. Norfolk, Conn.: New Directions, 1950.

The English Reports (House of Lords, Privy Council, Chancery, etc.). Continuous vols. London, Stevens, 1900–.

Evans, Maurice. *English Poetry in the Sixteenth Century*. London: Hutchinson U Library, 1967.

Eves, Charles Kenneth. *Matthew Prior, Poet and Diplomatist*. New York: Columbia UP, 1939.

Ezell, Margaret J. M. *The Patriarch's Wife: Literary Evidence and the History of the Family*. Chapel Hill: U of North Carolina P, 1987.

Fabricant, Carole. *Swift's Landscape*. Baltimore: Johns Hopkins UP, 1982.

Fairchild, Hoxie Neale. *Religious Trends in English Poetry*. New York: Columbia UP, 1939.

Farley-Hills, David, ed. *Rochester: The Critical Heritage*. New York: Barnes, 1972.

Fausset, Hugh l'Anson, ed. *Minor Poets of the Eighteenth Century*. London: Dutton, 1930.

Ferguson, Moira, ed. *First Feminists: British Women Writers, 1578–1799*. Bloomington: Indiana UP; Old Westbury: Feminist, 1985.

Finch, Anne, countess of Winchilsea. *Miscellany Poems, on Several Occasions: Written by a Lady*. London: printed for J[ohn] B[arber] and sold by Benj. Tooke at the Middle-Temple-Gate, William Taylor in Pater-Noster-Row, and James Round, in Exchange-Alley, Cornhil, 1713.

—————. *The Poems of Anne Countess of Winchilsea*. Ed. Myra Reynolds. Chicago: U of Chicago P, 1903.

—————. *Selected Poems*. Ed. Denys Thompson. Manchester, Eng.: Carcanet, 1987.

—————. *Selected Poems of Anne Finch, Countess of Winchilsea*. Ed. Katharine Rogers. New York: Ungar, 1979.

—————. *The Wellesley Manuscript Poems of Anne Countess of Winchilsea*. Ed. Jean M. Ellis D'Alessandro. Florence: privately printed, 1988.

Foucault, Michel. *Madness and Civilization: A History of Insanity in the Age of Reason*. Trans. Richard Howard. New York: Pantheon, 1965.

Fraser, Antonia. *The Weaker Vessel*. New York: Knopf, 1984.

Fuller, Francis. *Medicina Gymnastica*. N.p., 1704.

Fuller, Thomas. *The History of the Worthies of England*. 1662. A new ed. with a few explanatory notes, by John Nichols. 2 vols. London, 1811.

Fussell, Paul. *The Rhetorical World of Augustan Humanism: Ethics and Imagery from Swift to Burke*. Oxford: Clarendon, 1965.

Gagen, Jean. "Honor and Fame in the Works of the Duchess of Newcastle." *Studies in Philology* 56 (1965): 519–38.

Gardiner, Judith K. "Aphra Behn: Sexuality and Self-Respect." *Women's Studies* 7 (1980): 67–78.

Garrison, James. *Dryden and the Tradition of the Panegyric*. Berkeley: U of California P, 1975.

Gay, John. *The Beggar's Opera and Companion Pieces*. Ed. C. F. Burgess. Arlington Heights: AHM, 1966.

—————. *Poems of John Gay*. Ed. John Underhill. 2 vols. London: Routledge, 1893.

Gidnger, James. *Biographical Dictionary*. London, 1769.

Gilbert, Sandra M., and Susan Gubar. *The Madwoman in the Attic: The Woman Writer and the Nineteenth-Century Literary Imagination*. New Haven: Yale UP, 1979.

———, eds. *The Norton Anthology of Literature by Women*. New York: Norton, 1985.

———. "Introduction: Gender, Creativity, and the Woman Poet." *Shakespeare's Sisters: Feminist Essays on Women Poets*. Bloomington: Indiana UP, 1979.

Gildon, Charles. *A New Collection of Poems for Several Occasions*. London: Peter Back and George Strahan, 1701.

Gill, R. B. "Real People and Persuasion in Personal Satire." *South Atlantic Quarterly* 82 (1983): 165–78.

Gilligan, Carol. *In a Different Voice: Psychological Theory and Women's Development*. Cambridge: Harvard UP, 1982.

Goreau, Angeline. *Reconstructing Aphra*. New York: Dial, 1980.

———. *The Whole Duty of a Woman: Female Writers in Seventeenth Century England*. Garden City: Dial-Doubleday, 1985.

Gosse, Edmund. *Gossip in a Library*. 2 vols. New York: Dodd, 1891.

———. *A History of Eighteenth Century Literature (1660–1780)*. New York: Macmillan, 1901.

Gough, Richard. *Anecdotes of British Topography*. London, 1768.

Goulianos, Joan, ed. *"By a Woman writt": Literature from Six Centuries by and About Women*. New York: Bobbs, 1973.

Greenberg, Janelle. "The Legal Status of English Women in Early Eighteenth-Century Law and Equity." *Studies in Eighteenth-Century Culture* 4 (1975): 171–81.

Greer, Germaine. "Wordsworth and Winchilsea: The Progress of an Error." *The Nature of Identity: Essays Presented to Donald E. Hayden by the Graduate Faculty of Modern Letters*. Tulsa: U of Tulsa, 1981. 1–13.

Greer, Germaine, et al., eds. *Kissing the Rod: An Anthology of Seventeenth-Century Women's Verse*. London: Virago, 1988.

Greg, Walter W. *Pastoral Poetry and Pastoral Drama*. 1936. New York: Russell, 1959.

Gregg, Edward. *Queen Anne*. London: Routledge, 1980.

Haile, Martin. *Queen Mary of Modena: Her Life and Letters*. London: Dent, 1905.

Hale, Sara. *Women's Record*. New York, 1853.

Haley, H. D. "International Affairs." *The Age of William III and Mary II: Power, Politics and Patronage, 1688–1702*. Ed. Robert P. Maccubbin and Martha Hamilton. Williamsburg: College of William and Mary, 1988. 35–48.

Halifax, George Savile, marquis of. *Complete Works*. Ed. J. P. Kenyon. Baltimore: Penguin, 1969.

Hampsten, Elizabeth. "Petticoat Authors: 1660–1720." *Women's Studies* 7 (1980): 21–38.

——. Introduction. "Poems by Ann Finch." *Women's Studies* 7 (1980): 5–19. [Five prev. unpub. poems.]

Handasyde, Elizabeth. *Granville the Polite: The Life of George Granville, Lord Lansdowne, 1666–1735*. Oxford: Oxford UP, 1933.

Hart, A. Tindal. *The Life and Times of John Sharp, Archbishop of York*. London: SPCK, 1949.

Hasted, Edward. *The History and Topographical Survey of the County of Kent. Containing the Ancient and Present State of it, Civil and Ecclesiastical.* 3 vols. Canterbury, Eng.: Simmons and Kirkly, 1778.

Hatton. *Correspondence of the Family of Hatton. Being chiefly letters addressed to Christopher, First Viscount Hatton. A.D. 1601–1704.* Ed. Edward Maunde Thompson. 2 vols. London: Camden Society, 1878.

Hearne, Thomas. *Remarks and Collections of Thomas Hearne*. Ed. C. E. Doble, D. W. Rannie, and H. E. Salter. 11 vols. Oxford: Oxford UP, 1885–1921.

Heath-Stubbs, John. *The Pastoral*. Oxford: Oxford UP, 1969.

Hedley, Olwen. *Royal Palaces*. Andover, Eng.: Pitkin Pictorials, 1981.

Henning, Basil Duke. *The House of Commons, 1660–1690*. 3 vols. London: Secker, 1983.

Herrick, Robert. *The Complete Poetry of Robert Herrick*. Ed. J. Max Patrick. Garden City: Doubleday, 1963.

Hill, Bridget, ed. *Eighteenth Century Women: An Anthology*. London: Allen, 1984.

Hill, Christopher. *The Century of Revolution, 1603–1714*. New York: Norton, 1961.

——. *The World Turned Upside Down: Radical Ideas During the English Revolution*. London: Temple Smith, 1972.

Historical Manuscripts Commission. *Historical Manuscripts Commission Calendar of the Stuart Papers Belonging to His Majesty the King, Presented at Windsor Castle.* 7 vols. London: HMSO, 1902.

——. *Manuscripts of S. H. Le Fleming, Esq., of Rydal Hall*. London: HMSO, 1890.

——. *Report on the Manuscripts of Allan George Finch, Esq., of Burley-on-the-Hill, Rutland*. 4 vols. London: Hereford Times, 1913.

——. *Report on the Manuscripts of the Marquess of Downshire*. 4 vols. London: HMSO, 1924.

Hughes, Helen Sard. *The Gentle Hertford: Her Life and Letters*. New York: Macmillan, 1940.

———. "Lady Winchilsea and Her Friends." *London Mercury* 19 (1929): 624–35.

Humphreys, A. R. *The Augustan World: Society, Thought, and Letters in Eighteenth-Century England.* New York: Harper, 1963.

Hunt, Leigh. *Men, Women and Books.* New York: Harper, 1847.

I'Anson, Arthur Bryan. *The History of the Finch Family. With Plates, Including Portraits.* London: Janson, 1933.

Igglesden, Charles. *A Saunter Through Kent with Pen and Pencil.* Vol. 3. Ashford, Eng.: Kentish Express, 1901.

[Innes, Lewis?]. *The Life of James the Second, King of England, &c. Collected out of memoirs writ of his own hand. Together with the king's advice to his son, and His Majesty's will.* Ed. S. J. Clarke. N.p., 1816.

Isham, Thomas. *The Diary of Thomas Isham of Lamport (1658–81) Kept by Him in Latin from 1671 to 1673 at His Father's Command.* Trans. Norman Marlow. Introd. Sir Gyles Isham. Pref. Sir George Clark. Hants, Eng.: Gregg, 1971.

Johnson, Samuel. *Lives of the English Poets.* 2 vols. London: Oxford UP, 1906.

Johnstone, Lesley. "Winchilsea's 'Nocturnal Reverie,' Lines 4–6." *Explicator* 41 (1983): 20.

———. "Winchilsea's 'Nocturnal Reverie,' Lines 25–28." *Explicator* 41 (1983): 20–21.

Journals of the House of Lords. 66 vols. London: HMSO, 1509–1834.

Kamuf, Peggy. "Writing Like a Woman." *Women and Language in Literature and Society.* Ed. S. McConnell-Ginet et al. New York: Praeger, 1980. 284–99.

Kaplan, Cora, ed. *Salt and Bitter and Good: Three Centuries of English and American Women Poets.* New York: Paddington, 1975.

Kaplan, Harold, Alfred Freedman, and Benjamin Sadock, eds. *Comprehensive Textbook of Psychiatry.* 3 vols. Baltimore: Williams, 1980.

Kenny, Virginia C. *The Country House Ethos in English Literature, 1688–1750: Themes of Personal Retreat and National Expansion.* New York: St. Martin's, 1984.

Kermode, Frank. Introduction. *English Pastoral Poetry from the Beginnings to Marvell.* 1952. Freeport, N.Y.: Books for Libraries, 1969.

Kingsmill, J. T. *Chronicles of the Kingsmills.* 2nd ed. Bedford, Eng.: privately printed, 1919.

Kolodny, Annette. "Dancing Through the Minefield: Some Observations on the Theory, Practice, and Politics of a Feminist Literary Criticism." Showalter, *New Feminist Criticism* 144–67.

Kristeva, Julia. "Woman Can Never Be Defined." *New French Feminisms.* Ed. Elaine Marks and Isabelle de Courtivron. Amherst: U of Massachusetts P, 1980. 134–38.

Kuhn, A. J. "Nature Spiritualized: Aspects of Anti-Newtonianism." *ELH* 41 (1974): 400–12.

Leslett, Russell. *Family Life and Illicit Love in Earlier Generations.* Cambridge: Cambridge UP, 1977.

The Life and Character of John Barber, Esq, Late Lord-Mayor of London, Deceased. London, 1741.

Lipking, Lawrence K. *Abandoned Women and Poetic Tradition.* Chicago: U of Chicago P, 1988.

———. "The History of the Future." *New Approaches to Eighteenth-Century Literature.* Ed. Philip Harth. New York: Columbia UP, 1974. 157–76.

Lips, Hilary. *Sex and Gender.* Mountain View, Calif.: Mayfield, 1988.

Locke, John. *An Essay Concerning Human Understanding.* Ed. Alexander C. Fraser. 2 vols. Oxford: Clarendon, 1894.

London County Council. *Survey of London.* 31 vols. London: London County Council, 1900–63.

The London Encyclopedia. Ed. Ben Weinrab and Christopher Hibbert. London: Macmillan, 1983.

Longknife, Ann. "A Preface to an Edition of the Works of Anne Finch, Countess of Winchilsea." Diss. U of Houston, 1978.

Lonsdale, Roger, ed. *Eighteenth-Century Women Poets: An Oxford Anthology.* Oxford: Oxford UP, 1989.

Lunt, W. E. *History of England.* 3rd ed. New York: Harper, 1947.

Luttrell, Narcissus. *A Brief Historical Relation of State Affairs from September 1678 to April 1714.* 6 vols. Oxford: Oxford UP, 1857.

Lyons, Bridget Gellert. *Voices of Melancholy: Studies in Literary Treatments of Melancholy in Renaissance England.* New York: Barnes, 1971.

Maccubbin, Robert P., and Peter Martin. *British and American Gardens in the Eighteenth Century: Eighteen Illustrated Essays on Garden History.* Williamsburg: Colonial Williamsburg Foundation, 1984.

Macfarlane, Alan. *Marriage and Love in England: Models of Reproduction, 1300–1840.* London: Blackwell, 1986.

Mack, Maynard. *The Garden and the City.* Toronto: U of Toronto P, 1969.

———. "The Muse of Satire." *Satire: Modern Essays in Criticism.* Ed. Ronald Paulson. Englewood Cliffs: Prentice, 1971. 190–201.

Mahl, Mary R., and Helen Koon, eds. *The Female Spectator: English Women Writers Before 1800.* Bloomington: Indiana U; Old Westbury: Feminist, 1977.

Mallette, Richard. *Spenser, Milton, and Renaissance Pastoral.* Lewisburg: Bucknell UP, 1981.

Mallinson, Jean. "Anne Finch: A Woman Poet and the Tradition." *Gender at Work: Four Women Writers of the Eighteenth Century.* Ed. Ann Messenger.

Detroit: Wayne State UP, 1990. 34–76.

Mandeville, Bernard. *A Treatise of the Hypochondriack and Hysterick Passions.* London, 1711.

Manley, Mary de la Riviere. *Court Intrigues, in a Collection of Original Letters, from the Island of the New Atalantis.* London, 1711.

———. *Secret Memoirs from the New Atalantis.* Vols. 1 and 2. New York: Garland, 1972. A facsimile from a copy in the Beinecke Library of Yale University, *Secret Memoirs and Manners of Several Persons of Quality, of Both Sexes. From the New Atalantis, An Island in the Mediteranean.* London, 1709.

Marlborough, Lady Sarah. *An Account of the Conduct of the Dowager Duchess of Marlborough, From her first coming to Court, to the Year 1710, In a Letter from Herself to My Lord.* London: printed by James Bettenham, for George Hawkins, at Milton's Head, between the two Temple-Gates, 1742.

Martin, Peter. *Pursuing Innocent Pleasures: The Gardening World of Alexander Pope.* Hamden: Archon, 1984.

Marvell, Andrew. *The Poems and Letters of Andrew Marvell.* Ed. H. M. Margoliouth. Vol. 1. Oxford: Oxford UP, 1927.

Masek, Rosemary. "Women in an Age of Transition: 1485–1714." *The Women of England, from Anglo-Saxon Times to the Present: Interpretative Bibliographical Essays.* Ed. Barbara Kanner. Hamden: Archon, 1979. 138–82.

Meese, Elizabeth A. *Crossing the Double Cross: The Practice of Feminist Criticism.* Chapel Hill: U of North Carolina P, 1986.

Mermin, Dorothy. "Women Becoming Poets: Katherine Philips, Aphra Behn, Anne Finch." *ELH* 57 (1990): 335–55.

Messenger, Ann P. "'Adam Pos'd': Metaphysical and Augustan Satire." *West Coast Review* 8 (1974): 10–11.

———. "Lady Winchilsea and Twice-Fallen Women." *Atlantis* 3 (1978): 82–98.

———. "Publishing Without Perishing: Lady Winchilsea's *Miscellany Poems* of 1713." *Restoration: Studies in English Literary Culture, 1660–1700* 5 (1981): 27–37.

———. "Selected Nightingales and an 'Augustan' Sensibility." *English Studies in Canada* 6 (1980): 145–53. Rev. and rpt. as "Selected Nightingales: Anne Finch, Countess of Winchilsea, et al." *His and Hers: Essays in Restoration and Eighteenth-Century Literature.* Lexington: U of Kentucky P, 1986. 71–83.

Michael, Wolfgang. *England Under George I: The Beginnings of the Hanoverian Dynasty.* London: Macmillan, 1936.

Miller, Nancy K. "Arachnologies: The Woman, the Text, and the Critic." *The Poetics of Gender.* Ed. Nancy K. Miller. New York: Columbia UP, 1986. 270–95.

————. *The Heroine's Text: Readings in the French and English Novel, 1722–1782.* New York: Columbia UP, 1980.

Miner, Earl Roy. *The Restoration Mode from Milton to Dryden.* Princeton: Princeton UP, 1974.

Moers, Ellen. *Literary Women: The Great Writers.* Garden City: Doubleday, 1976.

Monod, Paul Kléber. *Jacobitism and the English People, 1688–1788.* Cambridge: Cambridge UP, 1989.

Moore, Cecil A. "The English Malady." *Backgrounds of English Literature, 1700–1760.* Minneapolis: U of Minnesota P, 1953. 179–235.

————. "Whig Panegyric Verse, 1700–1760: A Phase of Sentimentalism." *PMLA* 41 (1926): 362–401.

Morgan, Fidelis. *A Woman of No Character: An Autobiography of Mrs. Manley.* London: Faber, 1986.

Mullan, John. "Hypochondria and Hysteria: Sensibility and the Physicians." *Eighteenth Century: Theory and Interpretation* 25 (1984): 141–74.

Murry, John Middleton. "Anne Finch, Countess of Winchilsea." *New Adelphi* 1 (1927): 145–53.

————. "The Countess of Winchilsea." *Countries of the Mind.* London: Oxford UP, 1931. 166–80.

Neill, D. G. "Studies for an Edition of the Poems of Anne, Countess of Winchilsea, Consisting of a Bibliography of Her Poems and a Study of All Available Manuscripts." Thesis. New College, Oxford, 1954. [Unavailable to everyone by order of the author.]

Nenner, Harold. "The Rule of Monarchical Succession." *The Age of William III and Mary II: Power, Politics and Patronage, 1688–1702.* Ed. Robert P. Maccubbin and Martha Hamilton-Phillips. Williamsburg: College of William and Mary, 1989. 21–34.

A New Miscellany of Original Poems, On Several Occasions. Written by the E. of D., Sir Charles Sidley, Sir Fleetw. Shepheards, Mr. Wolesly, Mr. Granville the Hands. London, 1701.

Newton, Judith. "Making—and Remaking—History: Another Look at 'Patriarchy.'" *Tulsa Studies in Women's Literature* 3 (1984): 125–41.

Nichols, John. *Illustrations of the Literary History of the Eighteenth Century, consisting of authentic memoirs and original letters of eminent persons, and intended as a sequel to the "Literary Anecdotes."* 8 vols. London: Nichols, Son, and Bentley, 1817–58.

————. *Literary Anecdotes of the Eighteenth Century.* 9 vols. London: Nichols, Son, and Bentley, 1812–16.

Nussbaum, Felicity. *The Brink of All We Hate: English Satires on Women, 1660–1750.* Lexington: UP of Kentucky, 1984.

————. "The Politics of Difference." *Eighteenth-Century Studies* 23 (1990): 375–86.

————, ed. "The Politics of Difference." *Eighteenth-Century Studies* 23. whole no. 4 (1990).

Nussbaum, Felicity, and Laura Brown. "Revising Critical Practices: An Introductory Essay." *The New Eighteenth Century*. Ed. Felicity Nussbaum and Laura Brown. New York: Methuen, 1987.

Ober, William B. "Eighteenth-Century Spleen." *Psychology and Literature in the Eighteenth Century*. Ed. Christopher Fox. New York: AMS Press, 1987. 225–58.

Ogg, David. *England in the Reign of Charles II*. Oxford: Clarendon, 1935.

————. *England in the Reign of James II and William III*. Oxford: Clarendon, 1955.

Okin, Susan Moller. "Patriarchy and Married Women's Property in England: Questions on Some Current Views." *Eighteenth-Century Studies* 17 (1983–84): 121–38.

Oldmixon, John. *History of England, During the Reign of King William and Queen Mary, Queen Anne, King George*. N.p., 1735.

Oman, Carola. *Mary of Modena*. Bungay, Eng.: Hodder, 1962.

Overton, J. H. *The Nonjurors: Their Lives, Principles, and Writings*. London: Smith, Elder, 1902.

Ovid. *Metamorphoses*. Trans. Rolfe Humphries. Bloomington: Indiana UP, 1958.

Palmer, Thomas. *The Admirable Secrets of Physick and Chyrurgery*. Ed. Thomas Rogers Forbes. New Haven: Yale UP, 1984. [A transcription of the 1696 ms.]

Parkins, E. W. "The Vanishing Houses of Kent." *Archaeologica Cantiana* 83 (1968).

Paul, Herbert. *Queen Anne*. London: Goupil, 1906. New ed. London: Hodder, 1912.

Pearson, Hesketh. *Charles II: His Life and Likeness*. London: Heinemann, 1960.

Pearson, LuEmily. *Elizabethan Love Connections*. Berkeley: U of California P, 1932.

Peck, Francis. *Desiderata Curiosa; or, a collection of diverse scarce and curious pieces, relating chiefly to matters of English history. . . .* Ed. [T. Evans]. 2 vols. London, 1779.

Pepys, Samuel. *The Diary of Samuel Pepys*. Ed. Robert Latham and William Matthews. 10 vols. Berkeley: U of California P, 1974.

Perry, Ruth. *The Celebrated Mary Astell: An Early English Feminist*. Chicago: U of Chicago P, 1986.

————. "Mary Astell and the Feminist Critique of Possessive Individualism." *Eighteenth-Century Studies* 23 (1990): 444–57.

Philips, Katherine. *Selected Poems: The Orinda Booklets*. Ed. Louise I. Guiney. Vol. 1. Hull: Tutin, 1905.

Physick, John. *Five Monuments from Eastwell*. Brochure 3. London: Victoria and Albert Museum, 1973.

Piggott, Stuart. *William Stukeley: An Eighteenth-Century Antiquary*. 1950. London: Thames, 1985.

Pinto, Vivian de Sola. *Enthusiast in Wit: A Portrait of John Wilmot, Earl of Rochester, 1647–1680*. London: Routledge, 1962.

———, ed. *Poetry of the Restoration*. New York: Barnes, 1966.

Piper, William Bowman. *The Heroic Couplet*. Cleveland: Case Western Reserve U, 1969.

Plaisant, Michèle. "Sentiment et représentation de la mort chez quelques poètes anglais du XVIII siècle." *La mort, le fantastique, le surnaturel du XVIE a l'époque romantique*. Lille: U de Lille III, Centre de Recherches sur l'Angleterre, 1979. 67–76.

Plantagant, Richard. "Memoirs of Richard Plantagant (a Natural Son of King Richard III) Who Died at Eastwell, 22nd Dec. 1550, with an Extract from the Parish Register, by Drs. Brett, Pegge, and the Rev. Parsons, Rector of Eastwell." *Gentleman's Magazine* July, Aug., Sept., Dec. 1707.

Poggioli, Renato. *The Oaten Flute: Essays on Pastoral Poetry and the Pastoral Ideal*. Cambridge: Harvard UP, 1975.

Pope, Alexander. *The Correspondence of Alexander Pope*. Ed. George Sherburn. 3 vols. Oxford: Clarendon, 1956.

———. *Minor Poems*. Ed. Norman Ault and John Butt. London: Methuen, 1964. Vol. 6 of *The Poems of Alexander Pope*. Gen. ed. John Butt. 11 vols. 1939–69.

———. *Pope's Own Miscellany, Being a Reprint of Poems on Several Occasions, 1717, Containing New Poems by Alexander Pope and Others*. Ed. Norman Ault. London: Nonesuch, 1935.

———. *The Rape of the Lock and Other Poems*. Ed. Geoffrey Tillotson. London: Methuen, 1962. Vol. 2 of *The Poems of Alexander Pope*. Gen. ed. John Butt. 11 vols. 1939–69.

Pope, Alexander, John Gay, and John Arbuthnot. *Three Hours After Marriage*. Ed. Richard Morton and William M. Peterson. Lake Erie College Studies, vol. 1. Painesville, Ohio: Lake Erie College, 1961.

Porter, Roy. *English Society in the Eighteenth Century*. London: Allenhouse, 1982.

Prall, Stuart E. *The Bloodless Revolution: England, 1688*. Madison: U of Wisconsin P, 1985.

Prior, Mary, ed. *Women in English Society, 1500–1800*. London: Methuen, 1985.

Randolph, Mary Claire. "The Medical Concept in English Renaissance Satiric

Theory: Its Possible Relationships and Implications." *Studies in Philology* 38 (1941): 51–57.

Rawson, C. J. *Gulliver and the Gentle Reader: Studies in Swift and Our Time.* London: Routledge, 1973.

———. *Henry Fielding and the Augustan Ideal Under Stress.* London: Routledge, 1972.

———. "Order and Misrule: Eighteenth-Century Literature in the 1970's." *ELH* 42 (1972): 481–82.

Reed, Amy. *The Background of Gray's Elegy: A Study in the Taste for Melancholy Poetry, 1700–1751.* New York: Russell, 1962.

Rees, Christine. "Gay, Swift, and the Nymphs of Drury-Lane." *Essays in Criticism* 23 (1973): 1–21.

Reresby, John. *Memoirs of Sir John Reresby.* Ed. with introd. and notes by Andrew Browning. Glasgow: Jackson, 1936.

Reynolds, Myra. *The Learned Lady in England, 1650–1760.* Boston: Houghton, 1920.

———. *Nature in English Poetry.* Chicago: U of Chicago P, 1909.

Riddell, William R. "Dr. George Cheyne and the 'English Malady.'" *Annals of Medical History* (1922): 304–10.

Riedenauer, Annemarie. "Die Gedichte Der anne Finch, Countess of Winchilsea." Diss. U of Vienna, 1964.

Robinson, Mabel L. "Lady Winchilsea: A Modernist." *Sewanee Review* 25 (1917): 412–21.

Rochester, earl of (John Wilmot). *The Complete Poems of John Wilmot, Earl of Rochester.* Ed. David M. Vieth. New Haven: Yale UP, 1968.

Rogers, Katharine. "Anne Finch, Countess of Winchilsea: An Augustan Woman Poet." *Shakespeare's Sisters: Feminist Essays on Women Poets.* Ed. Sandra M. Gilbert and Susan Gubar. Bloomington: Indiana UP, 1979. 32–46.

———. *Feminism in Eighteenth-Century England.* Urbana: U of Illinois P, 1982.

———. "Finch's 'Candid Account' vs. Eighteenth-Century Theories of the Spleen." *Mosaic: A Journal for the Interdisciplinary Study of Literature* 22 (1989): 17–27.

———. *The Troublesome Helpmate: A History of Misogyny in Literature.* Seattle: U of Washington P, 1966.

Rogers, Katharine, and William McCarthy, eds. *The Meridian Anthology of Early Women Writers: British Women from Aphra Behn to Maria Edgeworth, 1660–1800.* New York: NAL, 1987.

Rogers, Nicholas. "Riot and Popular Jacobitism." *Ideology and Conspiracy: Aspects of Jacobitism, 1689–1759.* Ed. Eveline Cruickshanks. Edinburgh: John Donald, 1982. 76–81.

Rosenmeyer, Thomas G. *The Green Cabinet.* Berkeley: U of California P, 1969.

Rowe, Nicholas. *The Tragedy of Jane Shore*. Ed. Harry William Pedicord. Lincoln: U of Nebraska P, 1974.

Rowse, A. L. *Jonathan Swift: Major Prophet*. London: Thames, 1985.

Rowtons, Frederic. *The Female Poets of Great Britain*. Detroit: Wayne State UP, 1981.

Rupp, Gordon. *Religion in England, 1688–1791*. Oxford: Clarendon, 1986.

Rust, George. *A Discourse of the Use of Reason in Matters of Religion*. London, 1683.

Salvaggio, Ruth. *Enlightened Absence: Neoclassical Configurations of the Feminine*. Urbana: U of Illinois P, 1988.

Savage, Roger. "Swift's Fallen City: 'A Description of the Morning.'" *The World of Jonathan Swift*. Ed. Brian Vickers. Oxford: Basil Blackwell, 1968. 171–94.

Schenck, Celeste M. "Feminism and Deconstruction: Re-Constructing the Elegy." *Tulsa Studies in Women's Literature* 5 (1986): 13–27.

Sena, John F. "Belinda's Hysteria: The Medical Context of *The Rape of the Lock*." *Psychology and Literature in the Eighteenth Century*. Ed. Christopher Fox. New York: AMS, 1987. 129–47.

———. *A Bibliography of Melancholy: 1660–1800*. London: Nether, 1970.

———. "Melancholic Madness and the Puritans." *Harvard Theological Review* 66 (1973): 293–309.

———. "Melancholy in Anne Finch and Elizabeth Carter: The Ambivalence of an Idea." *Yearbook of English Studies* 1 (1971): 108–19.

Sharpe, Kevin, and Steven Zwicker. "Politics of Discourse." *Politics of Discourse*. Ed. Kevin Sharpe and Steven Zwicker. Berkeley: U of California P, 1987. 1–20.

Sherburn, George. *The Early Career of Alexander Pope*. New York: Russell, 1963.

Showalter, Elaine. *A Literature of Their Own: British Women Novelists from Bronte to Lessing*. Princeton: Princeton UP, 1977.

———, ed. *The New Feminist Criticism: Essays on Women, Literature, and Theory*. New York: Pantheon, 1985.

Sinclair-Stevenson, Christopher. *Inglorious Rebellion: The Jacobite Risings of 1708, 1715, and 1719*. New York: St. Martin's, 1971.

Smith, Hilda L. *Reason's Disciples: Seventeenth-Century English Feminists*. Urbana: U of Illinois P, 1982.

Smith-Rosenberg, Carroll. *Disorderly Conduct: Visions of Gender in Victorian America*. New York: Knopf, 1985.

Southey, Robert. *Specimen of Later English Poets*. London: Longmen, Hurst, Rees and Orve, 1807.

The Spectator. Ed. with introd. and notes by Donald F. Bond. 2 vols. Oxford: Clarendon, 1965.

Spenser, Edmund. *The Minor Poems*. Vol. 7 of *The Works of Edmund Spenser:*

A Variorum Edition. Eds. Edwin Greenlaw et al. 11 vols. Baltimore: Johns Hopkins P, 1943–66.

Stanford, Ann, ed. *The Women Poets in English*. New York: McGraw, 1972.

Staves, Susan. *Players' Scepters: Fictions of Authority in the Restoration*. Lincoln: U of Nebraska P, 1979.

Stead, Philip John, ed. *Songs of the Restoration Theatre*. London: Methuen, 1948.

Steele, Richard, ed. *Poetical Miscellanies, Consisting of Original Poems and Translations. By the Best Hands*. London: J. Tonson, 1714.

———. *The Tatler*. London: Dent, 1953.

Stone, Lawrence. *The Family, Sex and Marriage in England, 1500–1800*. New York: Harper, 1977.

———. "Social Mobility in England, 1500–1700." *Past and Present* 33 (1966): 40–41.

Strickland, Agnes. *Lives of the Queens of England, from the Norman Conquest; with Anecdotes of their Courts, now first Published from Official Records and Other Authentic Documents, Private as well as Public*. 12 vols. Philadelphia: Blanchard and Lea, 1852.

Stukeley, William. *Of the Spleen, Its Description and History, Uses and Diseases, Particularly the Vapours, with Their Remedy*. London: printed for the author, 1723.

The Survey of London. Ed. C. R. Ashlee et al. London: Joint Publishing Committee Representing the London County Council and the Committee for the Survey of the Memorials of Greater London. 1900–63.

Sussex Archaeological Collections, Relating to the History and Antiquities of the County. 127 vols. Sussex: George P. Bacon, 1863.

Swift, Jonathan. *The Account Books of Jonathan Swift*. Transcribed and introd. by Paul Thompson and Dorothy Jay Thompson. Newark: U of Delaware P, 1984.

———. *Collected Poems of Jonathan Swift*. Ed. Joseph Horrell. 2 vols. Cambridge: Harvard UP, 1958.

———. *The Complete Poems*. Ed. Pat Rogers. New York: Penguin, 1983.

———. *The Correspondence of Jonathan Swift*. Ed. Harold Williams. 5 vols. Oxford: Clarendon, 1963.

Thomas, Keith. "The Double Standard." *Journal of the History of Ideas* 20.2 (1959): 195–216.

Thompson, Denys. "Anne Finch." *PN Review* 8 (1982): 35–38.

Thompson, Roger. *Unfit for Modest Ears: A Study of Pornographic, Obscene, and Bawdy Works*. Totowa: Rowman, 1979.

———. *Women in Stuart England and America: A Comparative Study*. London: Routledge, 1974.

Tillotson, Geoffrey, Paul Fussell, Jr., and Marshall Waingrow, eds. *Eighteenth-Century English Literature*. New York: Harcourt, 1969.

Todd, Janet, ed. *British Women Writers*. New York: Ungar/Continuum, 1989.

——. *Dictionary of British and American Women Writers, 1660–1800*. Totowa: Rowman; London: Methuen, 1985.

——. *Women's Friendship in Literature*. New York: Columbia UP, 1980.

Toliver, Harold E. *Pastoral Forms and Attitudes*. Berkeley: U of California P, 1971.

Tonson, Jacob [comp.]. *Poetical Miscellanies: The Sixth Part, containing a Collection of Original Poems with Several New Translations by the Most Eminent Hands*. London: printed for Jacob Tonson, 1709.

Trumbach, Randolph. *The Rise of the Egalitarian Family: Aristocratic Kinship and Domestic Relations in Eighteenth-Century England*. New York: Academic, 1978.

Turco, Lewis. *The New Book of Forms: A Handbook of Poetics*. Hanover: UP of New England, 1986.

Tutin, J. R. *Four Early English Poetesses*. London: Hull, 1908.

Walpole, Horace. *A Catalogue of the Royal and Noble Authors*. London: R. and J. Dodsley, 1759.

Ward, Thomas H., ed. *The English Poets*. New York: Macmillan, 1880.

Wasserman, Earl R. "Nature Moralized." *ELH* 20 (1953): 39–76.

——. Rev. of *Pastoral Poetry and An Essay on Criticism*, by Alexander Pope. *Philological Quarterly* 41 (1962): 615–22.

Weber, Harold M. *The Restoration Rake-Hero: Transformation in Sexual Understanding in Seventeenth-Century England*. Madison: U of Wisconsin P, 1986.

Weinreb, Ben, and Christopher Hibbert, eds. *The London Encyclopedia*. London: Macmillan, 1984.

Williams, Iola A. *Points in Eighteenth-Century Verse: A Bibliographer's and Collector's Scrapbook*. London: Constable, 1934.

——. "Some Poetical Miscellanies of the Early Eighteenth Century." *Library* 10.4 (1930): 233–51.

Williams, Jane. *The Literary Women of England*. London: Saunders, Otley, 1861.

Williamson, Marilyn L. *Raising Their Voices: British Women Writers, 1650–1750*. Detroit: Wayne State UP, 1990.

Wilson, John Harold. *The Court Wits of the Restoration: An Introduction*. New York: Octagon, 1967.

Wittig, M. A. "Metatheoretical Dilemmas in the Psychology of Gender." *American Psychologist* 40 (1985): 800–11.

Wood, Anthony A. *Athenae Oxonienses, an Exact History of all the Writers and Bishops who have had their Education in the University of Oxford*. 3rd ed. 4 vols. London: printed for Lackington, Hughes, Harding, Mavor, and Jones, 1820.

Woolf, Virginia. "Professions for Women." *The Death of the Moth and Other*

Essays. New York: Harcourt, 1942. 235–42.

———. *A Room of One's Own*. New York: Harcourt, 1929.

Wordsworth, William, comp. *Poems and Extracts Chosen by William Wordsworth for an Album Presented to Lady Mary Lowther, Christmas, 1819*. Introd. Harold Littledale. London: Frowde, 1905.

———. *The Prose Works of William Wordsworth*. Ed. W. J. B. Owen and Jane W. Smyser. 3 vols. Oxford: Clarendon, 1974.

Wright, T. *The Female Vertuoso's, A Comedy*. London, 1693.

Wrigley, E. A. "Family Limitation in Pre-Industrial England." *Economic History Review* 2nd ser. 19 (1966): 82–109.

Wye College, 1447–1947. Kent: Wye College, 1947.

Yeager, Patricia. *Honey-Mad Women: Emancipatory Strategies in Women's Writing*. New York: Columbia UP, 1988.

Index